A Practical Guide To Quantitative Finance Interviews

First Edition

Xinfeng Zhou

Edited by Brett Jiu

To the memory of my sister, Xinli Zhou

Table of Contents

Contents

Contents

Preface

This book will prepare you for quantitative finance interviews by helping you zero in on the key concepts that are frequently tested in such interviews. In this book we analyze solutions to more than 200 *real* interview problems and provide valuable insights into how to ace quantitative interviews. The book covers a variety of topics that you are likely to encounter in quantitative interviews: brain teasers, calculus, linear algebra, probability, stochastic processes and stochastic calculus, finance and programming.

Professionals and students seeking to pursue a career in quantitative finance or related quantitative fields will benefit most from thoroughly reading this book. In recent years, we have seen a dramatic surge in demand for talents with strong quantitative skills from investment banks, investment management firms, hedge funds, financial software vendors and financial consulting companies. As a result, quant, an umbrella description that encompasses quantitative analysts, quantitative researchers, quantitative strategists, quantitative traders, and quantitative developers, has become an attractive career choice.

Dozens of financial engineering or computational finance programs have been established in the last few years to educate professionals for quantitative finance jobs. Graduates with backgrounds in finance, mathematics, physics, computer sciences, and various engineering majors are contending for quant jobs as well. Naturally, the competition is fierce. To be a successful candidate, you have to distinguish yourself from many other excellent applicants.

In general, a successful candidate for a quantitative finance position is expected to have a strong mathematics background (in probability, statistics, stochastic calculus, etc.), solid programming skills and basic to intermediate-level finance knowledge. Most candidates find quantitative interviews, or at least some interview problems, challenging.

Quantitative interviews cover a broad range of mathematics, finance and programming topics that the candidates may have never used or even encountered in their daily work or study. Moreover, most interview problems require strong problem-solving skills, beyond reciting formulas or doing simple calculations. A successful candidate needs a combination of knowledge and problem-solving skills in order to excel in quantitative interviews. This is precisely what this book provides!

This book addresses these aspects by reviewing the necessary finance and mathematical concepts that serve as tools to structure and solve interview problems. Since it includes most of the topics used by quantitative interviewers, it presupposes some basic preparation in mathematics, statistics, finance, and programming.

I also strongly recommend that you try to solve each problem on your own first before reading the answer. Working out solutions on your own will help you improve your problem-solving skills and help you quickly identify common approaches to tackling quantitative problems.

Needless to say, you are likely to encounter some problems in interviews that are similar to or exactly the same as the problems in this book. After all, the book covers many essential quantitative topics using real interview problems. However, the goal of the book is not to teach you how to game the system by remembering the answers! In fact, just memorizing answers may not help much in your interview process. Unless you truly understand the underlying concepts and can analyze the problems yourself, you will fail to elaborate on the solutions and will be ill-equipped to answer many other problems that use similar concepts. (Besides, many experienced quantitative interviewers are good at catching those who have simply memorized "canned" answers.)

This is exactly the reason why I make significant effort to review essential concepts, to present solution strategies, and to analyze the solutions in detail instead of simply providing answers to problems. Furthermore, although the building blocks can be learned, how one analyzes problems and implements these concepts usually makes a big difference—and these are the skills you can acquire through practice, practice and practice.

I realize that there may be better methods to solve some of the problems presented in this book. It is entirely possible that despite my best efforts some inadvertent errors may have crept in. Please email me at xinfeng@quantfinanceinterviews.com if you have a better approach to solving some of these problems or find errors. I will be grateful for your feedback and will post corrections and your constructive feedback on the book's companion website http://www.quantfinanceinterviews.com. The website is a joint venture with my editor, Brett Jiu. You will also find some extra interview problems with answers that we have gathered.

I sincerely hope that you enjoy solving these problems and are successful in your interviews.

Xinfeng Zhou

Notations

$\forall$	for each/for every/for all
$\exists$	there exists
$\therefore$	therefore
$A \Rightarrow B$	whenever A is true, B is also true
s.t.	such that
$a \wedge b$	the minimum of a and b
$a \vee b$	the maximum of a and b
$\sum_{i=1}^{n} x_i$	$x_1 + x_2 + \cdots + x_n$
$\prod_{i=1}^{n} x_i$	$x_1 \times x_2 \times \cdots \times x_n$
$n!$	factorial of nonnegative integer n, $n! = \prod_{i=1}^{n} i$ $(0! = 1)$
$x \% y$	modulo operation
Φ	empty set
$\int f(x)dx$	indefinite integral of $f(x)$
$\int_{a}^{b} f(x)dx$	definite integral of $f(x)$ from a to b
x^+	$\max(x, 0)$
$N(\mu, \sigma^2)$	normal distribution with mean μ and variance σ^2
cdf	cumulative density function
pdf	probability density function

Chapter 1 General Principles

Let us begin this book by exploring five general principles that will be extremely helpful in your interview process. From my experience on both sides of the interview table, these general guidelines will better prepare you for job interviews and will likely make you a successful candidate.

1. Build a broad knowledge base

The length and the style of quant interviews differ from firm to firm. Landing a quant job may mean enduring hours of bombardment with brain teaser, calculus, linear algebra, probability theory, statistics, derivative pricing, or programming problems. To be a successful candidate, you need to have broad knowledge in mathematics, finance and programming.

Will all these topics be relevant for your future quant job? Probably not. Each specific quant position often requires only limited knowledge in these domains. General problem solving skills may make more difference than specific knowledge. Then why are quantitative interviews so comprehensive? There are at least two reasons for this:

The first reason is that interviewers often have diverse backgrounds. Each interviewer has his or her own favorite topics that are often related to his or her own educational background or work experience. As a result, the topics you will be tested on are likely to be very broad. The second reason is more fundamental. Your problem solving skills—a crucial requirement for any quant job—is often positively correlated to the breadth of your knowledge. A basic understanding of a broad range of topics often helps you better analyze problems, explore alternative approaches, and come up with efficient solutions. Besides, your responsibility may not be restricted to your own projects. You will be expected to contribute as a member of a bigger team. Having broad knowledge will help you contribute to the team's success as well.

The key here is "basic understanding." Interviewers do not expect you to be an expert on a specific subject—unless it happens to be your PhD thesis. The knowledge used in interviews, although broad, covers mainly essential concepts. This is exactly the reason why most of the books I refer to in the following chapters have the word "introduction" or "first" in the title. If I am allowed to give only one suggestion to a candidate, it will be **know the basics very well**.

2. Practice your interview skills

The interview process starts long before you step into an interview room. In a sense, the success or failure of your interview is often determined before the first question is asked. Your solutions to interview problems may fail to reflect your true intelligence and knowledge if you are unprepared. Although a complete review of quant interview problems is impossible and unnecessary, practice does improve your interview skills. Furthermore, many of the behavioral, technical and resume-related questions can be anticipated. So prepare yourself for potential questions long before you enter an interview room.

3. Listen carefully

You should be an active listener in interviews so that you understand the problems well before you attempt to answer them. If any aspect of a problem is not clear to you, politely ask for clarification. If the problem is more than a couple of sentences, jot down the key words to help you remember all the information. For complex problems, interviewers often give away some clues when they explain the problem. Even the assumptions they give may include some information as to how to approach the problem. So listen carefully and make sure you get the necessary information.

4. Speak your mind

When you analyze a problem and explore different ways to solve it, never do it silently. Clearly demonstrate your analysis and write down the important steps involved if necessary. This conveys your intelligence to the interviewer and shows that you are methodical and thorough. In case that you go astray, the interaction will also give your interviewer the opportunity to correct the course and provide you with some hints.

Speaking your mind does not mean explaining every tiny detail. If some conclusions are obvious to you, simply state the conclusion without the trivial details. More often than not, the interviewer uses a problem to test a specific concept/approach. You should focus on demonstrating your understanding of the key concept/approach instead of dwelling on less relevant details.

5. Make reasonable assumptions

In real job settings, you are unlikely to have all the necessary information or data you'd prefer to have before you build a model and make a decision. In interviews, interviewers may not give you all the necessary assumptions either. So it is up to you to make reasonable assumptions. The keyword here is reasonable. Explain your assumptions to the interviewer so that you will get immediate feedback. To solve quantitative problems, it is crucial that you can quickly make reasonable assumptions and design appropriate frameworks to solve problems based on the assumptions.

We are now ready to review basic concepts in quantitative finance subject areas and have fun solving real-world interview problems!

Chapter 2 Brain Teasers

In this chapter, we cover problems that only require common sense, logic, reasoning, and basic—no more than high school level—math knowledge to solve. In a sense, they are real brain teasers as opposed to mathematical problems in disguise. Although these brain teasers do not require specific math knowledge, they are no less difficult than other quantitative interview problems. Some of these problems test your analytical and general problem-solving skills; some require you to think out of the box; while others ask you to solve the problems using fundamental math techniques in a creative way. In this chapter, we review some interview problems to explain the general themes of brain teasers that you are likely to encounter in quantitative interviews.

2.1 Problem Simplification

If the original problem is so complex that you cannot come up with an immediate solution, try to identify a simplified version of the problem and start with it. Usually you can start with the simplest sub-problem and gradually increase the complexity. You do not need to have a defined plan at the beginning. Just try to solve the simplest cases and analyze your reasoning. More often than not, you will find a pattern that will guide you through the whole problem.

Screwy pirates

Five pirates looted a chest full of 100 gold coins. Being a bunch of democratic pirates, they agree on the following method to divide the loot:

The most senior pirate will propose a distribution of the coins. All pirates, *including the most senior pirate*, will then vote. If at least 50% of the pirates (3 pirates in this case) accept the proposal, the gold is divided as proposed. If not, the most senior pirate will be fed to shark and the process starts over with the next most senior pirate… The process is repeated until a plan is approved. You can assume that all pirates are perfectly rational: they want to stay alive first and to get as much gold as possible second. Finally, being blood-thirsty pirates, they want to have fewer pirates on the boat if given a choice between otherwise equal outcomes.

How will the gold coins be divided in the end?

Solution: If you have not studied game theory or dynamic programming, this strategy problem may appear to be daunting. If the problem with 5 pirates seems complex, we can always *start with a simplified version of the problem* by reducing the number of pirates. Since the solution to 1-pirate case is trivial, let's start with 2 pirates. The senior pirate (labeled as 2) can claim all the gold since he will always get 50% of the votes from himself and pirate 1 is left with nothing.

Let's add a more senior pirate, 3. He knows that if his plan is voted down, pirate 1 will get nothing. But if he offers private 1 nothing, pirate 1 will be happy to kill him. So pirate 3 will offer private 1 one coin and keep the remaining 99 coins, in which strategy the plan will have 2 votes from pirate 1 and 3.

If pirate 4 is added, he knows that if his plan is voted down, pirate 2 will get nothing. So pirate 2 will settle for one coin if pirate 4 offers one. So pirate 4 should offer pirate 2 one coin and keep the remaining 99 coins and his plan will be approved with 50% of the votes from pirate 2 and 4.

Now we finally come to the 5-pirate case. He knows that if his plan is voted down, both pirate 3 and pirate 1 will get nothing. So he only needs to offer pirate 1 and pirate 3 one coin each to get their votes and keep the remaining 98 coins. If he divides the coins this way, he will have three out of the five votes: from pirates 1 and 3 as well as himself.

Once we start with a simplified version and add complexity to it, the answer becomes obvious. Actually after the case $n = 5$, a clear pattern has emerged and we do not need to stop at 5 pirates. For any $2n + 1$ pirate case (n should be less than 99 though), the most senior pirate will offer pirates 1, 3, $\cdots$, and $2n - 1$ each one coin and keep the rest for himself.

Tiger and sheep

One hundred tigers and one sheep are put on a magic island that only has grass. Tigers can eat grass, but they would rather eat sheep. Assume: *A*. Each time only one tiger can eat one sheep, and that tiger itself will become a sheep after it eats the sheep. *B*. All tigers are smart and perfectly rational and they want to survive. So will the sheep be eaten?

Solution: 100 is a large number, so again let's *start with a simplified version of the problem*. If there is only 1 tiger ($n = 1$), surely it will eat the sheep since it does not need to worry about being eaten. How about 2 tigers? Since both tigers are perfectly rational, either tiger probably would do some thinking as to what will happen if it eats the sheep. Either tiger is probably thinking: if I eat the sheep, I will become a sheep; and then I will be eaten by the other tiger. So to guarantee the highest likelihood of survival, neither tiger will eat the sheep.

If there are 3 tigers, the sheep will be eaten since each tiger will realize that once it changes to a sheep, there will be 2 tigers left and it will not be eaten. So the first tiger that thinks this through will eat the sheep. If there are 4 tigers, each tiger will understand that if it eats the sheep, it will turn to a sheep. Since there are 3 other tigers, it will be eaten. So to guarantee the highest likelihood of survival, no tiger will eat the sheep.

Following the same logic, we can naturally show that if the number of tigers is even, the sheep will not be eaten. If the number is odd, the sheep will be eaten. For the case $n = 100$, the sheep will not be eaten.

2.2 Logic Reasoning

River crossing

Four people, A, B, C and D need to get across a river. The only way to cross the river is by an old bridge, which holds at most 2 people at a time. Being dark, they can't cross the bridge without a torch, of which they only have one. So each pair can only walk at the speed of the slower person. They need to get all of them across to the other side as quickly as possible. A is the slowest and takes 10 minutes to cross; B takes 5 minutes; C takes 2 minutes; and D takes 1 minute.

What is the minimum time to get all of them across to the other side?[1]

Solution: The key point is to realize that the 10-minute person should go with the 5-minute person and this should not happen in the first crossing, otherwise one of them have to go back. So C and D should go across first (2 min); then send D back (1min); A and B go across (10 min); send C back (2min); C and D go across again (2 min).

It takes 17 minutes in total. Alternatively, we can send C back first and then D back in the second round, which takes 17 minutes as well.

Birthday problem

You and your colleagues know that your boss A's birthday is one of the following 10 dates:

Mar 4, Mar 5, Mar 8

Jun 4, Jun 7

Sep 1, Sep 5

Dec 1, Dec 2, Dec 8

A told you only the month of his birthday, and told your colleague C only the day. After that, you first said: "I don't know A's birthday; C doesn't know it either." After hearing

---

[1] Hint: The key is to realize that A and B should get across the bridge together.

what you said, C replied: "I didn't know A's birthday, but now I know it." You smiled and said: "Now I know it, too." After looking at the 10 dates and hearing your comments, your administrative assistant wrote down A's birthday without asking any questions. So what did the assistant write?

Solution: Don't let the "he said, she said" part confuses you. Just interpret the logic behind each individual's comments and try your best to derive useful information from these comments.

Let D be the day of the month of A's birthday, we have $D \in \{1, 2, 4, 5, 7, 8\}$. If the birthday is on a unique day, C will know the A's birthday immediately. Among possible Ds, 2 and 7 are unique days. Considering that you are sure that C does not know A's birthday, you must infer that the day the C was told of is not 2 or 7. Conclusion: the month is not June or December. (If the month had been June, the day C was told of may have been 2; if the month had been December, the day C was told of may have been 7.)

Now C knows that the month must be either March or September. He immediately figures out A's birthday, which means the day must be unique in the March and September list. It means A's birthday cannot be Mar 5, or Sep 5. Conclusion: the birthday must be Mar 4, Mar 8 or Sep 1.

Among these three possibilities left, Mar 4 and Mar 8 have the same month. So if the month you have is March, you still cannot figure out A's birthday. Since you can figure out A's birthday, A's birthday must be Sep 1. Hence, the assistant must have written Sep 1.

Card game

A casino offers a card game using a normal deck of 52 cards. The rule is that you turn over two cards each time. For each pair, if both are black, they go to the dealer's pile; if both are red, they go to your pile; if one black and one red, they are discarded. The process is repeated until you two go through all 52 cards. If you have more cards in your pile, you win $100; otherwise (including ties) you get nothing. The casino allows you to negotiate the price you want to pay for the game. How much would you be willing to pay to play this game?[2]

Solution: This surely is an insidious casino. No matter how the cards are arranged, you and the dealer will always have the same number of cards in your piles. Why? Because each pair of discarded cards have one black card and one red card, so equal number of

---

[2] Hint: Try to approach the problem using symmetry. Each discarded pair has one black and one red card. What does that tell you as to the number of black and red cards in the rest two piles?

red and black cards are discarded. As a result, the number of red cards left for you and the number of black cards left for the dealer are always the same. The dealer always wins! So we should not pay anything to play the game.

Burning ropes

You have two ropes, each of which takes 1 hour to burn. But either rope has different densities at different points, so there's no guarantee of consistency in the time it takes different sections within the rope to burn. How do you use these two ropes to measure 45 minutes?

Solution: This is a classic brain teaser question. For a rope that takes x minutes to burn, if you light both ends of the rope simultaneously, it takes $x/2$ minutes to burn. So we should light both ends of the first rope and light one end of the second rope. 30 minutes later, the first rope will get completely burned, while that second rope now becomes a 30-min rope. At that moment, we can light the second rope at the other end (with the first end still burning), and when it is burned out, the total time is exactly 45 minutes.

Defective ball

You have 12 identical balls. One of the balls is heavier OR lighter than the rest (you don't know which). Using just a balance that can only show you which side of the tray is heavier, how can you determine which ball is the defective one with 3 measurements?[3]

Solution: This weighing problem is another classic brain teaser and is still being asked by many interviewers. The total number of balls often ranges from 8 to more than 100. Here we use $n = 12$ to show the fundamental approach. The key is to separate the original group (as well as any intermediate subgroups) into three sets instead of two. The reason is that the comparison of the first two groups always gives information about the third group.

Considering that the solution is wordy to explain, I draw a tree diagram in Figure 2.1 to show the approach in detail. Label the balls 1 through 12 and separate them to three groups with 4 balls each. Weigh balls 1, 2, 3, 4 against balls 5, 6, 7, 8. Then we go on to explore two possible scenarios: two groups balance, as expressed using an "=" sign, or 1,

---

[3] Hint: First do it for 9 identical balls and use only 2 measurements, knowing that one is heavier than the rest.

2, 3, 4 are lighter than 5, 6, 7, 8, as expressed using an "<" sign. There is no need to explain the scenario that 1, 2, 3, 4 are heavier than 5, 6, 7, 8. (Why?[4])

If the two groups balance, this immediately tells us that the defective ball is in 9, 10, 11 and 12, and it is either lighter (*L*) or heavier (*H*) than other balls. Then we take 9, 10 and 11 from group 3 and compare balls 9, 10 with 8, 11. Here we have already figured out that 8 is a normal ball. If 9, 10 are lighter, it must mean either 9 or 10 is *L* or 11 is *H*. In which case, we just compare 9 with 10. If 9 is lighter, 9 is the defective one and it is *L*; if 9 and 10 balance, then 11 must be defective and *H*; If 9 is heavier, 10 is the defective one and it is *L*. If 9, 10 and 8, 11 balance, 12 is the defective one. If 9, 10 is heavier, than either 9 or 10 is *H*, or 11 is *L*.

You can easily follow the tree in Figure 2.1 for further analysis and it is clear from the tree that all possible scenarios can be resolved in 3 measurements.

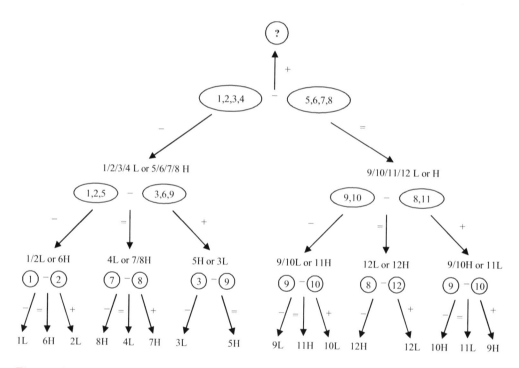

Figure 2.1 Tree diagram to identify the defective ball in 12 balls

In general if you have the information as to whether the defective ball is heavier or

---

[4] Here is where the symmetry idea comes in. Nothing makes the 1, 2, 3, 4 or 5, 6, 7, 8 labels special. If 1, 2, 3, 4 are heavier than 5, 6, 7, 8, let's just exchange the labels of these two groups. Again we have the case of 1, 2, 3, 4 being lighter than 5, 6, 7, 8.

lighter, you can identify the defective ball among up to 3^n balls using no more than n measurements since each weighing reduces the problem size by 2/3. If you have no information as to whether the defective ball is heavier or lighter, you can identify the defective ball among up to $(3^n - 3)/2$ balls using no more than n measurements.

Trailing zeros

How many trailing zeros are there in 100! (factorial of 100)?

Solution: This is an easy problem. We know that each pair of 2 and 5 will give a trailing zero. If we perform prime number decomposition on all the numbers in 100!, it is obvious that the frequency of 2 will far outnumber of the frequency of 5. So the frequency of 5 determines the number of trailing zeros. Among numbers $1, 2, \cdots, 99$, and 100, 20 numbers are divisible by 5 ($5, 10, \cdots, 100$). Among these 20 numbers, 4 are divisible by 5^2 ($25, 50, 75, 100$). So the total frequency of 5 is 24 and there are 24 trailing zeros.

Horse race

There are 25 horses, each of which runs at a constant speed that is different from the other horses'. Since the track only has 5 lanes, each race can have at most 5 horses. If you need to find the 3 fastest horses, what is the minimum number of races needed to identify them?

Solution: This problem tests your basic analytical skills. To find the 3 fastest horses, surely all horses need to be tested. So a natural first step is to divide the horses to 5 groups (with horses 1-5, 6-10, 11-15, 16-20, 21-25 in each group). After 5 races, we will have the order within each group, let's assume the order follows the order of numbers (e.g., 6 is the fastest and 10 is the slowest in the 6-10 group)[5]. That means 1, 6, 11, 16 and 21 are the fastest within each group.

Surely the last two horses within each group are eliminated. What else can we infer? We know that within each group, if the fastest horse ranks 5th or 4th among 25 horses, then all horses in that group cannot be in top 3; if it ranks the 3rd, no other horse in that group can be in the top 3; if it ranks the 2nd, then one other horse in that group may be in top 3; if it ranks the first, then two other horses in that group may be in top 3.

---

[5] Such an assumption does not affect the generality of the solution. If the order is not as described, just change the labels of the horses.

So let's race horses 1, 6, 11, 16 and 21. Again without loss of generality, let's assume the order is 1, 6, 11, 16 and 21. Then we immediately know that horses 4-5, 8-10, 12-15, 16-20 and 21-25 are eliminated. Since 1 is fastest among all the horses, 1 is in. We need to determine which two among horses 2, 3, 6, 7 and 11 are in top 3, which only takes one extra race.

So all together we need 7 races (in 3 rounds) to identify the 3 fastest horses.

Infinite sequence

If $x^\wedge x^\wedge x^\wedge x^\wedge x \cdots = 2$, where $x^\wedge y = x^y$, what is x?

Solution: This problem appears to be difficult, but a simple analysis will give an elegant solution. What do we have from the original equation?

$\lim_{n\to\infty} \underbrace{x^\wedge x^\wedge x^\wedge x^\wedge x \cdots}_{n\ terms} = 2 \Leftrightarrow \lim_{n\to\infty} \underbrace{x^\wedge x^\wedge x^\wedge x^\wedge x \cdots}_{n-1\ terms} = 2$. In other words, as $n \to \infty$, adding or minus one $x^\wedge$ should yield the same result.

so $x^\wedge x^\wedge x^\wedge x^\wedge x \cdots = x^\wedge (x^\wedge x^\wedge x^\wedge x \cdots) = x^\wedge 2 = 2 \Rightarrow x = \sqrt{2}$.

2.3 Thinking Out of the Box

Box packing

Can you pack 53 bricks of dimensions $1 \times 1 \times 4$ into a $6 \times 6 \times 6$ box?

Solution: This is a nice problem extended from a popular chess board problem. In that problem, you have a 8×8 chess board with two small squares at the opposite diagonal corners removed. You have many bricks with dimension 1×2. Can you pack 31 bricks into the remaining 62 squares? (An alternative question is whether you can cover all 62 squares using bricks without any bricks overlapping with each other or sticking out of the board, which requires a similar analysis.)

A real chess board figure surely helps the visualization. As shown in Figure 2.2, when a chess board is filled with alternative black and white squares, both squares at the opposite diagonal corners have the same color. If you put a 1×2 brick on the board, it will always cover one black square and one white square. Let's say it's the two black corner squares were removed, then the rest of the board can fit at most 30 bricks since we only have 30 black squares left (and each brick requires one black square). So to pack 31 bricks is out of the question. To cover all 62 squares without overlapping or overreaching, we must have exactly 31 bricks. Yet we have proved that 31 bricks cannot fit in the 62 squares left, so you cannot find a way to fill in all 62 squares without overlapping or overreaching.

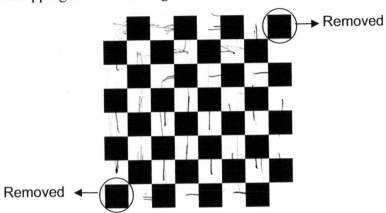

Figure 2.2 Chess board with alternative black and white squares

Just as any good trading strategy, if more and more people get to know it and replicate it, the effectiveness of such a strategy will disappear. As the chess board problem becomes popular, many interviewees simply commit it to memory (after all, it's easy to remember the answer). So some ingenious interviewer came up with the newer version to test your thinking process, or at least your ability to extend your knowledge to new problems.

If we look at the total volume in this 3D problem, 53 bricks have a volume of 212, which is smaller then the box's volume 216. Yet we can show it is impossible to pack all the bricks into the box using a similar approach as the chess board problem. Let's imagine that the $6\times6\times6$ box is actually comprised of small $2\times2\times2$ cubes. There should be 27 small cubes. Similar to the chess board (but in 3D), imagine that we have black cubes and white cubes alternates—it does take a little 3D visualization. So we have either 14 black cubes & 13 white cubes or 13 black cubes & 14 white cubes. For any $1\times1\times4$ brick that we pack into the box, half ($1\times1\times2$) of it must be in a black $2\times2\times2$ cube and the other half must be in a white $2\times2\times2$ cube. The problem is that each $2\times2\times2$ cube can only be used by 4 of the $1\times1\times4$ bricks. So for the color with 13 cubes, be it black or white, we can only use them for 52 $1\times1\times4$ tubes. There is no way to place the 53th brick. So we cannot pack 53 bricks of dimensions $1\times1\times4$ into a $6\times6\times6$ box.

Calendar cubes

You just had two dice custom-made. Instead of numbers $1-6$, you place single-digit numbers on the faces of each dice so that every morning you can arrange the dice in a way as to make the two front faces show the current day of the month. You must use both dice (in other words, days $1-9$ must be shown as $01-09$), but you can switch the order of the dice if you want. What numbers do you have to put on the six faces of each of the two dice to achieve that?

Solution: The days of a month include 11 and 22, so both dice must have 1 and 2. To express single-digit days, we need to have at least a 0 in one dice. Let's put a 0 in dice one first. Considering that we need to express all single digit days and dice two cannot have all the digits from 1 – 9, it's necessary to have a 0 in dice two as well in order to express all single-digit days.

So far we have assigned the following numbers:

Dice one	1	2	0	?	?	?
Dice two	1	2	0	?	?	?

If we can assign all the rest of digits 3, 4, 5, 6, 7, 8, and 9 to the rest of the faces, the problem is solved. But there are 7 digits left. What can we do? Here's where you need to think out of the box. We can use a 6 as a 9 since they will never be needed at the same time! So, simply put 3, 4, and 5 on one dice and 6, 7, and 8 on the other dice, and the final numbers on the two dice are:

Dice one	1	2	0	3	4	5
Dice two	1	2	0	6	7	8

Door to offer

You are facing two doors. One leads to your job offer and the other leads to exit. In front of either door is a guard. One guard always tells lies and the other always tells the truth. You can only ask one guard one yes/no question. Assuming you do want to get the job offer, what question will you ask?

Solution: This is another classic brain teaser (maybe a little out-of-date in my opinion). One popular answer is to ask one guard: "Would the other guard say that you are guarding the door to the offer?" If he answers yes, choose the other door; if he answers no, choose the door this guard is standing in front of.

There are two possible scenarios:

1. Truth teller guards the door to offer; Liar guards the door to exit.
2. Truth teller guards the door to exit; Liar guards the door to offer.

If we ask a guard a direct question such as "Are you guarding the door to the offer?" For scenario 1, both guards will answer yes; for scenario 2, both guards will answer no. So a direct question does not help us solve the problem. The key is to involve both guards in the questions as the popular answer does. For scenario 1, if we happen to choose the truth teller, he will answer no since the liar will say no; if we happen to choose the liar guard, he will answer yes since the truth teller will say no. For scenario 2, if we happen to choose the truth teller, he will answer yes since the liar will say yes; if we happen to choose the liar guard, he will answer no since the truth teller with say yes. So for both scenarios, if the answer is no, we choose that door; if the answer is yes, we choose the other door.

Message delivery

You need to communicate with your colleague in Greenwich via a messenger service. Your documents are sent in a padlock box. Unfortunately the messenger service is not secure, so anything inside an unlocked box will be lost (including any locks you place inside the box) during the delivery. The high-security padlocks you and your colleague each use have only one key which the person placing the lock owns. How can you securely send a document to your colleague?[6]

Solution: If you have a document to deliver, clearly you cannot deliver it in an unlocked box. So the first step is to deliver it to Greenwich in a locked box. Since you are the person who has the key to that lock, your colleague cannot open the box to get the document. Somehow you need to remove the lock before he can get the document, which means the box should be sent back to you before your colleague can get the document.

So what can he do before he sends back the box? He can place a second lock on the box, which he has the key to! Once the box is back to you, you remove your own lock and send the box back to your colleague. He opens his own lock and gets the document.

Last ball

A bag has 20 blue balls and 14 red balls. Each time you randomly take two balls out. (Assume each ball in the bag has equal probability of being taken). You do not put these two balls back. Instead, if both balls have the same color, you add a blue ball to the bag; if they have different colors, you add a red ball to the bag. Assume that you have an unlimited supply of blue and red balls, if you keep on repeating this process, what will be the color of the last ball left in the bag?[7] What if the bag has 20 blue balls and 13 red balls instead?

---

[6] Hint: You can have more than one lock on the box.
[7] Hint: Consider the changes in the number of red and blue balls after each step.

Solution: Once you understand the hint, this problem should be an easy one. Let (B, R) represent the number of blue balls and red balls in the bag. We can take a look what will happen after two balls are taken out.

Both balls are blue: $(B, R) \rightarrow (B-1, R)$

Both balls are red: $(B, R) \rightarrow (B+1, R-2)$

One red and one blue: $(B, R) \rightarrow (B-1, R)$

Notice that R either stays the same or decreases by 2, so the number of red balls will never become odd if we begin with 14 red balls. We also know that the total number of balls decreases by one each time until only one ball is left. Combining the information we have, the last ball must be a blue one. Similarly, when we start with odd number of red balls, the final ball must be a red one.

Light switches

There is a light bulb inside a room and four switches outside. All switches are currently at off state and only one switch controls the light bulb. You may turn any number of switches on or off any number of times you want. How many times do you need to go into the room to figure out which switch controls the light bulb?

Solution: You may have seen the classical version of this problem with 3 light bulbs inside the room and 3 switches outside. Although this problem is slightly modified, the approach is exact the same. Whether the light is on and off is binary, which only allows us to distinguish two switches. If we have another binary factor, there are $2 \times 2 = 4$ possible combinations of scenarios, so we can distinguish 4 switches. Besides light, a light bulb also emits heat and becomes hot after the bulb has been lit for some time. So we can use the on/off and cold/hot combination to decide which one of the four switches controls the light.

Turn on switches 1 and 2; move on to solve some other puzzles or do whatever you like for a while; turn off switch 2 and turn on switch 3; get into the room quickly, touch the bulb and observe whether the light is on or off.

The light bulb is on and hot → switch 1 controls the light;

The light bulb is off and hot → switch 2 controls the light;

The light bulb is on and cold → switch 3 controls the light;

The light bulb is off and cold → switch 4 controls the light.

Quant salary

Eight quants from different banks are getting together for drinks. They are all interested in knowing the average salary of the group. Nevertheless, being cautious and humble individuals, everyone prefers not to disclose his or her own salary to the group. Can you come up with a strategy for the quants to calculate the average salary without knowing other people's salaries?

Solution: This is a light-hearted problem and has more than one answer. One approach is for the first quant to choose a random number, adds it to his/her salary and gives it to the second quant. The second quant will add his/her own salary to the result and give it to the third quant; ...; the eighth quant will add his/her own salary to the result and give it back to the first quant. Then the first quant will deduct the "random" number from the total and divide the "real" total by 8 to yield the average salary.

You may be wondering whether this strategy has any use except being a good brain teaser to test interviewees. It does have applications in practice. For example, a third party data provider collect fund holding position data (securities owned by a fund and the number of shares) from all participating firms and then distribute the information back to participants. Surely most participants do not want others to figure out what they are holding. If each position in the fund has the same fund ID every day, it's easy to reverse-engineer the fund from the holdings and to replicate the strategy. So different random numbers (or more exactly pseudo-random numbers since the provider knows what number is added to the fund ID of each position and complicated algorithm is involved to make the mapping one to one) are added to the fund ID of each position in the funds before distribution. As a result, the positions in the same fund appear to have different fund IDs. That prevents participants from re-constructing other funds. Using this approach, the participants can share market information and remain anonymous at the same time.

2.4 Application of Symmetry

Coin piles

Suppose that you are blind-folded in a room and are told that there are 1000 coins on the floor. 980 of the coins have tails up and the other 20 coins have heads up. Can you separate the coins into two piles so to guarantee both piles have equal number of heads? Assume that you cannot tell a coin's side by touching it, but you are allowed to turn over any number of coins.

Solution: Let's say that we separate the 1000 coins into two piles with n coins in one pile and $1000 - n$ coins in the other. If there are m coins in the first pile with heads up, there must be $20 - m$ coins in the second pile with heads up. We also know that there are $n - m$ coins in the first pile with tails up. We clearly cannot guarantee that $m = 10$ by simply adjusting n.

What other options do we have? We can turn over coins if we want to. Since we have no way of knowing what a coin's side is, it won't guarantee anything if we selectively flip coins. However, if we flip all the coins in the first pile, all heads become tails and all tails become heads. As a result, it will have $n - m$ heads and m tails (symmetry). So, to start, we need to make the number of tails in the original first pile equal to the number of heads in the second pile; in other words, to make $n - m = 20 - m$. $n = 20$ makes the equation hold. If we take 20 coins at random and turn them all over, the number of heads among these turned-over 20 coins should be the same as the number of heads among the other 980 coins.

Mislabeled bags

You are given three bags of fruits. One has apples in it; one has oranges in it; and one has a mix of apples and oranges in it. Each bag has a label on it (apple, orange or mix). Unfortunately, your manager tells you that ALL bags are mislabeled. Develop a strategy to identify the bags by taking out minimum number of fruits? You can take any number of fruits from any bags.[8]

Solution: The key here is to use the fact that ALL bags are mislabeled. For example, a bag labeled with apple must contain either oranges only or a mix of oranges and apples. Let's look at the labels: orange, apple, mix (orange + apple). Have you realized that the orange label and the apple label are symmetric? If not, let me explain it in detail: If you pick a fruit from the bag with the orange label and it's an apple (orange $\rightarrow$ apple), then the bag is either all apples or a mix. If you pick a fruit from the bag with the apple label and it's an orange (apple $\rightarrow$ orange), then the bag is either an orange bag or a mix. Symmetric labels are not exciting and are unlikely to be the correct approach. So let's try the bag with the mix label and get one fruit from it. If the fruit we get is an orange, then we know that bag is actually orange (It cannot be a mix of oranges and apples since we know the bag's label is wrong). Since the bag with the apple label cannot be apple only, it must be the mix bag. And the bag with the orange label must be the apple bag. Similarly, for the case that apples are in the bag with the mix label, we can figure out all the bags using one single pick.

---

[8] The problem struck me as a word game when I first saw it. But it does test a candidate's attention to details besides his or her logic reasoning skills.

Wise men

A sultan has captured 50 wise men. He has a glass currently standing bottom down. Every minute he calls one of the wise men who can choose either to turn it over (set it upside down or bottom down) or to do nothing. The wise men will be called randomly, possibly for an infinite number of times. When someone called to the sultan correctly states that all wise men have already been called to the sultan at least once, everyone goes free. But if his statement is wrong, the sultan puts everyone to death. The wise men are allowed to communicate only once before they get imprisoned into separate rooms (one per room). Design a strategy that lets the wise men go free.

Solution: For the strategy to work, one wise man, let's call him the spokesman, will state that every one has been called. What does that tell us? 1. All the other 49 wise men are equivalent (symmetric). 2. The spokesman is different from the other 49 men. So naturally those 49 equivalent wise men should act in the same way and the spokesman should act differently.

Here is one of such strategies: Every one of the 49 (equivalent) wise men should flip the glass upside down the first time that he sees the glass bottom down. He does nothing if the glass is already upside down or he has flipped the glass once. The spokesman should flip the glass bottom down each time he sees the glass upside down and he should do nothing if the glass is already bottom down. After he does the 49th flip, which means all the other 49 wise men have been called, he can declare that all the wise men have been called.

2.5 Series Summation

Here is a famous story about the legendary mathematician/physicist Gauss: When he was a child, his teacher gave the children a boring assignment to add the numbers from 1 to 100. To the amazement of the teacher, Gauss turned in his answer in less than a minute. Here is his approach:

$$
\left.
\begin{array}{l}
\sum_{n=1}^{100} n = 1\ +\ 2 + \cdots + 99 + 100 \\
\qquad +\quad +\qquad\ +\quad\ + \\
\sum_{n=1}^{100} n = 100 + 99 + \cdots +\ 2\ +\ 1
\end{array}
\right\} \Rightarrow
$$

$$
2\sum_{n=1}^{100} n = 101 + 101 + \cdots + 101 + 101 = 101 \times 100 \Rightarrow \sum_{n=1}^{100} n = \frac{100 \times 101}{2}
$$

This approach can be generalized to any integer N: $\sum_{n=1}^{N} n = \dfrac{N(N+1)}{2}$

The summation formula for consecutive squares may not be as intuitive:

$$\sum_{n=1}^{N} n^2 = \frac{N(N+1)(2N+1)}{6} = \frac{N^3}{3} + \frac{N^2}{2} + \frac{N}{6}.$$

But if we correctly guess that $\sum_{n=1}^{N} n^2 = aN^3 + bN^2 + cN + d$ and apply the initial conditions

$N = 0 \Rightarrow 0 = d$

$N = 1 \Rightarrow 1 = a + b + c + d$

$N = 2 \Rightarrow 5 = 8a + 4b + 2c + d$

$N = 3 \Rightarrow 14 = 27a + 9b + 3c + d$

we will have the solution that a = 1/3, b = 1/2, c = 1/6, d = 0. We can then easily show that the same equation applies to all N by induction.

Clock pieces

A clock (numbered 1 – 12 clockwise) fell off the wall and broke into three pieces. You find that the sums of the numbers on each piece are equal. What are the numbers on each piece? (No strange-shaped piece is allowed.)

Solution: Using the summation equation, $\sum_{n=1}^{12} n = \dfrac{12 \times 13}{2} = 78$. So the numbers on each piece must sum up to 26. Some interviewees mistakenly assume that the numbers on each piece have to be continuous because no strange-shaped piece is allowed. It's easy to see that 5, 6, 7 and 8 add up to 26. Then the interviewees' thinking gets stuck because they cannot find more consecutive numbers that add up to 26.

Such an assumption is not correct since 12 and 1 are continuous on a clock. Once that wrong assumption is removed, it becomes clear that $12 + 1 = 13$ and $11 + 2 = 13$. So the second piece is 11, 12, 1 and 2; the third piece is 3, 4, 9 and 10.

Missing integers

Suppose we have 98 distinct integers from 1 to 100. What is a good way to find out the two missing integers (within [1, 100])?

Solution: Denote the missing integers as x and y, and the existing ones are $z_1, \cdots, z_{98}$. Applying the summation equations, we have

$$\sum_{n=1}^{100} n = x + y + \sum_{i=1}^{98} z_i \Rightarrow x + y = \frac{100 \times 101}{2} - \sum_{i=1}^{98} z_i$$

$$\sum_{n=1}^{100} n^2 = x^2 + y^2 + \sum_{i=1}^{98} z_i^2 \Rightarrow x^2 + y^2 = \frac{100^3}{3} + \frac{100^2}{2} + \frac{100}{6} - \sum_{i=1}^{98} z_i^2$$

Using these two equations, we can easily solve x and y. If you implement this strategy using a computer program, it is apparent that the algorithm has a complexity of $O(n)$ for two missing integers in 1 to n.

Counterfeit coins I

There are 10 bags with 100 identical coins in each bag. In all bags but one, each coin weighs 10 grams. However, all the coins in the counterfeit bag weigh either 9 or 11 grams. Can you find the counterfeit bag in only one weighing, using a digital scale that tells the exact weight? [9]

Solution: Yes, we can identify the counterfeit bag using one measurement. Take 1 coin out of the first bag, 2 out of the second bag, 3 out the third bag, $\cdots$, and 10 coins out of the tenth bag. All together, there are $\sum_{i=1}^{10} n = 55$ coins. If there were no counterfeit coins, they should weigh 550 grams. Let's assume the i-th bag is the counterfeit bag, there will be i counterfeit coins, so the final weight will be $550 \pm i$. Since i is distinct for each bag, we can identify the counterfeit coin bag as well as whether the counterfeit coins are lighter or heavier than the real coins using $550 \pm i$.

This is not the only answer: we can choose other numbers of coins from each bag as long as they are all different numbers.

Glass balls

You are holding two glass balls in a 100-story building. If a ball is thrown out of the window, it will not break if the floor number is less than X, and it will always break if

---

[9] Hint: In order to find the counterfeit coin bag in one weighing, the number of coins from each bag must be different. If we use the same number of coins from two bags, symmetry will prevent you from distinguish these two bags if one is the counterfeit coin bag.

the floor number is equal to or greater than X. You would like to determine X. What is the strategy that will minimize the number of drops for the worst case scenario? [10]

Solution: Suppose that we have a strategy with a maximum of N throws. For the first throw of ball one, we can try the N-th floor. If the ball breaks, we can start to try the second ball from the first floor and increase the floor number by one until the second ball breaks. At most, there are $N-1$ floors to test. So a maximum of N throws are enough to cover all possibilities. If the first ball thrown out of N-th floor does not break, we have $N-1$ throws left. This time we can only increase the floor number by $N-1$ for the first ball since the second ball can only cover $N-2$ floors if the first ball breaks. If the first ball thrown out of $(2N-1)$th floor does not break, we have $N-2$ throws left. So we can only increase the floor number by $N-2$ for the first ball since the second ball can only cover $N-3$ floors if the first ball breaks...

Using such logic, we can see that the number of floors that these two balls can cover with a maximum of N throws is $N+(N-1)+\cdots+1 = N(N+1)/2$. In order to cover 100 stories, we need to have $N(N+1)/2 \geq 100$. Taking the smallest integer, we have $N=14$.

Basically, we start the first ball on the 14th floor, if the ball breaks, we can use the second ball to try floors $1, 2, \cdots, 13$ with a maximum throws of 14 (when the 13th or the 14th floor is X). If the first ball does not break, we will try the first ball on the $14+(14-1)=27$th floor. If it breaks, we can use the second ball to cover floors $15, 16, \cdots, 26$ with a total maximum throws of 14 as well...

2.6 The Pigeon Hole Principle

Here is the basic version of the Pigeon Hole Principle: if you have fewer pigeon holes than pigeons and you put every pigeon in a pigeon hole, then at least one pigeon hole has more than one pigeon. Basically it says that if you have n holes and more than $n+1$ pigeons, at least 2 pigeons have to share one of the holes. The generalized version is that if you have n holes and at least $mn+1$ pigeons, at least $m+1$ pigeons have to share one of the holes. These simple and intuitive ideas are surprisingly useful in many problems. Here we will use some examples to show their applications.

---

[10] Hint: Assume we design a strategy with N maximum throws. If the first ball is thrown once, the second ball can cover $N-1$ floors; if the first ball is thrown twice, the second ball can cover $N-2$ floors...

Matching socks

Your drawer contains 2 red socks, 20 yellow socks and 31 blue socks. Being a busy and absent-minded MIT student, you just randomly grab a number of socks out of the draw and try to find a matching pair. Assume each sock has equal probability of being selected, what is the minimum number of socks you need to grab in order to guarantee a pair of socks of the same color?

Solution: This question is just a variation of the even simpler version of two-color-socks problem, in which case you only need 3. When you have 3 colors (3 pigeon holes), by the Pigeon Hole Principle, you will need to have $3+1=4$ socks (4 pigeons) to guarantee that at least two socks have the same color (2 pigeons share a hole).

Handshakes

You are invited to a welcome party with 25 fellow team members. Each of the fellow members shakes hands with you to welcome you. Since a number of people in the room haven't met each other, there's a lot of random handshaking among others as well. If you don't know the total number of handshakes, can you say with certainty that there are at least two people present who shook hands with exactly the same number of people?

Solution: There are 26 people at the party and each shakes hands with from 1—since everyone shakes hands with you—to 25 people. In other words, there are 26 pigeons and 25 holes. As a result, at least two people must have shaken hands with exactly the same number of people.

Have we met before?

Show me that, if there are 6 people at a party, then either at least 3 people met each other before the party, or at least 3 people were strangers before the party.

Solution: This question appears to be a complex one and interviewees often get puzzled by what the interviewer exactly wants. But once you start to analyze possible scenarios, the answer becomes obvious.

Let's say that you are the 6th person at the party. Then by generalized Pigeon Hole Principle (Do we even need that for such an intuitive conclusion?), among the remaining 5 people, we conclude that either at least 3 people met you or at least 3 people did not meet you. Now let's explore these two mutually exclusive and collectively exhaustive scenarios:

Case 1: Suppose that at least 3 people have met you before.

If two people in this group met each other, you and the pair (3 people) met each other. If no pair among these people met each other, then these people (≥ 3 people) did not meet each other. In either sub-case, the conclusion holds.

Case 2: Suppose at least 3 people have not met you before.

If two people in this group did not meet each other, you and the pair (3 people) did not meet each other. If all pairs among these people knew each other, then these people (≥ 3 people) met each other. Again, in either sub-case, the conclusion holds.

Ants on a square

There are 51 ants on a square with side length of 1. If you have a glass with a radius of 1/7, can you put your glass at a position on the square to guarantee that the glass encompasses at least 3 ants?[11]

Solution: To guarantee that the glass encompasses at least 3 ants, we can separate the square into 25 smaller areas. Applying the generalized Pigeon Hole Principle, we can show that at least one of the areas must have at least 3 ants. So we only need to make sure that the glass is large enough to cover any of the 25 smaller areas. Simply separate the area into 5×5 smaller squares with side length of 1/5 each will do since a circle with radius of 1/7 can cover a square[12] with side length 1/5.

Counterfeit coins II

There are 5 bags with 100 coins in each bag. A coin can weigh 9 grams, 10 grams or 11 grams. Each bag contains coins of equal weight, but we do not know what type of coins a bag contains. You have a digital scale (the kind that tells the exact weight). How many times do you need to use the scale to determine which type of coin each bag contains?[13]

Solution: If the answer for 5 bags is not obvious, let's start with the simplest version of the problem—1 bag. We only need to take one coin to weigh it. Now we can move on to 2 bags. How many coins do we need to take from bag 2 in order to determine the coin types of bag 1 and bag 2? Considering that there are three possible types for bag 1, we will need three coins from bag 2; two coins won't do. For notation simplicity, let's change the number/weight for three types to -1, 0 and 1 (by removing the mean 10). If

---

[11] Hint: Separate the square into 25 smaller areas; then at least one area has 3 ants in it.
[12] A circle with radius r can cover a square with side length up to $\sqrt{2} r$ and $\sqrt{2} \approx 1.414$.
[13] Hint: Start with a simpler problem. What if you have two bags of coins instead of 5, how many coins do you need from each bag to find the type of coins in either bag? What is the minimum difference in coin numbers? Then how about three bags?

we only use 2 coins from bag 2, the final sum for 1 coin from bag 1 and 2 coins from bag 2 ranges from -3 to 3 (7 pigeon holes). At the same time we have 9 (3×3) possible combinations for the weights of coins in bag 1 and bag 2 (9 pigeons). So at least two combinations will yield the same final sum (9>7, so at least two pigeons need to share one hole), and we can not distinguish them. If we use 3 coins from bag 2, then the sum ranges from -4 to 4, which is possible to cover all 9 combinations. The following table exactly shows that all possible combinations yield different sums:

Sum	1 coin, bag 1		
C2＼C1	-1	0	1
-1	-4	-3	-2
0	-1	0	1
1	2	3	4

(3 Coins, Bag 2)

C1and C2 represent the weights of coins from bag 1 and 2 respectively.

Then how about 3 bags? We are going to have $3^3 = 27$ possible combinations. Surely an indicator ranging from -13 to 13 will cover it and we will need 9 coins from bag 3. The possible combinations are shown in the following table:

Sum	C2 = -1			C2=0			C2=1		
C3＼C1	-1	0	1	-1	0	1	-1	0	1
-1	-13	-12	-11	-10	-9	-8	-7	-6	-5
0	-4	-3	-2	-1	0	1	2	3	4
1	5	6	7	8	9	10	11	12	13

(9 Coins, Bag 3)

C1, C2, and C3 represent the weights of coins from bag 1, 2, and 3 respectively.

Following this logic, it is easy to see that we will need 27 coins from bag 4 and 81 coins from bag 5. So the answer is to take 1, 3, 9, 27 and 81 coins from bags 1, 2, 3, 4, and 5, respectively, to determine which type of coins each bag contains using a single weighing.

2.7 Modular Arithmetic

The modulo operation—denoted as $x\%y$ or $x \bmod y$—finds the remainder of division of number x by another number y. For simpicility, we only consider the case where y is a positive integer. For example, $5\%3 = 2$. An intuitive property of modulo operation is that if $x_1 \% y = x_2 \% y$, then $(x_1 - x_2)\% y = 0$. From this property we can also show that $x\%y$, $(x+1)\%y$, $\cdots$, and $(x+y-1)\%y$ are all different numbers.

Prisoner problem

One hundred prisoners are given the chance to be set free tomorrow. They are all told that each will be given a red or blue hat to wear. Each prisoner can see everyone else's hat but not his own. The hat colors are assigned randomly and once the hats are placed on top of each prisoner's head they cannot communicate with one another in any form, or else they are immediately executed. The prisoners will be called out in random order and the prisoner called out will guess the color of his hat. Each prisoner declares the color of his hat so that everyone else can hear it. If a prisoner guesses correctly the color of his hat, he is set free immediately; otherwise he is executed.

They are given the night to come up with a strategy among themselves to save as many prisoners as possible. What is the best strategy they can adopt and how many prisoners can they guarantee to save?[14]

Solution: At least 99 prisoners can be saved.

The key lies in the first prisoner who can see everyone else's hat. He declares his hat to be red if the number of red hats he sees is odd. Otherwise he declares his hat to be blue. He will have a 1/2 chance of having guessed correctly. Everyone else is able to deduce his own hat color combining the knowledge whether the number of red hats is odd among 99 prisoners (excluding the first) and the color of the other 98 prisoners (excluding the first and himself). For example, if the number of red hats is odd among the other 99 prisoners. A prisoner wearing a red hat will see even number of red hats in the other 98 prisoners (excluding the first and himself) and deduce that he is wearing a red hat.

The two-color case is easy, isn't it? What if there are 3 possible hat colors: red, blue, and white? What is the best strategy they can adopt and how many prisoners can they guarantee to save?[15]

Solution: The answer is still that at least 99 prisoners will be saved. The difference is that the first prisoner now only has 1/3 chance of survival. Let's use the following scoring system: red=0, green=1, and blue=2. The first prisoner counts the total score for

---

[14] Hint: The first prisoner can see the number of red and blue hats of all other 99 prisoners. One color has odd number of counts and the other has even number of counts.

[15] Hint: That a number is odd simply means $x\%2 = 1$. Here we have 3 colors, so you may want to consider $x\%3$ instead.

the rest of 99 prisoners and calculates $s\%3$. If the remainder is 0, he announces red; if the remainder is 1, green; 2, blue. He has 1/3 chance of living, but all the rest of the prisoners can determine his own score (color) from the remainder. Let's consider a prisoner i among 99 prisoners (excluding the first prisoner). He can calculate the total score (x) of all other 98 prisoners. Since $(x+0)\%3$, $(x+1)\%3$, and $(x+2)\%3$ are all different, so from the remainder that the first prisoner gives (for the 99 prisoners including i), he can determine his own score (color). For example, if prisoner i sees that there are 32 red, 29 green and 37 blue in those 98 prisoners (excluding the first and himself). The total score of those 98 prisoners is 103. If the first prisoner announces that the remainder is 2 (green), then prisoner i knows his own color is green (1) since only $104\%3 = 2$ among 103, 104 and 105.

Theoretically, a similar strategy can be extended to any number of colors. Surely that requires all prisoners to have exceptional memory and calculation capability.

Division by 9

Given an arbitrary integer, come up with a rule to decide whether it is divisible by 9 and prove it.

Solution: Hopefully you still remember the rules from your high school math class. Add up all the digits of the integer. If the sum is divisible by 9, then the integer is divisible by 9; otherwise the integer is not divisible by 9. But how do we prove it?

Let's express the original integer as $a = a_n10^n + a_{n-1}10^{n-1} + \cdots + a_110^1 + a_0$. Basically we state that if $a_n + a_{n-1} + \cdots + a_1 + a_0 = 9x$ (x is a integer), then the a is divisible by 9 as well. The proof is straightforward:

For any $a = a_n10^n + a_{n-1}10^{n-1} + \cdots + a_110^1 + a_0$, let $b = a - (a_n + a_{n-1} + \cdots + a_1 + a_0)$. We have $b = a_n(10^n - 1) + a_{n-1}(10^{n-1} - 1) + \cdots + a_1(10^1 - 1) = a - 9x$, which is divisible by 9 since all $(10^k - 1)$, $k = 1, \cdots, n$ are divisible by 9. Because both b and $9x$ are divisible by 9, $a = b + 9x$ must be divisible by 9 as well.

(Similarly you can also show that $a = (-1)^n a_n + (-1)^{n-1} a_{n-1} + \cdots + (-1)^1 a_1 + a_0 = 11x$ is the necessary and sufficient condition for a to be divisible by 11.)

Chameleon colors

A remote island has three types of chameleons with the following population: 13 red chameleons, 15 green chameleons and 17 blue chameleons. Each time two chameleons with different colors meet, they would change their color to the third color. For example, if a green chameleon meets a red chameleon, they both change their color to blue. Is it ever possible for all chameleons to become the same color? Why or why not?[16]

Solution: It is not possible for all chameleons to become the same color. There are several approaches to proving this conclusion. Here we discuss two of them.

Approach 1. Since the numbers 13, 15 and 17 are "large" numbers, we can simplify the problem to 0, 2 and 4 for three colors. (To see this, you need to realize that if combination $(m+1, n+1, p+1)$ can be converted to the same color, combination (m, n, p) can be converted to the same color as well.) Can a combination $(0, 2, 4)$ be converted to a combination $(0, 0, 6)$? The answer is NO, as shown in Figure 2.3:

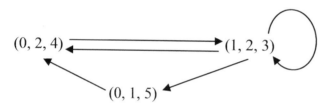

Figure 2.3 chameleon color combination transitions from (0, 2, 4)

Actually combination $(1, 2, 3)$ is equivalent to combination $(0, 1, 2)$, which can only be converted to another $(0, 1, 2)$ but will never reach $(0, 0, 3)$.

Approach 2. A different, and more fundamental approach, is to realize that in order for all the chameleons to become the same color, at certain intermediate stage, two colors must have the same number. To see this, just imagine the stage before a final stage. It must has the combination $(1, 1, x)$. For chameleons of two different colors to have the same number, their module of 3 must be the same as well. We start with $15 = 3x$, $13 = 3y + 1$, and $17 = 3z + 2$ chameleon, when two chameleons of different colors meet, we will have three possible scenarios:

---

[16] Hint: consider the numbers in module of 3.

$$(3x,3y+1,3z+2) \Rightarrow \begin{cases} (3x+2,3y,3z+1) = (3x',3y'+1,3z'+2), & \text{one } y \text{ meets one } z \\ (3(x-1)+2,3(y+1),3z+1) = (3x',3y'+1,3z'+2), & \text{one } x \text{ meets one } z \\ (3(x-1)+2,3y,3(z+1)+1) = (3x',3y'+1,3z'+2), & \text{one } x \text{ meets one } y \end{cases}$$

So the pattern is preserved and we will never get two colors to have the same module of 3. In other words, we cannot make two colors have the same number. As a result, the chameleons cannot become the same color. Essentially, the relative change of any pair of colors after two chameleons meet is either 0 or 3. In order for all the chameleons to become one color, at least one pair's difference must be a multiple of 3.

2.8 Math Induction

Induction is one of the most powerful and commonly-used proof techniques in mathematics, especially discrete mathematics. Many problems that involve integers can be solved using induction. The general steps for proof by induction are the following:

- State that the proof uses induction and define an appropriate predicate $P(n)$.

- Prove the base case $P(1)$, or any other smallest number n for the predicate to be true.

- Prove that $P(n)$ implies $P(n+1)$ for every integer n. Alternatively, in a strong induction argument, you prove that $P(1)$, $P(2)$, $\cdots$, and $P(n)$ together imply $P(n+1)$.

In most cases, the real difficulty lies not in the induction step, but to formulate the problem as an induction problem and come up with the appropriate predicate $P(n)$. The simplified version of the problem can often help you identify $P(n)$.

Coin split problem

You split 1000 coins into two piles and count the number of coins in each pile. If there are x coins in pile one and y coins in pile two, you multiple x by y to get xy. Then you split both piles further, repeat the same counting and multiplication process, and add the new multiplication results to the original. For example, you split x to x_1 and x_2, y to y_1 and y_2, then the sum is $xy+x_1x_2+y_1y_2$. The same process is repeated until you only have piles of 1 stone each. What is the final sum? (The final 1's are not included in the sum.) Prove that you always get the same answer no matter how the piles are divided.

Solution: Let n be the number of the coins and $f(n)$ be the final sum. It is unlikely that a solution will jump to our mind since the number $n = 1000$ is a large number. If you aren't sure how to approach the problem, it never hurts to begin with the simplest cases and try to find a pattern. For this problem, the base case has $n = 2$. Clearly the only split is $1+1$ and the final sum is 1. When $n = 3$, the first split is $2+1$ and we have $xy = 2$ and the 2-coin pile will further give an extra multiplication result 1, so the final sum is 3. This analysis also gives the hint that when n coins are split into x and $n-x$ coins, the total sum will be $f(n) = x(n-x) + f(x) + f(n-x)$. 4 coins can be split into $2+2$ or $3+1$. For either case we can apply $x(n-x) + f(x) + f(n-x)$ and yields the same final sum 6.

Claim: For n coins, independent of intermediate splits, the final sum is $\dfrac{n(n-1)}{2}$. [17]

So how do we prove it? The answer should be clear to you: by strong induction. We have proved the claim for the base cases $n = 2, 3, 4$. Assume the claim is true for $n = 2, \cdots, N-1$ coins, we need to prove that it holds for $n = N$ coins as well. Again we apply the equation $f(n) = x(n-x) + f(x) + f(n-x)$. If N coins are split into x coins and $N-x$ coins, we have

$$f(N) = x(N-x) + f(x) + f(N-x)$$
$$= x(N-x) + \frac{N(N-1)}{2} + \frac{(N-x)(N-x-1)}{2} = \frac{N(N-1)}{2}$$

So indeed it holds for $n = N$ as well and $f(n) = \dfrac{n(n-1)}{2}$ is true for any $n \geq 2$. Applying the conclusion to $n = 1000$, we have $f(n) = 1000 \times 999 / 2$.

Chocolate bar problem

A chocolate bar has 6 rows and 8 columns (48 small 1×1 squares). You break it into individual squares by making a number of breaks. Each time, break one rectangle into two smaller rectangles. For example, in the first step you can break the 6×8 chocolate bar into a 6×3 one and a 6×5 one. What is the total number of breaks needed in order to break the chocolate bar into 48 small squares?

---

[17] $f(2) = 1$, $f(3) - f(2) = 2$ and $f(4) - f(3) = 3$ should give you enough hint to realize the pattern is
$f(n) = 1 + 2 + \cdots + (n-1) = \dfrac{n(n-1)}{2}$.

Solution: Let m be the number of the rows of the chocolate bar and n be the number of columns. Since there is nothing special for the case $m=6$ and $n=8$, we should find a general solution for all m and n. Let's begin with the base case where $m=1$ and $n=1$. The number of breaks needed is clearly 0. For $m>1$ and $n=1$, the number of breaks is $m-1$; similarly for $m=1$ and $n>1$, the number of breaks is $n-1$. So for any m and n, if we break the chocolate into m rows first, which takes $m-1$ breaks, and then break each row into n small pieces, which takes $m(n-1)$ breaks, the total number of breaks is $(m-1)+m(n-1)=mn-1$. If we breaks it into n columns first and then break each column into m small pieces, the total number of breaks is also $mn-1$. But is the total number of breaks always $mn-1$ for other sequences of breaks? Of course it is. We can prove it using strong induction.

We have shown the number of breaks is $mn-1$ for base cases $m \geq 1, n=1$ and $m=1, n \geq 1$. To prove it for a general $m \times n$ case, let's assume the statement is true for cases where *rows* $< m$, *columns* $\leq n$ and *rows* $\leq m$, *columns* $< n$. If the first break is along a row and it is broken into two smaller pieces $m \times n_1$ and $m \times (n-n_1)$, then the total number of breaks is $1+(m \times n_1 -1)+(m \times (n-n_1)-1)=mn-1$. Here we use the results for *rows* $\leq m$, *columns* $< n$. Similarly, if it is broken into two pieces $m_1 \times n$ and $(m-m_1) \times n$, the total number of breaks is $1+(m_1 \times n-1)+((m-m_1) \times n-1)=mn-1$. So the total number of breaks is always $mn-1$ in order to break the chocolate bar into $m \times n$ small pieces. For the case $m=6$ and $n=8$, the number of breaks is 47.

Although induction is the standard approach used to solve this problem, there is actually a simpler solution if you've noticed an important fact: the number of pieces always increases by 1 with each break since it always breaks one piece into two. In the beginning, we have a single piece. In the end, we will have mn pieces. So the number of breaks must be $mn-1$.

Race track

Suppose that you are on a one-way circular race track. There are N gas cans randomly placed on different locations of the track and the total sum of the gas in these cans is enough for your car to run exactly one circle. Assume that your car has no gas in the gas tank initially, but you can put your car at any location on the track and you can pick up the gas cans along the way to fill in your gas tank. Can you always choose a starting position on the track so that your car can complete the entire circle?[18]

---

[18] Hint: Start with $N=1, 2$ and solve the problem using induction.

Solution: If you get stuck as to how to solve the problem, again start with the simplest cases ($N = 1, 2$) and consider using an induction approach. Without loss of generality, let's assume that the circle has circumference of 1. For $N = 1$, the problem is trivial. Just start at where the gas can is. For $N = 2$, The problem is still simple. Let's use a figure to visualize the approach. As shown in Figure 2.4A, the amount of gas in can 1 and can 2, expressed as the distance the car can travel, are x_1 and x_2 respectively, so $x_1 + x_2 = 1$. The corresponding segments are y_1 and y_2, so $y_1 + y_2 = 1$. Since $x_1 + x_2 = 1$ and $y_1 + y_2 = 1$, we must have $x_1 \geq y_1$ or $x_2 \geq y_2$ ($x_1 < y_1$ and $x_2 < y_2$ cannot both be true). If $x_1 \geq y_1$, we can start at gas can 1, which has enough gas to reach gas can 2, and get more gas from gas can 2 to finish the whole circle. Otherwise, we will just start at gas can 2 and pick up gas can 1 along the way to finish the whole circle.

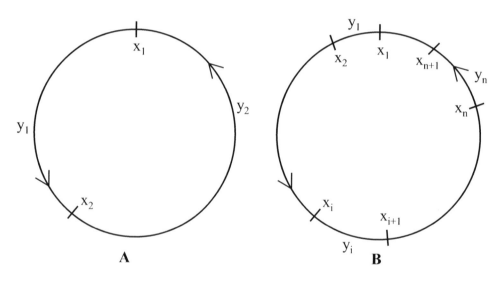

Figure 2.4 Gas can locations on the cycle and segments between gas cans

The argument for $N = 2$ also gives us the hint for the induction step. Now we want to show that if the statement holds for $N = n$, then the same statement also holds for $N = n+1$. As shown in Figure 2.4B, we have $x_1 + x_2 + \cdots + x_{n+1} = 1$ and $y_1 + y_2 + \cdots + y_{n+1} = 1$ for $N = n+1$. So there must exist at least one i, $1 \leq i \leq n+1$, that has $x_i \geq y_i$. That means whenever the car reaches x_i, it can reach x_{i+1} with more gas (For $i = n+1$, it goes to $i = 1$ instead). In other words, we can actually "combine" x_i and x_{i+1} to one gas can at the position of x_i with an amount of gas $x_i + x_{i+1}$ (and eliminate the gas can $i+1$). But such combination reduces the $N = n+1$ problem to $N = n$, for which the statement holds. So the statement also holds for $N = n+1$. Hence we can always choose a starting position on the track to complete the entire circle for any N.

There is also an alternative approach to this problem that provides a solution to the starting point. Let's imagine that you have another car with enough gas to finish the circle. You put that car at the position of a randomly chosen gas can and drive the car for a full circle. Whenever you reach a gas can (including at the initial position), you measure the amount of gas in your gas tank before you add the gas from the can to your gas tank. After you finish the circle, read through your measurement records and find the lowest measurement. The gas can position corresponding to the lowest measurement should be your starting position if the car has no gas initially. (It may take some thinking to fully understand this argument. I'd recommend that you again draw a figure and give this argument some careful thoughts if you don't find the reasoning obvious.)

2.9 Proof by Contradiction

In a **proof by contradiction** or **indirect proof**, you show that if a proposition were false, then some logical contradiction or absurdity would follow. Thus, the proposition must be true.

Irrational number

Can you prove that $\sqrt{2}$ is an irrational number? A rational number is a number that can be expressed as a ratio of two integers; otherwise it is irrational.

Solution: This is a classical example of proof by contradiction. If $\sqrt{2}$ is not an irrational number, it can be expressed as a ratio of two integers m and n. If m and n have any common factor, we can remove it by dividing both m and n by the common factor. So in the end, we will have a pair of m and n that have no common factors. (It is called irreducible fraction.) Since $m/n = \sqrt{2}$, we have $m^2 = 2n^2$. So m^2 must be an even number and m must be an even number as well. Let's express m as $2x$, where x is an integer, since m is even. Then $m^2 = 4x^2$ and we also have $n^2 = 2x^2$, which means n must be even as well. But that both m and n are even contradicts the earlier statement that m and n have no common factors. So $\sqrt{2}$ must be an irrational number.

Rainbow hats

Seven prisoners are given the chance to be set free tomorrow. An executioner will put a hat on each prisoner's head. Each hat can be one of the seven colors of the rainbow and the hat colors are assigned completely at the executioner's discretion. Every prisoner can see the hat colors of the other six prisoners, but not his own. They cannot communicate with others in any form, or else they are immediately executed. Then each prisoner writes down his guess of his own hat color. If at least one prisoner correctly guesses the color of his hat, they all will be set free immediately; otherwise they will be executed.

They are given the night to come up with a strategy. Is there a strategy that they can guarantee that they will be set free?[19]

Solution: This problem is often perceived to be more difficult than the prisoner problem in the modular arithmetic section. In the previous prisoner problem, the prisoners can hear others' guesses. So one prisoner's declaration gives all the necessary information other prisoners need. In this problem, prisoners won't know what others' guesses are. To solve the problem, it does require an aha moment. The key to the aha moment is given by the hint. Once you realize that if we code the colors to 0-6, $\left(\sum_{i=1}^{7} x_i\right)\%7$ must be among 0, 1, 2, 3, 4, 5 or 6 as well. Then each prisoner i—let's label them as 0-6 as well—should give a guess g_i so that the sum of g_i and the rest of 6 prisoners' hat color codes will give a remainder of i when divided by 7, where g_i is a unique number between 0 and 6. For example, prisoner 0's guess should make $\left(g_0 + \sum_{k \neq 0} x_k\right)\%7 = 0$. This way, we can guarantee at least one of $g_i = x_i$ for $i = 0,1,2,3,4,5,6$.

We can easily prove this conclusion by contradiction. If $g_i \neq x_i$, then $\left(\sum_{i=1}^{7} x_i\right)\%7 \neq i$ (since $\left(g_i + \sum_{k \neq i} x_k\right)\%7 \neq i$ and g_i and x_i are both between 0 and 6). But if $g_i \neq x_i$ for all $i = 0,1,2,3,4,5,$ and 6, then $\left(\sum_{i=1}^{7} x_i\right)\%7 \neq 0,1,2,3,4,5,6$, which is clearly impossible. So at least one of g_i must equal to x_i. As a result, using this strategy, they are guaranteed to be set free.

---

[19] Hint: Let's assign the 7 colors of rainbow with code 0-6 and x_i be the color code of prisoner i. Then $\left(\sum_{i=1}^{7} x_i\right)\%7$ must be 0, 1, 2, 3, 4, 5 or 6. How many guesses can 7 prisoners make?

Chapter 3 Calculus and Linear Algebra

Calculus and linear algebra lay the foundation for many advanced math topics used in quantitative finance. So be prepared to answer some calculus or linear algebra problems—many of them may be incorporated into more complex problems—in quantitative interviews. Since most of the tested calculus and linear algebra knowledge is easy to grasp, the marginal benefit far outweighs the time you spend brushing up your knowledge on key subjects. If your memory of calculus or linear algebra is a little rusty, spend some time reviewing your college textbooks!

Needless to say, it is extremely difficult to condense any calculus/linear algebra books into one chapter. Neither is it my intention to do so. This chapter focuses only on some of the core concepts of calculus/linear algebra that are frequently occurring in quantitative interviews. And unless necessary, it does so without covering the proof, details or even caveats of these concepts. If you are not familiar with any of the concepts, please refer to your favorite calculus/linear algebra books for details.

3.1 Limits and Derivatives

Basics of derivatives

Let's begin with some basic definitions and equations used in limits and derivatives. Although the notations may be different, you can find these materials in any calculus textbook.

Derivative: Let $y = f(x)$, then $f'(x) = \dfrac{dy}{dx} = \lim_{\Delta x \to 0} \dfrac{\Delta y}{\Delta x} = \lim_{\Delta x \to 0} \dfrac{f(x + \Delta x) - f(x)}{\Delta x}$

The product rule: If $u = u(x)$ and $v = v(x)$ and their respective derivatives exist,
$$\frac{d(uv)}{dx} = u\frac{dv}{dx} + v\frac{du}{dx}, \quad (uv)' = u'v + uv'$$

The quotient rule: $\dfrac{d}{dx}\left(\dfrac{u}{v}\right) = \left(v\dfrac{du}{dx} - u\dfrac{dv}{dx}\right)\bigg/ v^2$, $\quad \left(\dfrac{u}{v}\right)' = \dfrac{u'v - uv'}{v^2}$

The chain rule: If $y = f(u(x))$ and $u = u(x)$, then $\dfrac{dy}{dx} = \dfrac{dy}{du}\dfrac{du}{dx}$

The generalized power rule: $\dfrac{dy^n}{dx} = ny^{n-1}\dfrac{dy}{dx}$ for $\forall n \neq 0$

Some useful equations:

$$a^x = e^{x \ln a} \qquad \ln(ab) = \ln a + \ln b \qquad e^x = \lim_{n \to \infty} (1 + \tfrac{x}{n})^n$$

$$\lim_{x \to 0} \tfrac{\sin x}{x} = 1 \qquad \lim_{x \to 0} (1 + x)^k = 1 + kx \text{ for any } k$$

$$\lim_{x \to \infty} (\ln x / x^r) = 0 \text{ for any } r > 0 \qquad\qquad \lim_{x \to \infty} x^r e^{-x} = 0 \text{ for any } r$$

$$\frac{d}{dx} e^u = e^u \frac{du}{dx} \qquad\qquad \frac{d a^u}{dx} = (a^u \ln a) \frac{du}{dx} \qquad\qquad \frac{d}{dx} \ln u = \frac{1}{u} \frac{du}{dx} = \frac{u'}{u}$$

$$\frac{d}{dx} \sin x = \cos x, \quad \frac{d}{dx} \cos x = -\sin x, \quad \frac{d}{dx} \tan x = \sec^2 x$$

What is the derivative of $y = \ln x^{\ln x}$?[1]

Solution: This is a good problem to test your knowledge of basic derivative formulas—specifically, the chain rule and the product rule.

Let $u = \ln y = \ln \left(\ln x^{\ln x} \right) = \ln x \times \ln (\ln x)$. Applying the chain rule and the product rule, we have

$$\frac{du}{dx} = \frac{d(\ln y)}{dx} = \frac{1}{y} \frac{dy}{dx} = \frac{d(\ln x)}{dx} \times \ln(\ln x) + \ln x \times \frac{d \left(\ln(\ln x) \right)}{dx} = \frac{\ln(\ln x)}{x} + \frac{\ln x}{x \ln x},$$

To derive $\dfrac{d \left(\ln(\ln x) \right)}{dx}$, we again use the chain rule by setting $v = \ln x$:

$$\frac{d \left(\ln(\ln x) \right)}{dx} = \frac{d(\ln v)}{dv} \frac{dv}{dx} = \frac{1}{v} \times \frac{1}{x} = \frac{1}{x \ln x}.$$

$$\therefore \quad \frac{1}{y} \frac{dy}{dx} = \frac{\ln(\ln x)}{x} + \frac{\ln x}{x \ln x} \Rightarrow \frac{dy}{dx} = \frac{y}{x} \left(\ln(\ln x) + 1 \right) = \frac{\ln x^{\ln x}}{x} \left(\ln(\ln x) + 1 \right).$$

Maximum and minimum

Derivative $f'(x)$ is essentially the slope of the tangent line to the curve $y = f(x)$ and the instantaneous rate of change (velocity) of y with respect to x. At point $x = c$, if

---

[1] Hint: To calculate the derivative of functions with the format $y = f(x)^z$, it is common to take natural logs on both sides and then take the derivative, since $d(\ln y) / dx = 1 / y \times dy / dx$.

$f'(c) > 0$, $f(x)$ is an increasing function at c; if $f'(c) < 0$, $f(x)$ is a decreasing function at c.

Local maximum or minimum: suppose that $f(x)$ is differentiable at c and is defined on an open interval containing c. If $f(c)$ is either a local maximum value or a local minimum value of $f(x)$, then $f'(c) = 0$.

Second Derivative test: Suppose the secondary derivative of $f(x)$, $f''(x)$, is continuous near c. If $f'(c) = 0$ and $f''(c) > 0$, then $f(x)$ has a local minimum at c; if $f'(c) = 0$ and $f''(c) < 0$, then $f(x)$ has a local maximum at c.

Without calculating the numerical results, can you tell me which number is larger, e^π or π^e?[2]

Solution: Let's take natural logs of e^π and π^e. On the left side we have $\pi \ln e$, on the right side we have $e \ln \pi$. If $e^\pi > \pi^e$, $e^\pi > \pi^e \Leftrightarrow \pi \times \ln e > e \times \ln \pi \Leftrightarrow \dfrac{\ln e}{e} > \dfrac{\ln \pi}{\pi}$.

Is it true? That depends on whether $f(x) = \dfrac{\ln x}{x}$ is an increasing or decreasing function from e to π. Taking the derivative of $f(x)$, we have $f'(x) = \dfrac{1/x \times x - \ln x}{x^2} = \dfrac{1 - \ln x}{x^2}$, which is less than 0 when $x > e$ ($\ln x > 1$). In fact, $f(x)$ has global maximum when $x = e$ for all $x > 0$. So $\dfrac{\ln e}{e} > \dfrac{\ln \pi}{\pi}$ and $e^\pi > \pi^e$.

Alternative approach: If you are familiar with the Taylor's series, which we will discuss in Section 3.4, you can apply Taylor's series to e^x: $e^x = \sum\limits_{n=0}^{\infty} \dfrac{1}{n!} = 1 + \dfrac{x}{1!} + \dfrac{x^2}{2!} + \dfrac{x^3}{3!} + \cdots$ So $e^x > 1 + x$, $\forall x > 0$. Let $x = \pi/e - 1$, then $e^{\pi/e}/e > \pi/e \Leftrightarrow e^{\pi/e} > \pi \Leftrightarrow e^\pi > \pi^e$.

L'Hospital's rule

Suppose that functions $f(x)$ and $g(x)$ are differentiable at $x \to a$ and that $\lim\limits_{x \to a} g'(a) \neq 0$.
Further suppose that $\lim\limits_{x \to a} f(a) = 0$ and $\lim\limits_{x \to a} g(a) = 0$ or that $\lim\limits_{x \to a} f(a) \to \pm\infty$ and

---

[2] Hint: Again consider taking natural logs on both sides; $\ln a > \ln b \Rightarrow a > b$ since $\ln x$ is a monotonously increasing function.

$\lim\limits_{x \to a} g(a) \to \pm\infty$, then $\lim\limits_{x \to a} \dfrac{f(x)}{g(x)} = \lim\limits_{x \to a} \dfrac{f'(x)}{g'(x)}$. L'Hospital's rule converts the limit from an indeterminate form to a determinate form.

What is the limit of e^x / x^2 as $x \to \infty$, and what is the limit of $x^2 \ln x$ as $x \to 0^+$?

Solution: $\lim\limits_{x \to \infty} \dfrac{e^x}{x^2}$ is a typical example of L'Hospital's rule since $\lim\limits_{x \to \infty} e^x = \infty$ and $\lim\limits_{x \to \infty} x^2 = \infty$. Applying L'Hospital's rule, we have

$$\lim\limits_{x \to a} \dfrac{f(x)}{g(x)} = \lim\limits_{x \to \infty} \dfrac{e^x}{x^2} = \lim\limits_{x \to \infty} \dfrac{f'(x)}{g'(x)} = \lim\limits_{x \to \infty} \dfrac{e^x}{2x}.$$

The result still has the property that $\lim\limits_{x \to \infty} f(x) = \lim\limits_{x \to \infty} e^x = \infty$ and $\lim\limits_{x \to \infty} g(x) = \lim\limits_{x \to \infty} 2x = \infty$, so we can apply the L' Hospital's rule again:

$$\lim\limits_{x \to \infty} \dfrac{f(x)}{g(x)} = \lim\limits_{x \to \infty} \dfrac{e^x}{x^2} = \lim\limits_{x \to \infty} \dfrac{f'(x)}{g'(x)} = \lim\limits_{x \to \infty} \dfrac{e^x}{2x} = \lim\limits_{x \to \infty} \dfrac{d(e^x)/dx}{d(2x)/dx} = \lim\limits_{x \to \infty} \dfrac{e^x}{2} = \infty.$$

At first look, L'Hospital's rule does not appear to be applicable to $\lim\limits_{x \to 0^+} x^2 \ln x$ since it's not in the format of $\lim\limits_{x \to a} \dfrac{f(x)}{g(x)}$. However, we can rewrite the original limit as $\lim\limits_{x \to 0^+} \dfrac{\ln x}{x^{-2}}$ and it becomes obvious that $\lim\limits_{x \to 0^+} x^{-2} = \infty$ and $\lim\limits_{x \to 0^+} \ln x = -\infty$. So we can now apply L'Hospital's rule:

$$\lim\limits_{x \to 0^+} x^2 \ln x = \lim\limits_{x \to 0^+} \dfrac{\ln x}{x^{-2}} = \lim\limits_{x \to 0^+} \dfrac{d(\ln x)/dx}{d(x^{-2})/dx} = \lim\limits_{x \to 0^+} \dfrac{1/x}{-2/x^3} = \lim\limits_{x \to 0^+} \dfrac{x^2}{-2} = 0$$

3.2 Integration

Basics of integration

Again, let's begin with some basic definitions and equations used in integration.

If we can find a function $F(x)$ with derivative $f(x)$, then we call $F(x)$ an **antiderivative** of $f(x)$.

If $f(x) = F'(x)$, $\displaystyle\int_a^b f(x) = \int_a^b F'(x)dx = [F(x)]_a^b = F(b) - F(a)$

$$\frac{dF(x)}{dx} = f(x), \quad F(a) = y_a \Rightarrow F(x) = y_a + \int_a^x f(t)dt$$

The generalized power rule in reverse: $\int u^k du = \dfrac{u^{k+1}}{k+1} + c \quad (k \neq 1)$, where c is any constant.

Integration by substitution:

$$\int f(g(x)) \cdot g'(x)dx = \int f(u)du \text{ with } u = g(x), \quad du = g'(x)dx$$

Substitution in definite integrals: $\displaystyle\int_a^b f(g(x)) \cdot g'(x)dx = \int_{g(a)}^{g(b)} f(u)du$

Integration by parts: $\int udv = uv - \int vdu$

A. What is the integral of $\ln(x)$?

Solution: This is an example of integration by parts. Let $u = \ln x$ and $v = x$, we have $d(uv) = vdu + udv = (x \times 1/x)dx + \ln xdx$,

$\therefore \int \ln xdx = x\ln x - \int dx = x\ln x - x + c$, where c is any constant.

B. What is the integral of $\sec(x)$ from $x = 0$ to $x = \pi/6$?

Solution: Clearly this problem is directly related to differentiation/integration of trigonometric functions. Although there are derivative functions for all basic trigonometric functions, we only need to remember two of them: $\dfrac{d}{dx}\sin x = \cos x$, $\dfrac{d}{dx}\cos x = -\sin x$. The rest can be derived using the product rule or the quotient rule. For example,

$$\frac{d\sec x}{dx} = \frac{d(1/\cos x)}{dx} = \frac{\sin x}{\cos^2 x} = \sec x \tan x,$$

$$\frac{d\tan x}{dx} = \frac{d(\sin x/\cos x)}{dx} = \frac{\cos^2 x + \sin^2 x}{\cos^2 x} = \sec^2 x.$$

$$\therefore \frac{d(\sec x + \tan x)}{dx} = \sec x(\sec x + \tan x).$$

Since the $(\sec x + \tan x)$ term occurs in the derivative, we also have

$$\frac{d \ln|\sec x + \tan x|}{dx} = \frac{\sec x(\sec x + \tan x)}{(\sec x + \tan x)} = \sec x$$

$$\Rightarrow \int \sec x = \ln|\sec x + \tan x| + c$$

and $\displaystyle\int_0^{\pi/6} \sec x = \ln(\sec(\pi/6) + \tan(\pi/6)) - \ln(\sec(0) + \tan(0)) = \ln(\sqrt{3})$

Applications of integration

A. Suppose that two cylinders each with radius 1 intersect at right angles and their centers also intersect. What is the volume of the intersection?

Solution: This problem is an application of integration to volume calculation. For these applied problems, the most difficult part is to correctly formulate the integration. The general integration function to calculate 3D volume is $V = \displaystyle\int_{z_1}^{z_2} A(z)\,dz$ where $A(z)$ is the cross-sectional area of the solid cut by a plane perpendicular to the z-axis at coordinate z. The key here is to find the right expression for cross-sectional area A as a function of z.

Figure 3.1 gives us a clue. If you cut the intersection by a horizontal plane, the cut will be a square with side-length $\sqrt{(2r)^2 - (2z)^2}$. Taking advantage of symmetry, we can calculate the total volume as

$$2 \times \int_0^r \left[(2r)^2 - (2z)^2\right] dz = 8 \times \left[r^2 z - z^3/3\right]_0^r = 16/3 r^3 = 16/3.$$

An alternative approach requires even better 3D imagination. Let's imagine a sphere that is inscribed inside both cylinders, so it is inscribed inside the intersection as well. The sphere should have a radius of $r/2$. At each cut perpendicular to the z-axis, the circle from the sphere is inscribed in the square from the intersection as well. So $A_{circle} = \frac{\pi}{4} A_{square}$. Since it's true for all z values, we have

$$V_{sphere} = \frac{4}{3}\pi\left(\frac{r}{2}\right)^3 = \frac{\pi}{4} V_{intersection} \Rightarrow V_{intersection} = 16/3 r^3 = 16/3.$$

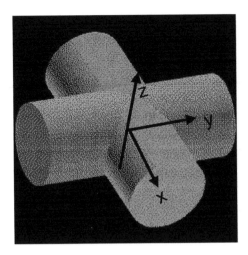

Figure 3.1 Interaction of two cylinders

B. The snow began to fall some time before noon at a constant rate. The city of Cambridge sent out a snow plow at noon to clear Massachusetts Avenue from MIT to Harvard. The plow removed snow at a constant volume per minute. At 1 pm, it had moved 2 miles and at 2 pm, 3 miles. When did the snow begin to fall?

Solution: Let's denote noon as time 0 and assume snow began to fall T hours before noon. The speed at which the plow moves is inversely related to the vertical cross-sectional area of the snow: $v = c_1 / A(t)$, where v is the speed of the plow, c_1 is a constant representing the volume of snow that the plow can remove every hour and $A(t)$ is the cross-sectional area of the snow. If t is defined as the time after noon, we also have $A(t) = c_2(t + T)$, where c_2 is the rate of cross-sectional area increase per hour (since the snow falls at a constant rate). So $v = \dfrac{c_1}{c_2(t + T)} = \dfrac{c}{t + T}$ where $c = \dfrac{c_1}{c_2}$. Taking the integration, we have

$$\int_0^1 \frac{c}{T + t} dt = c \ln(1 + T) - c \ln T = c \ln\left(\frac{1 + T}{T}\right) = 2,$$

$$\int_0^2 \frac{c}{T + t} dt = c \ln(2 + T) - c \ln T = c \ln\left(\frac{2 + T}{T}\right) = 3$$

From these two equations, we get

$$\left(\frac{1 + T}{T}\right)^3 = \left(\frac{2 + T}{T}\right)^2 \Rightarrow T^2 - T + 1 = 0 \Rightarrow T = \left(\sqrt{5} - 1\right)/2.$$

Overall, this question, although fairly straightforward, tests analytical skills, integration knowledge and algebra knowledge.

Expected value using integration

Integration is used extensively to calculate the unconditional or conditional expected value of continuous random variables. In Chapter 4, we will demonstrate its value in probability and statistics. Here we just use one example to show its application:

If X is a standard normal random variable, $X \sim N(0, 1)$, what is $E[X \mid X > 0]$?

Solution: Since $X \sim N(0, 1)$, the probability density function of x is $f(x) = \frac{1}{\sqrt{2\pi}} e^{-1/2x^2}$

and we have $E[X \mid X > 0] = \int_0^\infty xf(x)dx = \int_0^\infty x\frac{1}{\sqrt{2\pi}} e^{-1/2x^2} dx$.

Because $d(-1/2x^2) = -x$ and $\int e^u dy = e^u + c$, where c is an arbitrary constant, it is obvious that we can use **integration by substitution** by letting $u = -1/2x^2$. Replace $e^{-1/2x^2}$ with e^u and xdx with $-du$, we have

$\int_0^\infty x\frac{1}{\sqrt{2\pi}} e^{-1/2x^2} dx = \int_0^{-\infty} -\frac{1}{\sqrt{2\pi}} e^u du = -\frac{1}{\sqrt{2\pi}}\left[e^u\right]_0^{-\infty} = -\frac{1}{\sqrt{2\pi}}(0-1) = \frac{1}{\sqrt{2\pi}}$, where $\left[e^u\right]_0^{-\infty}$ is determined by $x = 0 \Rightarrow u = 0$ and $x = \infty \Rightarrow u = -\infty$.

$\therefore\ E[X \mid X > 0] = 1/\sqrt{2\pi}$

3.3 Partial Derivatives and Multiple Integrals

Partial derivative: $w = f(x, y) \Rightarrow \frac{\partial f}{\partial x}(x_0, y_0) = \lim_{\Delta x \to 0} \frac{f(x_0 + \Delta x, y_0) - f(x_0, y_0)}{\Delta x} = f_x$

Second order partial derivatives: $\frac{\partial^2 f}{\partial x^2} = \frac{\partial}{\partial x}(\frac{\partial f}{\partial x}),\quad \frac{\partial^2 f}{\partial x \partial y} = \frac{\partial}{\partial x}(\frac{\partial f}{\partial y}) = \frac{\partial}{\partial y}(\frac{\partial f}{\partial x})$

The general chain rule: Suppose that $w = f(x_1, x_2, \cdots, x_m)$ and that each of variables x_1, x_2, $\cdots$, x_m is a function of the variables t_1, t_2, $\cdots$, t_n. If all these functions have continuous first-order partial derivatives, then $\frac{\partial w}{\partial t_i} = \frac{\partial w}{\partial x_1}\frac{\partial x_1}{\partial t_i} + \frac{\partial w}{\partial x_2}\frac{\partial x_2}{\partial t_i} + \cdots + \frac{\partial w}{\partial x_m}\frac{\partial x_m}{\partial t_i}$ for each i, $1 \le i \le n$.

Changing Cartesian integrals into polar integrals: The variables in two-dimension plane can be mapped into polar coordinates: $x = r\cos\theta$, $y = r\sin\theta$. Tthe integration in a continuous polar region R is converted to

$$\iint\limits_R f(x,y)dxdy = \iint\limits_R f(r\cos\theta, r\sin\theta)r\,dr\,d\theta.$$

Calculate $\int_0^\infty e^{-x^2/2}dx$.

Solution: Hopefully you happen to remember that the probability density function (pdf) of the standard normal distribution is $f(x) = \dfrac{1}{\sqrt{2\pi}}e^{-x^2/2}$. By definition, we have

$$\int_{-\infty}^\infty f(x)dx = \int_{-\infty}^\infty \frac{1}{\sqrt{2\pi}}e^{-x^2/2}dx = 2\int_0^\infty \frac{1}{\sqrt{2\pi}}e^{-x^2/2}dx = 1 \Rightarrow \int_0^\infty e^{-x^2/2}dx = \sqrt{\frac{\pi}{2}}.$$

If you've forgotten the pdf of the standard normal distribution or if you are specifically asked to prove $\int_{-\infty}^\infty \dfrac{1}{\sqrt{2\pi}}e^{-x^2/2}dx = 1$, you will need to use polar integrals to solve the problem:

$$\int_{-\infty}^\infty e^{-x^2/2}dx \int_{-\infty}^\infty e^{-y^2/2}dy = \int_{-\infty}^\infty \int_{-\infty}^\infty e^{-(x^2+y^2)/2}dxdy = \int_0^\infty \int_0^{2\pi} e^{-(r^2\cos^2\theta + r^2\sin^2\theta)/2}r\,dr\,d\theta$$

$$= \int_0^\infty \int_0^{2\pi} e^{-r^2/2}r\,dr\,d\theta = -\int_0^\infty e^{-r^2/2}d(-r^2/2)\int_0^{2\pi}d\theta$$

$$= -\left[e^{-r^2/2}\right]_0^\infty \left[\theta\right]_0^{2\pi} = 2\pi$$

Since $\int_{-\infty}^\infty e^{-x^2/2}dx = \int_{-\infty}^\infty e^{-y^2/2}dy$, we have $\int_{-\infty}^\infty e^{-x^2/2}dx = \sqrt{2\pi} \Rightarrow \int_0^\infty e^{-x^2/2}dx = \sqrt{\dfrac{\pi}{2}}$.

3.4 Important Calculus Methods

Taylor's series

One-dimensional Taylor's series expands function $f(x)$ as the sum of a series using the derivatives at a point $x = x_0$:

$$f(x) = f(x_0) + f'(x_0)(x - x_0) + \frac{f''(x_0)}{2!}(x - x_0)^2 + \cdots + \frac{f^{(n)}(x_0)}{n!}(x - x_0)^n + \cdots$$

If $x_0 = 0$, $f(x) = f(0) + f'(0)x + \dfrac{f''(0)}{2!}x^2 + \cdots + \dfrac{f^{(n)}(0)}{n!}x^n + \cdots$

Taylor's series are often used to represent functions in power series terms. For example, Taylor's series for three common transcendental functions, e^x, $\sin x$ and $\cos x$, at $x_0 = 0$ are

$$e^x = \sum_{n=0}^{\infty} \frac{1}{n!} = 1 + \frac{x}{1!} + \frac{x^2}{2!} + \frac{x^3}{3!} + \cdots,$$

$$\sin x = \sum_{n=0}^{\infty} \frac{(-1)^n x^{2n+1}}{(2n+1)!} = x - \frac{x^3}{3!} + \frac{x^5}{5!} - \frac{x^7}{7!} + \cdots,$$

$$\cos x = \sum_{n=0}^{\infty} \frac{(-1)^n x^{2n}}{(2n)!} = 1 - \frac{x^2}{2!} + \frac{x^4}{4!} - \frac{x^6}{6!} + \cdots$$

The Taylor's series can also be expressed as the sum of the nth-degree Taylor polynomial $T_n(x) = f(x_0) + f'(x_0)(x - x_0) + \dfrac{f''(x_0)}{2!}(x - x_0)^2 + \cdots + \dfrac{f^{(n)}(x_0)}{n!}(x - x_0)^n$ and a remainder $R_n(x)$: $f(x) = T_n(x) + R_n(x)$.

For some $\tilde{x}$ between x_0 and x, $R_n(x) = \dfrac{f^{(n+1)}(\tilde{x})}{(n+1)!} |x - x_0|^{n+1}$. Let M be the maximum of $\left| f^{(n+1)}(\tilde{x}) \right|$ for all $\tilde{x}$ between x_0 and x, we get constraint $\left| R_n(x) \right| \le \dfrac{M \times |x - x_0|^{n+1}}{(n+1)!}$.

A. What is i^i ?

Solution: The solution to this problem uses Euler's formula, $e^{i\theta} = \cos\theta + i\sin\theta$, which can be proven using Taylor's series. Let's look at the proof. Applying Taylor's series to $e^{i\theta}$, $\cos\theta$ and $\sin\theta$, we have

$$e^{i\theta} = 1 + \frac{i\theta}{1!} + \frac{(i\theta)^2}{2!} + \frac{(i\theta)^3}{3!} + \frac{(i\theta)^4}{4!} + \cdots = 1 + i\frac{\theta}{1!} - \frac{\theta^2}{2!} - i\frac{\theta^3}{3!} + \frac{\theta^4}{4!} + i\frac{\theta^5}{5!} + \cdots$$

$$\cos\theta = 1 - \frac{\theta^2}{2!} + \frac{\theta^4}{4!} - \frac{\theta^6}{6!} + \cdots$$

$$\sin\theta = \theta - \frac{\theta^3}{3!} + \frac{\theta^5}{5!} - \frac{\theta^7}{7!} + \cdots \Rightarrow i\sin\theta = i\frac{\theta}{1!} - i\frac{\theta^3}{3!} + i\frac{\theta^5}{5!} - i\frac{\theta^7}{7!} + \cdots$$

Combining these three series, it is apparent that $e^{i\theta} = \cos\theta + i\sin\theta$.

When $\theta = \pi$, the equation becomes $e^{i\pi} = \cos\pi + i\sin\pi = -1$. When $\theta = \pi/2$, the equation becomes $e^{i\pi/2} = \cos(\pi/2) + i\sin(\pi/2) = i.$[3] So $\ln i = \ln\left(e^{i\pi/2}\right) = i\pi/2$.

Hence, $\ln\left(i^i\right) = i\ln i = i(i\pi/2) = -\pi/2 \Rightarrow i^i = e^{-\pi/2}$.

B. Prove $(1+x)^n \geq 1 + nx$ for all $x > -1$ and for all integers $n \geq 2$.

Solution: Let $f(x) = (1+x)^n$. It is clear that $1 + nx$ is the first two terms in the Taylor's series of $f(x)$ with $x_0 = 0$. So we can consider solving this problem using Taylor's series.

For $x_0 = 0$ we have $(1+x)^n = 1$ for $\forall n \geq 2$. The first and secondary derivatives of $f(x)$ are $f'(x) = n(1+x)^{n-1}$ and $f''(x) = n(n-1)(1+x)^{n-2}$. Applying Taylor's series, we have

$$f(x) = f(x_0) + f'(x_0)(x-x_0) + \frac{f''(\tilde{x})}{2!}(x-x_0)^2 = f(0) + f'(0)x + \frac{f''(\tilde{x})}{2!}x^2 ,$$

$$= 1 + nx + n(n-1)(1+\tilde{x})^{n-2}x^2$$

where $x \leq \tilde{x} \leq 0$ if $x < 0$ and $x \geq \tilde{x} \geq 0$ if $x > 0$.

Since $x > -1$ and $n \geq 2$, we have $n > 0$, $(n-1) > 0$, $(1+\tilde{x})^{n-2} > 0$, $x^2 \geq 0$.

Hence, $n(n-1)(1+\tilde{x})^{n-2}x^2 \geq 0$ and $f(x) = (1+x)^n > 1 + nx$.

If Taylor's series does not jump to your mind, the condition that n is an integer may give you the hint that you can try the induction method. We can rephrase the problem as: for every integer $n \geq 2$, prove $(1+x)^n \geq 1 + nx$ for $x > -1$.

The base case: show $(1+x)^n \geq 1 + nx, \forall x > -1$ when $n = 2$, which can be easily proven since $(1+x)^2 \geq 1 + 2x + x^2 \geq 1 + 2x, \forall x > -1$.

The induction step: show that if $(1+x)^n \geq 1 + nx, \forall x > -1$ when $n = k$, the same statement holds for $n = k+1$: $(1+x)^{k+1} \geq 1 + (k+1)x, \forall x > -1$. This step is straightforward as well.

---

[3] Clearly they satisfy equation $\left(e^{i\pi/2}\right)^2 = i^2 = e^{i\pi} = -1$.

$$(1+x)^{k+1} = (1+x)^k (1+x)$$
$$\geq (1+kx)(1+x) = 1+(k+1)x + kx^2, \quad \forall x > -1$$
$$\geq 1+(k+1)x$$

So the statement holds for all integers $n \geq 2$ when $x > -1$.

Newton's method

Newton's method, also known as the Newton-Raphson method or the Newton-Fourier method, is an iterative process for solving the equation $f(x) = 0$. It begins with an initial value x_0 and applies the iterative step $x_{n+1} = x_n - \dfrac{f(x_n)}{f'(x_n)}$ to solve $f(x) = 0$ if $x_1, x_2, \cdots$ converge.[4]

Convergence of Newton's method is not guaranteed, especially when the starting point is far away from the correct solution. For Newton's method to converge, it is often necessary that the initial point is sufficiently close to the root; $f(x)$ must be differentiable around the root. When it does converge, the convergence rate is quadratic, which means $\dfrac{|x_{n+1} - x_f|}{(x_n - x_f)^2} \leq \delta < 1$, where x_f is the solution to $f(x) = 0$.

A. Solve $x^2 = 37$ to the third digit.

Solution: Let $f(x) = x^2 - 37$, the original problem is equivalent to solving $f(x) = 0$. $x_0 = 6$ is a natural initial guess. Applying Newton's method, we have

$$x_1 = x_0 - \frac{f(x_0)}{f'(x_0)} = x_0 - \frac{x_0^2 - 37}{2x_0} = 6 - \frac{36 - 37}{2 \times 6} = 6.083.$$

($6.083^2 = 37.00289$, which is very close to 37.)

If you do not remember Newton's method, you can directly apply Taylor's series for function $f(x) = \sqrt{x}$ with $f'(x) = \frac{1}{2}x^{-1/2}$:

$$f(37) \approx f(36) + f'(36)(37 - 36) = 6 + 1/12 = 6.083.$$

---

[4] The iteration equation comes from the first-order Taylor's series:

$$f(x_{n+1}) \approx f(x_n) + f'(x_n)(x_{n+1} - x_n) = 0 \Rightarrow x_{n+1} = x_n - \frac{f(x_n)}{f'(x_n)}$$

Alternatively, we can use algebra since it is obvious that the solution should be slightly higher than 6. We have $(6+y)^2 = 37 \Rightarrow y^2 + 12y - 1 = 0$. If we ignore the y^2 term, which is small, then $y = 0.083$ and $x = 6 + y = 6.083$.

B. Could you explain some root-finding algorithms to solve $f(x) = 0$? Assume $f(x)$ is a differentiable function.

Solution: Besides Newton's method, the bisection method and the secant method are two alternative methods for root-finding. [5]

Bisection method is an intuitive root-finding algorithm. It starts with two initial values a_0 and b_0 such that $f(a_0) < 0$ and $f(b_0) > 0$. Since $f(x)$ is differentiable, there must be an x between a_0 and b_0 that makes $f(x) = 0$. At each step, we check the sign of $f\left((a_n + b_n)/2\right)$. If $f\left((a_n + b_n)/2\right) < 0$, we set $b_{n+1} = b_n$ and $a_{n+1} = (a_n + b_n)/2$; If $f\left((a_n + b_n)/2\right) > 0$, we set $a_{n+1} = a_n$ and $b_{n+1} = (a_n + b_n)/2$; If $f\left((a_n + b_n)/2\right) = 0$, or its absolute value is within allowable error, the iteration stops and $x = (a_n + b_n)/2$. The bisection method converges linearly, $\dfrac{x_{n+1} - x_f}{x_n - x_f} \leq \delta < 1$, which means it is slower than Newton's method. But once you find an a_0/b_0 pair, convergence is guaranteed.

Secant method starts with two initial values x_0, x_1 and applies the iterative step $x_{n+1} = x_n - \dfrac{x_n - x_{n-1}}{f(x_n) - f(x_{n-1})} f(x_n)$. It replaces the $f'(x_n)$ in Newton's method with a linear approximation $\dfrac{f(x_n) - f(x_{n-1})}{x_n - x_{n-1}}$. Compared with Newton's method, it does not require the calculation of derivative $f'(x_n)$, which makes it valuable if $f'(x)$ is difficult to calculate. Its convergence rate is $\left(1 + \sqrt{5}\right)/2$, which makes it faster than the bisection method but slower than Newton's method. Similar to Newton's method, convergence is not guaranteed if initial values are not close to the root.

Lagrange multipliers

The method of Lagrange multipliers is a common technique used to find local maximums/minimums of a multivariate function with one or more constraints. [6]

---

[5] Newton's method is also used in optimization—including multi-dimensional optimization problems—to find local minimums or maximums.

Let $f(x_1, x_2, \cdots, x_n)$ be a function of n variables $x = (x_1, x_2, \cdots, x_n)$ with gradient vector $\nabla f(x) = \left\langle \frac{\partial f}{\partial x_1}, \frac{\partial f}{\partial x_2}, \cdots, \frac{\partial f}{\partial x_n} \right\rangle$. The necessary condition for maximizing or minimizing $f(x)$ subject to a set of k constraints

$$g_1(x_1, x_2, \cdots, x_n) = 0, \quad g_2(x_1, x_2, \cdots, x_n) = 0, \quad \cdots, \quad g_k(x_1, x_2, \cdots, x_n) = 0$$

is that $\nabla f(x) + \lambda_1 \nabla g_1(x) + \lambda_2 \nabla g_2(x) + \cdots + \lambda_k \nabla g_k(x) = 0$, where $\lambda_1, \cdots, \lambda_k$ are called the Lagrange multipliers.

What is the distance from the origin to the plane $2x + 3y + 4z = 12$?

Solution: The distance (D) from the origin to a plane is the minimum distance between the origin and points on the plane. Mathematically, the problem can be expressed as

$$\min D^2 = f(x, y, z) = x^2 + y^2 + z^2$$
$$s.t. \quad g(x, y, z) = 2x + 3y + 4z - 12 = 0$$

Applying the Lagrange multipliers, we have

$$\left. \begin{array}{l} \frac{\partial f}{\partial x} + \lambda \frac{\partial f}{\partial x} = 2x + 2\lambda = 0 \\ \frac{\partial f}{\partial y} + \lambda \frac{\partial f}{\partial y} = 2y + 3\lambda = 0 \\ \frac{\partial f}{\partial z} + \lambda \frac{\partial f}{\partial z} = 2x + 4\lambda = 0 \\ 2x + 3y + 4z - 12 = 0 \end{array} \right\} \Rightarrow \left\{ \begin{array}{l} \lambda = -24/29 \\ x = 24/29 \\ y = 36/29 \\ z = 48/29 \end{array} \right. \Rightarrow D = \sqrt{\left(\frac{24}{29}\right)^2 + \left(\frac{36}{29}\right)^2 + \left(\frac{48}{29}\right)^2} = \frac{12}{\sqrt{29}}$$

In general, for a plane with equation $ax + by + cz = d$, the distance to the origin is

$$D = \frac{|d|}{\sqrt{a^2 + b^2 + c^2}}.$$

3.5 Ordinary Differential Equations

In this section, we cover four typical differential equation patterns that are commonly seen in interviews.

---

[6] The method of Lagrange multipliers is a special case of Karush-Kuhn-Tucker (KKT) conditions, which reveals the necessary conditions for the solutions to constrained nonlinear optimization problems.

Separable differential equations

A separable differential equation has the form $\dfrac{dy}{dx} = g(x)h(y)$. Since it is separable, we can express the original equation as $\dfrac{dy}{h(y)} = g(x)dx$. Integrating both sides, we have the solution $\int \dfrac{dy}{h(y)} = \int g(x)dx$.

A. Solve ordinary differential equation $y' + 6xy = 0, \ y(0) = 1$

Solution: Let $g(x) = -6x$ and $h(y) = y$, we have $\dfrac{dy}{y} = -6xdx$. Integrate both sides of the equation: $\int \dfrac{dy}{y} = \int -6xdx \Rightarrow \ln y = -3x^2 + c \Rightarrow y = e^{-3x^2 + c}$, where c is a constant. Plugging in the initial condition $y(0) = 1$, we have $c = 0$ and $y = e^{-3x^2}$.

B. Solve ordinary differential equation $y' = \dfrac{x - y}{x + y}.$[7]

Solution: Unlike the last example, this equation is not separable in its current form. But we can use a change of variable to turn it into a separable differential equation. Let $z = x + y$, then the original differential equation is converted to

$$\dfrac{d(z - x)}{dx} = \dfrac{x - (z - x)}{z} \Rightarrow \dfrac{dz}{dx} - 1 = \dfrac{2x}{z} - 1 \Rightarrow zdz = 2xdx \Rightarrow \int zdz = \int 2xdx + c$$
$$\Rightarrow (x + y)^2 = z^2 = 2x^2 + c \Rightarrow y^2 + 2xy - x^2 = c$$

First-order linear differential equations

A first-order differential linear equation has the form $\dfrac{dy}{dx} + P(x)y = Q(x)$. The standard approach to solving a first-order differential equation is to identify a suitable function $I(x)$, called an integrating factor, such that $I(x)(y' + P(x)y) = I(x)y' + I(x)P(x)y$

---

[7] Hint: Introduce variable $z = x + y$.

$= \big(I(x)y \big)'$; Then we have $\big(I(x)y \big)' = I(x)Q(x)$ and we can integrate both sides to solve

for y: $I(x)y = \int I(x)Q(x)dx \Rightarrow y = \dfrac{\int I(x)Q(x)dx}{I(x)}$.

The integrating factor, $I(x)$, must satisfy $\dfrac{dI(x)}{dx} = I(x)P(x)$, which means $I(x)$ is a

separable differential equation with general solution $I(x) = e^{\int P(x)dx}$. [8]

Solve ordinary different equation $y' + \dfrac{y}{x} = \dfrac{1}{x^2}$, $y(1) = 1$, where $x > 0$.

Solution: This is a typical example of first-order linear equations with $P(x) = \dfrac{1}{x}$ and

$Q(x) = \dfrac{1}{x^2}$. So $I(x) = e^{\int P(x)dx} = e^{\int (1/x)dx} = e^{\ln x} = x$ and we have $I(x)Q(x) = \dfrac{1}{x}$.

$\therefore I(x)\big(y' + P(x)y \big) = (xy)' = I(x)Q(x) = 1/x$

Taking integration on both sides, $xy = \int (1/x)dx = \ln x + c \Rightarrow y = \dfrac{\ln x + c}{x}$.

Plugging in $y(1) = 1$, we get $c = 1$ and $y = \dfrac{\ln x + 1}{x}$.

Homogeneous linear equations

A homogenous linear equation is a second-order differential equation with the form $a(x)\dfrac{d^2 y}{dx^2} + b(x)\dfrac{dy}{dx} + c(x)y = 0.$

It is easy to show that, if y_1 and y_2 are linearly independent solutions to the homogeneous linear equation, then any $y(x) = c_1 y_1(x) + c_2 y_2(x)$, where c_1 and c_2 are arbitrary constants, is a solution to the homogeneous linear equation as well.

When a, b and c ($a \neq 0$) are constants instead of functions of x, the homogenous linear equation has closed form solutions:

Let r_1 and r_2 be the roots of the characteristic equation $ar^2 + br + c = 0$, [9]

---

[8] The constant c is not needed in this case since it just scales both sides of the equation by a factor.

1. If r_1 and r_2 are real and $r_1 \neq r_2$, then the general solution is $y = c_1 e^{r_1 x} + c_2 e^{r_2 x}$;

2. If r_1 and r_2 are real and $r_1 = r_2 = r$, then the general solution is $y = c_1 e^{rx} + c_2 x e^{rx}$;

3. If r_1 and r_2 are complex numbers $\alpha \pm i\beta$, then the general solution is $y = e^{\alpha x}(c_1 \cos \beta x + c_2 \sin \beta x)$.

It is easy to verify that the general solutions indeed satisfy the homogeneous linear solutions by taking the first and secondary derivatives of the general solutions.

What is the solution of ordinary differential equation $y'' + y' + y = 0$?

Solution: In this specific case, we have $a = b = c = 1$ and $b^2 - 4ac = -3 < 0$, so we have complex roots $r = -1/2 \pm \sqrt{3}/2 i$ ($\alpha = -1/2$, $\beta = \sqrt{3}/2$), and the general solution to the differential equation is therefore

$$y = e^{\alpha x}(c_1 \cos \beta x + c_2 \sin \beta x) = e^{-1/2x}\left(c_1 \cos(\sqrt{3}/2x) + c_2 \sin(\sqrt{3}/2x)\right).$$

Nonhomogeneous linear equations

Unlike a homogenous linear equation $a\dfrac{d^2 y}{dx^2} + b\dfrac{dy}{dx} + cy = 0$, a nonhomogeneous linear

equation $a\dfrac{d^2 y}{dx^2} + b\dfrac{dy}{dx} + cy = d(x)$ has no closed-form solution. But if we can find a

particular solution $y_p(x)$ for $a\dfrac{d^2 y}{dx^2} + b\dfrac{dy}{dx} + cy = d(x)$, then $y = y_p(x) + y_g(x)$, where

$y_g(x)$ is the general solution of the homogeneous equation $a\dfrac{d^2 y}{dx^2} + b\dfrac{dy}{dx} + cy = 0$, is a

general solution of the nonhomogeneous equation $a\dfrac{d^2 y}{dx^2} + b\dfrac{dy}{dx} + cy = d(x)$.

---

[9] A quadratic equation $ar^2 + br + c = 0$ has roots given by quadratic formula $r = \dfrac{-b \pm \sqrt{b^2 - 4ac}}{2a}$. You should either commit the formula to memory or be able to derive it using $(r + b/2a)^2 = (b^2 - 4ac)/4a^2$.

Although it may be difficult to identify a particular solution $y_p(x)$ in general, in the special case when $d(x)$ is a simple polynomial, the particular solution is often a polynomial of the same degree.

What is the solution of ODEs $y'' + y' + y = 1$ and $y'' + y' + y = x$?

Solution: In these ODEs, we again have $a = b = c = 1$ and $b^2 - 4ac = -3 < 0$, so we have complex solutions $r = -1/2 \pm \sqrt{3}/2i$ ($\alpha = -1/2$, $\beta = \sqrt{3}/2$) and the general solution is $y = e^{-1/2x}\left(c_1\cos(\sqrt{3}/2x) + c_2\sin(\sqrt{3}/2x)\right)$.

What is a particular solution for $y'' + y' + y = 1$? Clearly $y = 1$ is. So the solution to $y'' + y' + y = 1$ is

$$y = y_p(x) + y_g(x) = e^{-1/2x}\left(c_1\cos(\sqrt{3}/2x) + c_2\sin(\sqrt{3}/2x)\right) + 1.$$

To find a particular solution for $y'' + y' + y = x$, Let $y_p(x) = mx + n$, then we have

$y'' + y' + y = 0 + m + (mx + n) = x \Rightarrow m = 1, n = -1$. So the particular solution is $x - 1$ and the solution to $y'' + y' + y = x$ is

$$y = y_p(x) + y_g(x) = e^{-1/2x}\left(c_1\cos(\sqrt{3}/2x) + c_2\sin(\sqrt{3}/2x)\right) + (x - 1).$$

3.6 Linear Algebra

Linear algebra is extensively used in applied quantitative finance because of its role in statistics, optimization, Monte Carlo simulation, signal processing, etc. Not surprisingly, it is also a comprehensive mathematical field that covers many topics. In this section, we discuss several topics that have significant applications in statistics and numerical methods.

Vectors

An $n \times 1$ (column) vector is a one-dimensional array. It can represent the coordinates of a point in the R^n (n-dimensional) Euclidean space.

Inner product/dot product: the inner product (or dot product) of two R^n vectors x and y is defined as $\sum_{i=1}^{n} x_i y_i = x^T y$

Euclidean norm: $\|x\| = \sqrt{\sum_{i=1}^{n} x_i^2} = \sqrt{x^T x}; \|x - y\| = \sqrt{(x-y)^T (x-y)}$

Then angle θ between R^n vectors x and y has the property that $\cos\theta = \dfrac{x^T y}{\|x\|\|y\|}$. x and y are orthogonal if $x^T y = 0$. The correlation coefficient of two random variables can be viewed as the cosine of the angle between them in Euclidean space ($\rho = \cos\theta$).

There are 3 random variables x, y and z. The correlation between x and y is 0.8 and the correlation between x and z is 0.8. What is the maximum and minimum correlation between y and z?

Solution: We can consider random variables x, y and z as vectors. Let θ be the angle between x and y, then we have $\cos\theta = \rho_{x,y} = 0.8$. Similarly the angle between x and z is θ as well. For y and z to have the maximum correlation, the angle between them needs to be the smallest. In this case, the minimum angle is 0 (when vector y and z are in the same direction) and the correlation is 1. For the minimum correlation, we want the maximum angle between y and z, which is the case shown in Figure 3.2.

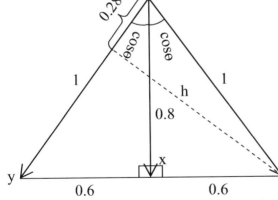

If you still remember some trigonometry, all you need is that

$$\cos(2\theta) = (\cos\theta)^2 - (\sin\theta)^2$$
$$= 0.8^2 - 0.6^2 = 0.28$$

Otherwise, you can solve the problem using Pythagoras's Theorem:

$$0.8 \times 1.2 = 1 \times h \Rightarrow h = 0.96$$
$$\cos 2\theta = \sqrt{1^2 - 0.96^2} = 0.28$$

Figure 3.2 Minimum correlation and maximum angle between vectors y and z

QR decomposition

QR decomposition: For each non-singular $n \times n$ matrix A, there is a unique pair of orthogonal matrix Q and upper-triangular matrix R with positive diagonal elements such that $A = QR$. [10]

QR decomposition is often used to solve linear systems $Ax = b$ when A is a non-singular matrix. Since Q is an orthogonal matrix, $Q^{-1} = Q^T$ and $QRx = b \Rightarrow Rx = Q^T b$. Because R is an upper-triangular matrix, we can begin with x_n (the equation is simply $R_{n,n} x_n = (Q^T b)_n$), and recursively calculate all x_i, $\forall i = n, n-1, \cdots, 1$.

If the programming language you are using does not have a function for the linear least squares regression, how would you design an algorithm to do so?

Solution: The linear least squares regression is probably the most widely used statistical analysis method. Let's go over a standard approach to solving linear least squares regressions using matrices. A simple linear regression with n observations can be expressed as

$$y_i = \beta_0 x_{i,0} + \beta_1 x_{i,1} + \cdots + \beta_{p-1} x_{i,p-1} + \varepsilon_i, \ \forall i = 1, \cdots, n, \text{ where } x_{i0} \equiv 1, \ \forall i, \text{ is the intercept}$$

term and $x_{i,1}, \cdots, x_{i,p-1}$ are $p-1$ exogenous regressors.

The goal of the linear least squares regression is to find a set of $\beta = [\beta_0, \beta_1, \cdots, \beta_{p-1}]^T$

that makes $\sum_{i=1}^{n} \varepsilon_i^2$ the smallest. Let's express the linear regression in matrix format:

$Y = X\beta + \varepsilon$, where $Y = [Y_1, Y_2, \cdots, Y_n]^T$ and $\varepsilon = [\varepsilon_1, \varepsilon_2, \cdots, \varepsilon_n]^T$ are both $n \times 1$ column vectors; X is a $n \times p$ matrix with each column representing a regressor (including the intercept) and each row representing an observation. Then the problem becomes

$$\min_{\beta} f(\beta) = \min_{\beta} \sum_{i=1}^{n} \varepsilon_i^2 = \min_{\beta} (Y - X\beta)^T (Y - X\beta)$$

---

[10] A nonsingular matrix Q is called an orthogonal matrix if $Q^{-1} = Q^T$. Q is orthogonal if and only if the columns (and rows) of Q form an orthonormal set of vectors in R^n. The Gram-Schmidt orthonormalization process (often improved to increase numerical stability) is often used for QR decomposition. Please refer to a linear algebra textbook if you are interested in the Gram-Schmidt process.

To minimize the function $f(\beta)$, taking the first derivative[11] of $f(\beta)$ with respect to β, we have $f'(\beta) = 2X^T(Y - X\hat{\beta}) = 0 \Rightarrow (X^T X)\hat{\beta} = X^T Y$, where $(X^T X)$ is a $p \times p$ symmetric matrix and $X^T Y$ is a $p \times 1$ column vector.

Let $A = (X^T X)$ and $b = X^T Y$, then the problem becomes $A\hat{\beta} = b$, which can be solved using QR decomposition as we described.

Alternatively, if the programming language has a function for matrix inverse, we can directly calculate $\hat{\beta}$ as $\hat{\beta} = (X^T X)^{-1} X^T Y$.[12]

Since we are discussing linear regressions, it's worthwhile to point out the assumptions behind the linear least squares regression (a common statistics question at interviews):

1. The relationship between Y and X is linear: $Y = X\beta + \varepsilon$.

2. $E[\varepsilon_i] = 0, \forall i = 1, \cdots, n$.

3. $\text{var}(\varepsilon_i) = \sigma^2, i = 1, \cdots, n$ (constant variance), and $E[\varepsilon_i \varepsilon_j] = 0, i \neq j$ (uncorrelated errors).

4. No perfect multicollinearity: $\rho(x_i, x_j) \neq \pm 1, i \neq j$ where $\rho(x_i, x_j)$ is the correlation of regressors x_i and x_j.

5. ε and x_i are independent.

Surely in practice, some of these assumptions are violated and the simple linear least squares regression is no longer the best linear unbiased estimator (BLUE). Many econometrics books dedicate significant chapters to addressing the effects of assumption violations and corresponding remedies.

Determinant, eigenvalue and eigenvector

Determinant: Let A be an $n \times n$ matrix with elements $\{A_{i,j}\}$, where $i, j = 1, \cdots, n$. The determinant of A is defined as a scalar: $\det(A) = \sum_p \psi(p) a_{1,p_1} a_{2,p_2} \cdots a_{n,p_n}$, where $p = (p_1, p_2, \cdots, p_n)$ is any permutation of $(1, 2, \cdots, n)$; the sum is taken over all $n!$ possible permutations; and

---

[11] To do that, you do need a little knowledge about matrix derivatives. Some of the important derivative equations for vectors/matrices are $\dfrac{\partial a^T x}{\partial x} = \dfrac{\partial x^T a}{\partial x} = a$, $\dfrac{\partial Ax}{\partial x} = A$, $\dfrac{\partial x^T Ax}{\partial x} = (A^T + A)x$, $\dfrac{\partial^2 x^T Ax}{\partial x \partial x^T} = 2A$,

$\dfrac{\partial (Ax + b)^T C(Dx + e)}{\partial x} = A^T C(Dx + e) + D^T C^T (Ax + b)$,

[12] The matrix inverse introduces large numerical error if the matrix is close to singular or badly scaled.

$$\psi(p) = \begin{cases} 1, & \text{if } p \text{ can be coverted to natural order by even number of exchanges} \\ -1, & \text{if } p \text{ can be coverted to natural order by odd number of exchanges} \end{cases}.$$

For example, determinants of 2×2 and 3×3 matrices can be calculated as

$$\det\left(\begin{bmatrix} a & b \\ c & d \end{bmatrix}\right) = ad - bc, \quad \det\left(\begin{bmatrix} a & b & c \\ d & e & f \\ g & h & i \end{bmatrix}\right) = aei + bfg + cdh - ceg - afh - bdi.[13]$$

Determinant properties: $\det(A^T) = \det(A)$, $\det(AB) = \det(A)\det(B)$, $\det(A^{-1}) = \dfrac{1}{\det(A)}$

Eigenvalue: Let A be an $n \times n$ matrix. A real number λ is called an eigenvalue of A if there exists a nonzero vector x in R^n such that $Ax = \lambda x$. Every nonzero vector x satisfying this equation is called an **eigenvector** of A associated with the eigenvalue λ.

Eigenvalues and eigenvectors are crucial concepts in a variety of subjects such as ordinary differential equations, Markov chains, principal component analysis (PCA), etc. The importance of determinant lies in its relationship to eigenvalues/eigenvectors.[14]

The determinant of matrix $A - \lambda I$, where I is an $n \times n$ identity matrix with ones on the main diagonal and zeros elsewhere, is called the **characteristic polynomial of A**. The equation $\det(A - \lambda I) = 0$ is called the **characteristic equation of A**. The eigenvalues of A are the real roots of the characteristic equation of A. Using the characteristic equation, we can also show that $\lambda_1 \lambda_2 \cdots \lambda_n = \det(A)$ and $\sum_{i=1}^{n} \lambda_i = trace(A) = \sum_{i=1}^{n} A_{i,i}$.

A is **diagonalizable** if and only if it has linearly independent eigenvectors.[15] Let $\lambda_1, \lambda_2, \cdots, \lambda_n$ be the eigenvalues of A, $x_1, x_2, \cdots, x_n$ be the corresponding eigenvectors. and $X = [x_1 \mid x_2 \mid \cdots \mid x_n]$, then

$$X^{-1}AX = \begin{bmatrix} \lambda_1 & & & \\ & \lambda_2 & & \\ & & \ddots & \\ & & & \lambda_n \end{bmatrix} = D \Rightarrow A = XDX^{-1} \Rightarrow A^k = XD^k X^{-1}.$$

---

[13] In practice, determinant is usually not solved by the sum of all permutations because it is computationally inefficient. LU decomposition and cofactors are often used to calculate determinants instead.

[14] Determinant can also be applied to matrix inverse and linear equations as well.

[15] If all n eigenvalues are real and distinct, then the eigenvectors are independent and A is diagonalizable.

If matrix $A = \begin{bmatrix} 2 & 1 \\ 1 & 2 \end{bmatrix}$, what are the eigenvalues and eigenvectors of A?

Solution: This is a simple example of eigenvalues and eigenvectors. It can be solved using three related approaches:

Approach A: Apply the definition of eigenvalues and eigenvectors directly.

Let λ be an eigenvalue and $x = \begin{bmatrix} x_1 \\ x_2 \end{bmatrix}$ be its corresponding eigenvector. By definition, we have

$$Ax = \begin{bmatrix} 2 & 1 \\ 1 & 2 \end{bmatrix}\begin{bmatrix} x_1 \\ x_2 \end{bmatrix} = \begin{bmatrix} 2x_1 + x_2 \\ x_1 + 2x_2 \end{bmatrix} = \lambda x = \begin{bmatrix} \lambda x_1 \\ \lambda x_2 \end{bmatrix} \Rightarrow \begin{cases} 2x_1 + x_2 = \lambda x_1 \\ x_1 + 2x_2 = \lambda x_2 \end{cases} \Rightarrow 3(x_1 + x_2) = \lambda(x_1 + x_2)$$

So either $\lambda = 3$, in which case $x_1 = x_2$ (plug $\lambda = 3$ into equation $2x_1 + x_2 = \lambda x_1$) and the corresponding normalized eigenvector is $\begin{bmatrix} 1/\sqrt{2} \\ 1/\sqrt{2} \end{bmatrix}$, or $x_1 + x_2 = 0$, in which case the normalized eigenvector is $\begin{bmatrix} 1/\sqrt{2} \\ -1/\sqrt{2} \end{bmatrix}$ and $\lambda = 1$ (plug $x_2 = -x_1$ into equation $2x_1 + x_2 = \lambda x_1$).

Approach B: Use equation $\det(A - \lambda I) = 0$.

$\det(A - \lambda I) = 0 \Rightarrow (2 - \lambda)(2 - \lambda) - 1 = 0$. Solving the equation, we have $\lambda_1 = 1$ and $\lambda_2 = 3$. Applying the eigenvalues to $Ax = \lambda x$, we can get the corresponding eigenvectors.

Approach C: Use equations $\lambda_1 \cdot \lambda_2 \cdots \lambda_n = \det(A)$ and $\sum_{i=1}^{n} \lambda_i = trace(A) = \sum_{i=1}^{n} A_{i,i}$.

$\det(A) = 2 \times 2 - 1 \times 1 = 3$ and $trace(A) = 2 \times 2 = 4$.

So we have $\left.\begin{array}{r} \lambda_1 \times \lambda_2 = 3 \\ \lambda_1 + \lambda_2 = 4 \end{array}\right\} \Rightarrow \begin{cases} \lambda_1 = 1 \\ \lambda_2 = 3 \end{cases}$. Again apply the eigenvalues to $Ax = \lambda x$, and we can get the corresponding eigenvectors.

Positive semidefinite/definite matrix

When A is a symmetric $n \times n$ matrix, as in the cases of covariance and correlation matrices, all the eigenvalues of A are real numbers. Furthermore, all eigenvectors that belong to distinct eigenvalues of A are orthogonal.

Each of the following conditions is a necessary and sufficient condition to make a symmetric matrix A **positive semidefinite**:

1. $x^T A x \geq 0$ for any $n \times 1$ vector x.

2. All eigenvalues of A are nonnegative.

3. All the upper left (or lower right) submatrices A_K, $K = 1, \cdots, n$ have nonnegative determinants.[16]

Covariance/correlation matrices must also be positive semidefinite. If there is no perfect linear dependence among random variables, the covariance/correlation matrix must also be positive definite. Each of the following conditions is a necessary and sufficient condition to make a symmetric matrix A **positive definite**:

1. $x^T A x > 0$ for any nonzero $n \times 1$ vector x.

2. All eigenvalues of A are positive.

3. All the upper left (or lower right) submatrices A_K, $K = 1, \cdots, n$ have positive determinants.

There are 3 random variables x, y and z. The correlation between x and y is 0.8 and the correlation between x and z is 0.8. What is the maximum and minimum correlation between y and z?

Solution: The problem can be solved using the positive semidefiniteness property of the correlation matrix.

Let the correlation between y and z be ρ, then the correlation matrix for x, y and z is

$$P = \begin{bmatrix} 1 & 0.8 & 0.8 \\ 0.8 & 1 & \rho \\ 0.8 & \rho & 1 \end{bmatrix}.$$

---

[16] A necessary, but not sufficient, condition for matrix A to be positive semidifinite is that A has no negative diagonal elements.

$$\det(P) = 1 \times \det\left(\begin{bmatrix} 1 & \rho \\ \rho & 1 \end{bmatrix}\right) - 0.8 \times \det\left(\begin{bmatrix} 0.8 & 0.8 \\ \rho & 1 \end{bmatrix}\right) + 0.8 \times \det\left(\begin{bmatrix} 0.8 & 0.8 \\ 1 & \rho \end{bmatrix}\right)$$

$$= (1-\rho^2) - 0.8 \times (0.8 - 0.8\rho) + 0.8 \times (0.8\rho - 0.8) = -0.28 + 1.28\rho - \rho^2 \geq 0$$

$$\Rightarrow (\rho-1)(\rho-0.28) \leq 0 \Rightarrow 0.28 \leq \rho \leq 1$$

So the maximum correlation between y and z is 1, the minimum is 0.28.

LU decomposition and Cholesky decomposition

Let A be a nonsingular $n \times n$ matrix. **LU decomposition** expresses A as the product of a lower and upper triangular matrix: $A = LU$.[17]

LU decomposition can be use to solve $Ax = b$ and calculate the determinant of A:

$$LUx = b \Rightarrow Ux = y, \ Ly = b; \ \det(A) = \det(L)\det(U) = \prod_{i=1}^{n} L_{i,i} \prod_{j=1}^{n} U_{j,j}.$$

When A is a symmetric positive definite matrix, **Cholesky decomposition** expresses A as $A = R^T R$, where R is a unique upper-triangular matrix with positive diagonal entries. Essentially, it is a LU decomposition with the property $L = U^T$.

Cholesky decomposition is useful in Monte Carlo simulation to generate correlated random variables as shown in the following problem:

How do you generate two $N(0,1)$ (standard normal distribution) random variables with correlation ρ if you have a random number generator for standard normal distribution?

Solution: Two $N(0,1)$ random variables x_1, x_2 with a correlation ρ can be generated from independent $N(0,1)$ random variables z_1, z_2 using the following equations:

$$x_1 = z_1$$
$$x_2 = \rho z_1 + \sqrt{1-\rho^2} z_2$$

It is easy to confirm that $\text{var}(x_1) = \text{var}(z_1) = 1$, $\text{var}(x_2) = \rho^2 \text{var}(z_1) + (1-\rho^2)\text{var}(z_2) = 1$, and $\text{cov}(x_1, x_2) = \text{cov}(z_1, \rho z_1 + \sqrt{1-\rho^2} z_2) = \text{cov}(z_1, \rho z_1) = \rho$.

This approach is a basic example using Cholesky decomposition to generate correlated random numbers. To generate correlated random variables that follow a n-dimensional

---

[17] LU decomposition occurs naturally in Gaussian elimination.

multivariate normal distribution $X = [X_1, X_2, \cdots, X_n]^T \sim N(\mu, \Sigma)$ with mean $\mu = [\mu_1, \mu_2, \cdots, \mu_n]^T$ and covariance matrix Σ (a $n \times n$ positive definite matrix)[18], we can decompose the covariance matrix Σ into $R^T R$ and generate n independent $N(0, 1)$ random variables z_1, z_2, $\cdots$, z_n. Let vector $Z = [z_1, z_2, \cdots, z_n]^T$, then X can be generated as $X = \mu + R^T Z$.[19]

Alternatively, X can also be generated using another important matrix decomposition called **singular value decomposition (SVD)**: For any $n \times p$ matrix X, there exists a factorization of the form $X = UDV^T$, where U and V are $n \times p$ and $p \times p$ orthogonal matrices, with columns of U spanning the column space of X, and the columns of V spanning the row space; D is a $p \times p$ diagonal matrix called the singular values of X. For a positive definite covariance matrix, we have $V = U$ and $\Sigma = UDU^T$. Furthermore, D is the diagonal matrix of eigenvalues λ_1, λ_2, $\cdots$, λ_n and U is the matrix of n corresponding eigenvectors. Let $D^{1/2}$ be a diagonal matrix with diagonal elements $\sqrt{\lambda_1}$, $\sqrt{\lambda_2}$, $\cdots$, $\sqrt{\lambda_n}$, then it is clear that $D = (D^{1/2})^2 = (D^{1/2})(D^{1/2})^T$ and $\Sigma = UD^{1/2}(UD^{1/2})^T$. Again, if we generate a vector of n independent $N(0, 1)$ random variables $Z = [z_1, z_2, \cdots, z_n]^T$, X can be generated as $X = \mu + (UD^{1/2})Z$.

---

[18] The probability density of multivariate normal distribution is $f(x) = \dfrac{\exp\left(-\frac{1}{2}(x-\mu)^T \Sigma^{-1}(x-\mu)\right)}{(2\pi)^{n/2} \det(\Sigma)^{1/2}}$

[19] In general, if $Y = AX + b$, where A and b are constant, then the covariance matrice $\Sigma_{YY} = A\Sigma_{XX}A^T$.

Chapter 4 Probability Theory

Chances are that you will face at least a couple of probability problems in most quantitative interviews. Probability theory is the foundation of every aspect of quantitative finance. As a result, it has become a popular topic in quantitative interviews.

Although good intuition and logic can help you solve many of the probability problems, having a thorough understanding of basic probability theory will provide you with clear and concise solutions to most of the problems you are likely to encounter. Furthermore, probability theory is extremely valuable in explaining some of the seemingly-counterintuitive results. Armed with a little knowledge, you will find that many of the interview problems are no more than disguised textbook problems.

So we dedicate this chapter to reviewing basic probability theory that is not only broadly tested in interviews but also likely to be helpful for your future career.[1] The knowledge is applied to real interview problems to demonstrate the power of probability theory. Nevertheless, the necessity of knowledge in no way downplays the role of intuition and logic. Quite the contrary, common sense and sound judgment are always crucial for analyzing and solving either interview or real-life problems. As you will see in the following sections, all the techniques we discussed in Chapter 2 still play a vital role in solving many of the probability problems.

Let's have some fun playing the odds.

4.1 Basic Probability Definitions and Set Operations

First let's begin with some basic definitions and notations used in probability. These definitions and notations may seem dry without examples—which we will present momentarily—yet they are crucial to our understanding of probability theory. In addition, it will lay a solid ground for us to systematically approach probability problems.

Outcome (ω): the outcome of an experiment or trial.

Sample space/Probability space (Ω): the set of all possible outcomes of an experiment.

---

[1] As I have emphasized in Chapter 3, this book does not teach probability or any other math topics due to the space limit—it is not my goal to do so, either. The book gives a summary of the frequently-tested knowledge and shows how it can be applied to a wide range of real interview problems. The knowledge used in this chapter is covered by most introductory probability books. It is always helpful to pick up one or two classic probability books in case you want to refresh your memory on some of the topics. My personal favorites are *First Course in Probability* by Sheldon Ross and *Introduction to Probability* by Dimitri P. Bertsekas and John N. Tsitsiklis.

$P(\omega)$: Probability of an outcome ($P(\omega) \geq 0$, $\forall \omega \in \Omega$, $\sum_{\omega \in \Omega} P(\omega) = 1$).

Event: A set of outcomes and a subset of the sample space.

$P(A)$: Probability of an event A, $P(A) = \sum_{\omega \in A} P(\omega)$.

$A \cup B$: Union $A \cup B$ is the set of outcomes in event A or in event B (or both).

$A \cap B$ or AB : Intersection $A \cap B$ (or AB) is the set of outcomes in both A and B.

A^c : The complement of A, which is the event "not A".

Mutually Exclusive: $A \cap B = \Phi$ where Φ is an empty set.

For any mutually exclusive events $E_1, E_2, \cdots E_N$, $P\left(\bigcup_{i=1}^{N} E_i\right) = \sum_{i=1}^{N} P(E_i)$.

Random variable: A **function** that maps each outcome (ω) in the sample space (Ω) into the set of real numbers.

Let's use the rolling of a six-sided dice to explain these definitions and notations. A roll of a dice has 6 possible outcomes (mapped to a random variable): 1, 2, 3, 4, 5, or 6. So the sample space Ω is $\{1,2,3,4,5,6\}$ and the probability of each outcome is 1/6 (assuming a fair dice). We can define an event A representing the event that the outcome is an odd number $A = \{1, 3, 5\}$, then the complement of A is $A^c = \{2, 4, 6\}$. Clearly $P(A) = P(1) + P(3) + P(5) = 1/2$. Let B be the event that the outcome is larger than 3: $B = \{4, 5, 6\}$. Then the union is $A \cup B = \{1, 3, 4, 5, 6\}$ and the intersection is $A \cap B = \{5\}$. One popular random variable called indicator variable (a binary dummy variable) for event A is defined as the following:

$I_A = \begin{cases} 1, & \text{if } x \in \{1, 3, 5\} \\ 0, & \text{if } x \notin \{1, 3, 5\} \end{cases}$. Basically $I_A = 1$ when A occurs and $I_A = 0$ if A^c occurs. The expected value of I_A is $E[I_A] = P(A)$.

Now, time for some examples.

Coin toss game

Two gamblers are playing a coin toss game. Gambler A has $(n+1)$ fair coins; B has n fair coins. What is the probability that A will have more heads than B if both flip all their coins?[2]

Solution: We have yet to cover all the powerful tools probability theory offers. What do we have now? Outcomes, events, event probabilities, and surely our reasoning capabilities! The one extra coin makes A different from B. If we remove a coin from A, A and B will become symmetric. Not surprisingly, the symmetry will give us a lot of nice properties. So let's remove the last coin of A and compare the number of heads in A's first n coins with B's n coins. There are three possible outcomes:

E_1 : A's n coins have more heads than B's n coins;

E_2 : A's n coins have equal number of heads as B's n coins;

E_3 : A's n coins have fewer heads than B's n coins.

By symmetry, the probability that A has more heads is equal to the probability that B has more heads. So we have $P(E_1) = P(E_3)$. Let's denote $P(E_1) = P(E_3) = x$ and $P(E_2) = y$. Since $\sum_{\omega \in \Omega} P(\omega) = 1$, we have $2x + y = 1$. For event E_1, A will always have more heads than B no matter what A's $(n+1)th$ coin's side is; for event E_3, A will have no more heads than B no matter what A's $(n+1)th$ coin's side is. For event E_2, A's $(n+1)th$ coin does make a difference. If it's a head, which happens with probability 0.5, it will make A have more heads than B. So the $(n+1)th$ coin increases the probability that A has more heads than B by $0.5y$ and the total probability that A has more heads is $x + 0.5y = x + 0.5(1 - 2x) = 0.5$ when A has $(n+1)$ coins.

Card game

A casino offers a simple card game. There are 52 cards in a deck with 4 cards for each value $2, 3, 4, 5, 6, 7, 8, 9, 10, J, Q, K, A$. Each time the cards are thoroughly shuffled (so each card has equal probability of being selected). You pick up a card from the deck and the dealer picks another one without replacement. If you have a larger number, you win; if the numbers are equal or yours is smaller, the house wins—as in all other casinos, the house always has better odds of winning. What is your probability of winning?

jack queen king ace

---

[2] Hint: What are the possible results (events) if we compare the number of heads in A's first n coins with B's n coins? By making the number of coins equal, we can take advantage of symmetry. For each event, what will happen if A's last coin is a head? Or a tail?

Solution: One answer to this problem is to consider all 13 different outcomes of your card. The card can have a value 2, 3, $\cdots$, A and each has 1/13 of probability. With a value of 2, the probability of winning is 0/51; with a value of 3, the probability of winning is 4/51 (when the dealer picks a 2); ...; with a value of A, the probability of winning is 48/51 (when the dealer picks a 2, 3, $\cdots$, or K). So your probability of winning is

$$\frac{1}{13} \times \left(\frac{0}{51} + \frac{4}{51} + \cdots + \frac{48}{51} \right) = \frac{4}{13 \times 51} \times (0 + 1 + \cdots + 12) = \frac{4}{13 \times 51} \times \frac{12 \times 13}{2} = \frac{8}{17}.$$

Although this is a straightforward solution and it elegantly uses the sum of an integer sequence, it is not the most efficient way to solve the problem. If you have got the core spirits of the coin tossing problem, you may approach the problem by considering three different outcomes:

E_1: Your card has a number larger than the dealer's;

E_2: Your card has a number equal to the dealer's;

E_3: Your card has a number lower than the dealer's.

Again by symmetry, $P(E_1) = P(E_3)$. So we only need to figure out $P(E_2)$, the probability that two cards have equal value. Let's say you have randomly selected a card. Among the remaining 51 cards, only 3 cards will have the same value as your card. So the probability that the two cards have equal value is 3/51. As a result, the probability that you win is $P(E_1) = (1 - P(E_2))/2 = (1 - 3/51)/2 = 8/17$.

Drunk passenger

A line of 100 airline passengers are waiting to board a plane. They each hold a ticket to one of the 100 seats on that flight. For convenience, let's say that the n-th passenger in line has a ticket for the seat number n. Being drunk, the first person in line picks a random seat (equally likely for each seat). All of the other passengers are sober, and will go to their proper seats unless it is already occupied; In that case, they will randomly choose a free seat. You're person number 100. What is the probability that you end up in your seat (i.e., seat #100) ?[3]

Solution: Let's consider seats #1 and #100. There are two possible outcomes:

---

[3] Hint: If you are trying to use complicated conditional probability to solve the problem, go back and think again. If you decide to start with a simpler version of the problem, starting with two passengers and increasing the number of passengers to show a pattern by induction, you can solve the problem more efficiently. But the problem is much simpler than that. Focus on events and symmetry and you will have an intuitive answer.

E_1 : Seat #1 is taken before #100;

E_2 : Seat #100 is taken before #1.

If any passenger takes seat #100 before #1 is taken, surely you will not end up in you own seat. But if any passenger takes #1 before #100 is taken, you will definitely end up in you own seat. By symmetry, either outcome has a probability of 0.5. So the probability that you end up in your seat is 50%.

In case this over-simplified version of reasoning is not clear to you, consider the following detailed explanation: If the drunk passenger takes #1 by chance, then it's clear all the rest of the passengers will have the correct seats. If he takes #100, then you will not get your seat. The probabilities that he takes #1 or #100 are equal. Otherwise assume that he takes the n-th seat, where n is a number between 2 and 99. Everyone between 2 and $(n-1)$ will get his own seat. That means the n-th passenger essentially becomes the new "drunk" guy with designated seat #1. If he chooses #1, all the rest of the passengers will have the correct seats. If he takes #100, then you will not get your seat. (The probabilities that he takes #1 or #100 are again equal.) Otherwise he will just make another passenger down the line the new "drunk" guy with designated seat #1 and each new "drunk" guy has equal probability of taking #1 or #100. Since at all jump points there's an equal probability for the "drunk" guy to choose seat #1 or 100, by symmetry, the probability that you, as the $100th$ passenger, will seat in #100 is 0.5.

N points on a circle

Given N points drawn randomly on the circumference of a circle, what is the probability that they are all within a semicircle?[4]

Solution: Let's start at one point and clockwise label the points as $1, 2, \cdots, N$. The probability that all the remaining $N-1$ points from 2 to N are in the clockwise semicircle starting at point 1 (That is, if point 1 is at 12:00, points 2 to N are all between 12:00 and 6:00) is $1/2^{N-1}$. Similarly the probability that a clockwise semicircle starting at any point i, where $i \in \{2, \cdots, N\}$ contains all the other $N-1$ points is also $1/2^{N-1}$.

Claim: the events that all the other $N-1$ points are in the clockwise semicircle starting at point i, $i = 1, 2, \cdots, N$ are mutually exclusive. In other words, if we, starting at point i and proceeding clockwise along the circle, sequentially encounters points $i+1, i+2, \cdots,$ $N, 1, \cdots, i-1$ in half a circle, then starting at any other point j, we cannot encounter all

---

[4] Hint: Consider the events that starting from a point n, you can reach all the rest of the points on the circle clockwise, $n \in \{1, \cdots, N\}$ in a semicircle. Are these events mutually exclusive?

other points within a clockwise semicircle. Figure 4.1 clearly demonstrates this conclusion. If starting at point i and proceeding clockwise along the circle, we sequentially encounter points $i+1, i+2, \cdots, N, 1, \cdots, i-1$ within half a circle, the clockwise arc between $i-1$ and i must be no less than half a circle. If we start at any other point, in order to reach all other points clockwise, the clockwise arc between $i-1$ and i are always included. So we cannot reach all points within a clockwise semicircle starting from any other points. Hence, all these events are mutually exclusive and we have

$$P\left(\bigcup_{i=1}^{N} E_i\right) = \sum_{i=1}^{N} P(E_i) \Rightarrow P\left(\bigcup_{i=1}^{N} E_i\right) = N \times 1/2^{N-1} = N/2^{N-1}$$

The same argument can be extended to any arcs that have a length less than half a circle. If the ratio of the arc length to the circumference of the circle is x ($x \le 1/2$), then the probability of all N points fitting into the arc is $N \times x^{N-1}$.

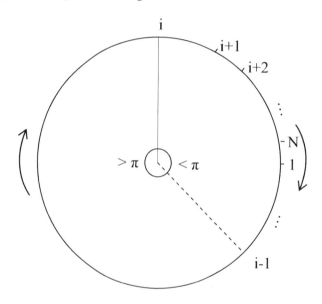

Figure 4.1 N points fall in a clockwise semicircle starting from i

4.2 Combinatorial Analysis

Many problems in probability theory can be solved by simply counting the number of different ways that a certain event can occur. The mathematic theory of counting is often referred to as combinatorial analysis (or combinatorics). In this section, we will cover the basics of combinatorial analysis.

Basic principle of counting: Let S be a set of length-k sequences. If there are

- n_1 possible first entries,
- n_2 possible second entries for each first entry,
- n_3 possible third entries for each combination of first and second entries, etc.

Then there are a total of $n_1 \cdot n_2 \cdots n_k$ possible outcomes.

Permutation: A rearrangement of objects into distinct sequence (i.e., order matters).

Property: There are $\dfrac{n!}{n_1! n_2! ... n_r!}$ different permutations of n objects, of which n_1 are alike, n_2 are alike, $\cdots$, n_r are alike.

Combination: An unordered collection of objects (i.e., order doesn't matter).

Property: There are $\dbinom{n}{r} = \dfrac{n!}{(n-r)! r!}$ different combinations of n distinct objects taken r at a time.

Binomial theorem: $(x+y)^n = \sum\limits_{k=0}^{n} \dbinom{n}{k} x^k y^{n-k}$

Inclusion-Exclusion Principle: $P(E_1 \cup E_2) = P(E_1) + P(E_2) - P(E_1 E_2)$

$P(E_1 \cup E_2 \cup E_3) = P(E_1) + P(E_2) + P(E_3) - P(E_1 E_2) - P(E_1 E_3) - P(E_2 E_3) + P(E_1 E_2 E_3)$

and more generally,

$$P(E_1 \cup E_2 \cup ... \cup E_N) = \sum_{i=1}^{N} P(E_i) - \sum_{i_1 < i_2} P(E_{i_1} E_{i_2}) + \cdots + (-1)^{r+1} \sum_{i_1 < i_2 < ... i_r} P(E_{i_1} E_{i_2} ... E_{i_r}) + \cdots$$
$$+ (-1)^{N+1} P(E_1 E_2 \cdots E_N)$$

where $\sum\limits_{i_1 < i_2 < ... i_r} P(E_{i_1} E_{i_2} \cdots E_{i_r})$ has $\dbinom{N}{r}$ terms.

Poker hands

Poker is a card game in which each player gets a hand of 5 cards. There are 52 cards in a deck. Each card has a value and belongs to a suit. There are 13 values, 2, 3, 4, 5, 6, 7, 8, 9, 10, J (jack), Q (queen), K (king), A (ace), and four suits, ♠ (spade), ♣ (club), ♥ (heart), ♦ (diamond).

What are the probabilities of getting hands with four-of-a-kind (four of the five cards with the same value)? Hands with a full house (three cards of one value and two cards of another value)? Hands with two pairs?

Solution: The number of different hands of a five-card draw is the number of 5-element subsets of a 52-element set, so total number of hands $= \binom{52}{5} = 2,598,960$.

Hands with a four-of-a-kind: First we can choose the value of the four cards with the same value, there are 13 choices. The 5th card can be any of the rest 48 cards (12 choices for values and 4 choices for suits). So the number of hands with four-of-a kind is $13 \times 48 = 624$.

Hands with a Full House: In sequence we need to choose the value of the triple, 13 choices; the suits of the triple, $\binom{4}{3}$ choices; the value of the pair, 12 choices; and the suits of the pair, $\binom{4}{2}$ choices. So the number of hands with full house is

$$13 \times \binom{4}{3} \times 12 \times \binom{4}{2} = 13 \times 4 \times 12 \times 6 = 3,744.$$

Hands with Two Pairs: In sequence we need to choose the values of the two pairs, $\binom{13}{2}$ choices; the suits of the first pair, $\binom{4}{2}$ choices; the suits of the second pair, $\binom{4}{2}$ choices; and the remaining card, 44 ($52 - 4 \times 2$, since the last cards can not have the same value as either pair) choices. So the number of hands with two pairs is

$$\binom{13}{2} \times \binom{4}{2} \times \binom{4}{2} \times 44 = 78 \times 6 \times 6 \times 44 = 123,552.$$

To calculate the probability of each, we only need to divide the number of hands of each kind by the total possible number of hands.

Hopping rabbit

A rabbit sits at the bottom of a staircase with n stairs. The rabbit can hop up only one or two stairs at a time. How many different ways are there for the rabbit to ascend to the top of the stairs?[5]

---

[5] Hint: Consider an induction approach. Before the final hop to reach the n-th stair, the rabbit can be at either the $(n-1)$th stair or the $(n-2)$th stair assuming $n > 2$.

Solution: Let's begin with the simplest cases and consider solving the problem for any number of stairs using induction. For $n = 1$, there is only one way and $f(1) = 1$. For $n = 2$, we can have one 2-stair hop or two 1-stair hops. So $f(2) = 2$. For any $n > 2$, there are always two possibilities for the last hop, either it's a 1-stair hop or a 2-stair hop. In the former case, the rabbit is at $(n-1)$ before reaching n, and it has $f(n-1)$ ways to reach $(n-1)$. In the latter case, the rabbit is at $(n-2)$ before reaching n, and it has $f(n-2)$ ways to reach $(n-2)$. So we have $f(n) = f(n-2) + f(n-1)$. Using this function we can calculate $f(n)$ for $n = 3, 4, \cdots$[6]

Screwy pirates 2

Having peacefully divided the loot (in chapter 2), the pirate team goes on for more looting and expands the group to 11 pirates. To protect their hard-won treasure, they gather together to put all the loot in a safe. Still being a democratic bunch, they decide that only a majority – any majority – of them (≥ 6) together can open the safe. So they ask a locksmith to put a certain number of locks on the safe. To access the treasure, every lock needs to be opened. Each lock can have multiple keys; but each key only opens one lock. The locksmith can give more than one key to each pirate.

What is the smallest number of locks needed? And how many keys must each pirate carry?[7]

Solution: This problem is a good example of the application of combinatorial analysis in information sharing and cryptography. A general version of the problem was explained in a 1979 paper *"How to Share a Secret"* by Adi Shamir. Let's randomly select 5 pirates from the 11-member group; there must be a lock that none of them has the key to. Yet any of the other 6 pirates must have the key to this lock since any 6 pirates can open all locks. In other words, we must have a "special" lock to which none of the 5 selected pirates has a key and the other 6 pirates all have keys. Such 5-pirate groups are randomly selected. So for each combination of 5 pirates, there must be such a "special" lock. The minimum number of locks needed is $\begin{pmatrix} 11 \\ 5 \end{pmatrix} = \dfrac{11!}{5!6!} = 462$ locks. Each lock has 6 keys, which are given to a unique 6-member subgroup. So each pirate must have $\dfrac{462 \times 6}{11} = 252$ keys. That's surely a lot of locks to put on a safe and a lot of keys for each pirate to carry.

---

[6] You may have recognized that the sequence is a sequence of Fibonacci numbers.
[7] Hint: every subgroup of 6 pirates should have the same key to a unique lock that the other 5 pirates do not have.

Chess tournament

A chess tournament has 2^n players with skills $1 > 2 > \cdots > 2^n$. It is organized as a knockout tournament, so that after each round only the winner proceeds to the next round. Except for the final, opponents in each round are drawn at random. Let's also assume that when two players meet in a game, the player with better skills always wins. What's the probability that players 1 and 2 will meet in the final?[8]

Solution: There are at least two approaches to solve the problem. The standard approach applies multiplication rule based on conditional probability, while a counting approach is far more efficient. (We will cover conditional probability in detail in the next section.)

Let's begin with the conditional probability approach, which is easier to grasp. Since there are 2^n players, the tournament will have n rounds (including the final). For round 1, players $2, 3, \cdots, 2^n$ each have $\dfrac{1}{2^n - 1}$ probability to be 1's rival, so the probability that 1 and 2 do not meet in round 1 is $\dfrac{2^n - 2}{2^n - 1} = \dfrac{2 \times (2^{n-1} - 1)}{2^n - 1}$. Condition on that 1 and 2 do not meet in round 1, 2^{n-1} players proceed to the 2nd round and the conditional probability that 1 and 2 will not meet in round 2 is $\dfrac{2^{n-1} - 2}{2^{n-1} - 1} = \dfrac{2 \times (2^{n-2} - 1)}{2^{n-1} - 1}$. We can repeat the same process until the $(n-1)th$ round, in which there are $2^2 \ (= 2^n / 2^{n-2})$ players left and the conditional probability that 1 and 2 will not meet in round $(n-1)$ is $\dfrac{2^2 - 2}{2^2 - 1} = \dfrac{2 \times (2^{2-1} - 1)}{2^2 - 1}$.

Let E_1 be the event that 1 and 2 do not meet in round 1;

$\quad$ E_2 be the event that 1 and 2 do not meet in rounds 1 and 2;

$\quad$ $\ldots$

$\quad$ E_{n-1} be the event that 1 and 2 do not meet in round $1, 2, \cdots, n-1$.

Apply the multiplication rule, we have

$P(1 \text{ and } 2 \text{ meet in the nth game}) = P(E_1) \times P(E_2 \mid E_1) \times \cdots \times P(E_{n-1} \mid E_1 E_2 \cdots E_{n-2})$

$= \dfrac{2 \times (2^{n-1} - 1)}{2^n - 1} \times \dfrac{2 \times (2^{n-2} - 1)}{2^{n-1} - 1} \times \cdots \times \dfrac{2 \times (2^{2-1} - 1)}{2^2 - 1} = \dfrac{2^{n-1}}{2^n - 1}$

---

[8] Hint: Consider separating the players to two 2^{n-1} subgroups. What will happen if player 1 and 2 in the same group? Or not in the same group?

Now let's move on to the counting approach. Figure 4.2A is the general case of what happens in the final. Player 1 always wins, so he will be in the final. From the figure, it is obvious that 2^n players are separated to two 2^{n-1}-player subgroups and each group will have one player reaching the final. As shown in Figure 4.2B, for player 2 to reach the final, he/she must be in a different subgroup from 1. Since any of the remaining players in $2, 3, \cdots, 2^n$ are likely to be one of the $(2^{n-1} - 1)$ players in the same subgroup as player 1 or one of the 2^{n-1} players in the subgroup different from player 1, the probability that 2 is in a different subgroup from 1 and that 1 and 2 will meet in the final is simply $\dfrac{2^{n-1}}{2^n - 1}$. Clearly, the counting approach provides not only a simpler solution but also more insight to the problem.

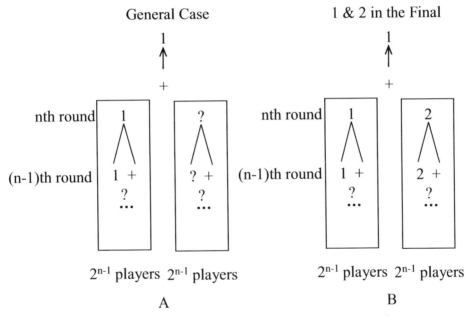

Figure 4.2A The general case of separating 2^n players into 2^{n-1}-player subgroups; 4.2B The special case with players 1 and 2 in different groups

Application letters

You're sending job applications to 5 firms: Morgan Stanley, Lehman Brothers, UBS, Goldman Sachs, and Merrill Lynch. You have 5 envelopes on the table neatly typed with names and addresses of people at these 5 firms. You even have 5 cover letters personalized to each of these firms. Your 3-year-old tried to be helpful and stuffed each cover letter into each of the envelopes for you. Unfortunately she randomly put letters into envelopes without realizing that the letters are personalized. What is the probability that all 5 cover letters are mailed to the wrong firms?[9]

Solution: This problem is a classic example for the Inclusion-Exclusion Principle. In fact, a more general case is an example in Ross' textbook *First Course in Probability*.

Let's denote by $E_i, i = 1, \cdots, 5$ the event that the *i*-th letter has the correct envelope. Then $P\left(\bigcup\limits_{i=1}^{5} E_i\right)$ is the probability that at least one letter has the correct envelope and $1 - P\left(\bigcup\limits_{i=1}^{5} E_i\right)$ is the probability that all letters have the wrong envelopes. $P\left(\bigcup\limits_{i=1}^{5} E_i\right)$ can be calculated using the Inclusion-Exclusion Principle:

$$P\left(\bigcup_{i=1}^{5} E_i\right) = \sum_{i=1}^{5} P(E_i) - \sum_{i_1 < i_2} P(E_{i_1} E_{i_2}) + \cdots + (-1)^6 P(E_1 E_2 \cdots E_5)$$

It's obvious that $P(E_i) = \dfrac{1}{5}, \forall i = 1, \cdots, 5$. So $\sum\limits_{i=1}^{5} P(E_i) = 1$.

$P(E_{i_1} E_{i_2})$ is the event that both letter i_1 and letter i_2 have the correct envelope. The probability that i_1 has the correct envelope is $1/5$; Conditioned on that i_1 has the correct envelope, the probability that i_2 has the correct envelope is $1/4$ (there are only 4 envelopes left). So $P(E_{i_1} E_{i_2}) = \dfrac{1}{5} \times \dfrac{1}{5-1} = \dfrac{(5-2)!}{5!}$.

There are $\dbinom{5}{2} = \dfrac{5!}{2!(5-2)!}$ members of $P(E_{i_1} E_{i_2})$ in $\sum\limits_{i_1 < i_2} P(E_{i_1} E_{i_2})$, so we have

$$\sum_{i_1 < i_2} P(E_{i_1} E_{i_2}) = \frac{(5-2)!}{5!} \times \frac{5!}{2!(5-2)!} = \frac{1}{2!}$$

Similarly we have $\sum\limits_{i_1 < i_2 < i_3} P(E_{i_1} E_{i_2} E_{i_3}) = \dfrac{1}{3!}$, $\sum\limits_{i_1 < i_2 < i_3 < i_4} P(E_{i_1} E_{i_2} E_{i_3} E_{i_4}) = \dfrac{1}{4!}$, and

$$P(E_1 E_2 \cdots E_5) = \frac{1}{5!}$$

---

[9] Hint: The complement is that at least one letter is mailed to the correct firm.

$$\therefore \ P\left(\bigcup_{i=1}^{5} E_i\right) = 1 - \frac{1}{2!} + \frac{1}{3!} - \frac{1}{4!} + \frac{1}{5!} = \frac{19}{30}$$

So the probability that all 5 letters are mailed to the wrong firms is $1 - P\left(\bigcup_{i=1}^{5} E_i\right) = \frac{11}{30}$.

Birthday problem

How many people do we need in a class to make the probability that two people have the same birthday more than 1/2? (For simplicity, assume 365 days a year.)

Solution: The number is surprisingly small: 23. Let's say we have n people in the class. Without any restrictions, we have 365 possibilities for each individual's birthday. The basic principle of counting tells us that there are 365^n possible sequences.

We want to find the number of those sequences that have no duplication of birthdays. For the first individual, we can choose any of the 365 days; but for the second, only 364 remaining choices left, ..., for the *r*th individual, there are $365 - r + 1$ choices. So for n people there are $365 \times 364 \times \cdots \times (365 - n + 1)$ possible sequences where no two individuals have the same birthday. We need to have $\dfrac{365 \times 364 \times \cdots \times (365 - n + 1)}{365^n} < 1/2$

for the odds to be in our favor. The smallest such n is 23.

100th digit

What is the 100th digit to the right of the decimal point in the decimal representation of $(1 + \sqrt{2})^{3000}$?[10]

Solution: If you still have not figure out the solution from the hint, here is one more hint: $(1 + \sqrt{2})^n + (1 - \sqrt{2})^n$ is an integer when $n = 3000$.

Applying the binomial theorem for $(x + y)^n$, we have

$$(1 + \sqrt{2})^n = \sum_{k=0}^{n} \binom{n}{k} 1^{n-k} \sqrt{2}^k = \sum_{k=2j,0 \le j \le \frac{n}{2}} \binom{n}{k} 1^{n-k} \sqrt{2}^k + \sum_{k=2j+1,0 \le j < \frac{n}{2}} \binom{n}{k} 1^{n-k} \sqrt{2}^k$$

---

[10] Hint: $(1 + \sqrt{2})^2 + (1 - \sqrt{2})^2 = 6$. What will happen to $(1 - \sqrt{2})^{2n}$ as n becomes large?

$$(1-\sqrt{2})^n = \sum_{k=0}^{n} \binom{n}{k} 1^{n-k} \left(-\sqrt{2}\right)^k = \sum_{k=2j, 0 \le j \le \frac{n}{2}} \binom{n}{k} 1^{n-k} \sqrt{2}^k - \sum_{k=2j+1, 0 \le j < \frac{n}{2}} \binom{n}{k} 1^{n-k} \sqrt{2}^k$$

So $(1+\sqrt{2})^n + (1-\sqrt{2})^n = 2 \sum_{k=2j, 0 \le j \le \frac{n}{2}} \binom{n}{k} 1^{n-k} \sqrt{2}^k$, which is always an integer. It is easy to

see that $0 < (1-\sqrt{2})^{3000} \ll 10^{-100}$. So the 100th digit of $(1+\sqrt{2})^n$ must be 9.

Cubic of integer

Let x be an integer between 1 and 10^{12}, what is the probability that the cubic of x ends with 11?[11]

Solution: All integers can be expressed as $x = a + 10b$, where a is the last digit of x. Applying the binomial theorem, we have $x^3 = (a+10b)^3 = a^3 + 30a^2b + 300ab^2 + 1000b^3$.

The unit digit of x^3 only depends on a^3. So a^3 has a unit digit of 1. Only $a = 1$ satisfies this requirement and $a^3 = 1$. Since $a^3 = 1$, the tenth digit only depends on $30a^2b = 30b$. So we must have that $3b$ ends in 1, which requires the last digit of b to be 7. Consequently, the last two digits of x should be 71, which has a probability of 1% for integers between 1 and 10^{12}.

4.3 Conditional Probability and Bayes' formula

Many financial transactions are responses to probability adjustments based on new—and most likely incomplete—information. Conditional probability surely is one of the most popular test subjects in quantitative interviews. So in this section, we focus on basic conditional probability definitions and theorems.

Conditional probability $P(A|B)$: If $P(B) > 0$, then $P(A|B) = \dfrac{P(AB)}{P(B)}$ is the fraction

of B outcomes that are also A outcomes.

Multiplication Rule: $P(E_1 E_2 \cdots E_n) = P(E_1)P(E_2 | E_1)P(E_3 | E_1 E_2) \cdots P(E_n | E_1 \cdots E_{n-1})$.

---

[11] Hint: The last two digits of x^3 only depend on the last two digits of x.

Law of total probability: for any mutually exclusive events $\{F_i\}$, $i = 1, 2, \cdots, n$, whose union is the entire sample space ($F_i \cap F_j = \Phi, \forall i \neq j; \bigcup_{i=1}^{n} F_i = \Omega$), we have

$$P(E) = P(EF_1) + P(EF_2) + \cdots + P(EF_n) = \sum_{i=1}^{n} P(E \mid F_i) P(F_i)$$

$$= P(E \mid F_1) P(F_1) + P(E \mid F_2) P(F_2) + \cdots + P(E \mid F_n) P(F_n)$$

Independent events: $P(EF) = P(E)P(F) \implies P(EF^C) = P(E)P(F^C)$.

Independence is a symmetric relation: X is independent of Y $\iff$ Y is independent of X.

Bayes' Formula: $P(F_j \mid E) = \dfrac{P(E \mid F_j)P(F_j)}{\sum_{i=1}^{n} P(E \mid F_i)P(F_i)}$ if F_i, $i = 1, \cdots, n$, are mutually exclusive events whose union is the entire sample space.

As the following examples will demonstrate, not all conditional probability problems have intuitive solutions. Many demand logical analysis instead.

Boys and girls

Part A. A company is holding a dinner for working mothers with at least one son. Ms. Jackson, a mother with two children, is invited. What is the probability that both children are boys?

Solution: The sample space of two children is given by $\Omega = \{(b,b), (b,g), (g,b), (g,g)\}$ (e.g., (g,b) means the older child is a girl and the younger child a boy), and each outcome has the same probability. Since Ms. Jackson is invited, she has at least one son. Let B be the event that at least one of the children is a boy and A be the event that both children are boys, we have

$$P(A \mid B) = \frac{P(A \cap B)}{P(B)} = \frac{P(\{(b,b)\})}{P(\{(b,b),(b,g),(g,b)\})} = \frac{1/4}{3/4} = \frac{1}{3}.$$

Part B. Your new colleague, Ms. Parker is known to have two children. If you see her walking with one of her children and that child is a boy, what is the probability that both children are boys?

Solution: the other child is equally likely to be a boy or a girl (independent of the boy you've seen), so the probability that both children are boys is 1/2.

Notice the subtle difference between part *A* and part *B*. In part *A*, the problem essentially asks given there is at least one boy in two children, what is the conditional probability that both children are boys. Part *B* asks that given one child is a boy, what is the conditional probability that the other child is also a boy. For both parts, we need to assume that each child is equal likely to be a boy or a girl.

All-girl world?

In a primitive society, every couple prefers to have a baby girl. There is a 50% chance that each child they have is a girl, and the genders of their children are mutually independent. If each couple insists on having more children until they get a girl and once they have a girl they will stop having more children, what will eventually happen to the fraction of girls in this society?

Solution: It was surprising that many interviewees—include many who studied probability—have the misconception that there will be more girls. Do not let the word "prefer" and a wrong intuition misguide you. The fraction of baby girls are driven by nature, or at least the X and Y chromosomes, not by the couples' preference. You only need to look at the key information: 50% and independence. Every new-born child has equal probability of being a boy or a girl regardless of the gender of any other children. So the fraction of girls born is always 50% and the fractions of girls in the society will stay stable at 50%.

Unfair coin

You are given 1000 coins. Among them, 1 coin has heads on both sides. The other 999 coins are fair coins. You randomly choose a coin and toss it 10 times. Each time, the coin turns up heads. What is the probability that the coin you choose is the unfair one?

Solution: This is a classic conditional probability question that uses Bayes' theorem. Let A be the event that the chosen coin is the unfair one, then A^c is the event that the chosen coin is a fair one. Let B be the event that all ten tosses turn up heads. Apply Bayes' theorem we have $P(A|B) = \dfrac{P(B|A)P(A)}{P(B)} = \dfrac{P(B|A)P(A)}{P(B|A)P(A) + P(B|A^c)P(A^c)}$.

The priors are $P(A) = 1/1000$ and $P(A^c) = 999/1000$. If the coin is unfair, it always turns up heads, so $P(B|A) = 1$. If the coin is fair, each time it has 1/2 probability turning up heads. So $P(B\,|\,A^c) = (1/2)^{10} = 1/1024$. Plug in all the available information and we have the answer:

$$P(A\,|\,B) = \frac{P(B\,|\,A)P(A)}{P(B\,|\,A)P(A) + P(B\,|\,A^c)P(A^c)} = \frac{1/1000 \times 1}{1/1000 \times 1 + 999/1000 \times 1/1024} \approx 0.5.$$

Fair probability from an unfair coin

If you have an unfair coin, which may bias toward either heads or tails at an unknown probability, can you generate even odds using this coin?

Solution: Unlike fair coins, we clearly can not generate even odds with one toss using an unfair coin. How about using 2 tosses? Let p_H be the probability the coin will yield head, and p_T be the probability the coin will yield tails ($p_H + p_T = 1$). Consider two independent tosses. We have four possible outcomes *HH, HT, TH* and *TT* with probabilities $P(HH) = p_H p_H$, $P(HT) = p_H p_T$, $P(TH) = p_T p_H$, and $P(TT) = p_T p_T$.

So we have $P(HT) = P(TH)$. By assigning *HT* to winning and *TH* to losing, we can generate even odds.[12]

Dart game

Jason throws two darts at a dartboard, aiming for the center. The second dart lands farther from the center than the first. If Jason throws a third dart aiming for the center, what is the probability that the third throw is farther from the center than the first? Assume Jason's skillfulness is constant.

Solution: A standard answer directly applies the conditional probability by enumerating all possible outcomes. If we rank the three darts' results from the best (A) to the worst (C), there are 6 possible outcomes with equal probability:

---

[12] I should point out that this simple approach is not the most efficient approach since I am disregarding the cases HH and TT. When the coin has high bias (one side is far more likely than the other side to occur), the method may take many runs to generate one useful result. For more complex algorithm that increasing efficiency, please refer to *Tree Algorithms for Unbiased Coin Tossing with a Biased Coin* by Quentin F. Stout and Bette L. Warren, Annals of Probability 12 (1984), pp. 212-222.

Outcome	1	2	3	4	5	6
1st throw	A	B	A	C	B	C
2nd throw	B	A	C	A	C	B
3rd throw	C	C	B	B	A	A

The information from the first two throws eliminates outcomes 2, 4 and 6. Conditioned on outcomes 1, 3, and 5, the outcomes that the 3rd throw is worse than the 1st throw are outcomes 1 and 3. So there is 2/3 probability that the third throw is farther from the center than the first.

This approach surely is reasonable. Nevertheless, it is not an efficient approach. When the number of darts is small, we can easily enumerate all outcomes. What if it is a more complex version of the original problem:

Jason throws n ($n \geq 5$) darts at a dartboard, aiming for the center. Each subsequent dart is farther from the center than the first dart. If Jason throws the $(n+1)$th dart, what is the probability that it is also farther from the center than his first?

This question is equivalent to a simple question: what is the probability that the $(n+1)th$ throw is not the best among all $(n+1)$ throws? Since the 1st throw is the best among the first n throws, essentially I am saying the event that the $(n+1)$th throw is the best of all $(n+1)$ throws (let's call it A_{n+1}) is independent of the event that the 1st throw is the best of the first n throws (let's call it A_1). In fact, A_{n+1} is independent of the order of the first n throws. Are these two events really independent? The answer is a resounding yes. If it is not obvious to you that A_{n+1} is independent of the order of the first n throws, let's look at it another way: the order of the first n throws is independent of A_{n+1}. Surely this claim is conspicuous. But independence is symmetric! Since the probability of A_{n+1} is $1/(n+1)$, the probability that $(n+1)th$ throw is not the best is $n/(n+1)$.[13]

For the original version, three darts are thrown independently, they each have a 1/3 chance of being the best throw. As long as the third dart is not the best throw, it will be worse than the first dart. Therefore the answer is 2/3.

Birthday line

At a movie theater, a whimsical manager announces that she will give a free ticket to the first person in line whose birthday is the same as someone who has already bought a ticket. You are given the opportunity to choose any position in line. Assuming that you

---

[13] Here you can again use symmetry argument: each throw is equally likely to be the best.

don't know anyone else's birthday and all birthdays are distributed randomly throughout the year (assuming 365 days in a year), what position in line gives you the largest chance of getting the free ticket?[14]

Solution: If you have solved the problem that no two people have the same birthday in an *n*-people group, this new problem is just a small extension. Assume that you choose to be the *n*-th person in line. In order for you to get the free ticket, all of the first $n-1$ individuals in line must have different birthdays and your birthday needs to be the same as one of those $n-1$ individuals.

$$p(n) = p\left(first\ n-1\ people\ have\ no\ same\ birthday\right) \times p\left(yours\ among\ those\ n-1\ birthdays\right)$$
$$= \frac{365 \times 364 \times \cdots (365-n+2)}{365^{n-1}} \times \frac{n-1}{365}$$

It is intuitive to argue that when *n* is small, increasing *n* will increase your chance of getting the free ticket since the increase of $p\left(yours\ among\ those\ n-1\ birthdays\right)$ is more significant than the decrease in $p\left(first\ n-1\ people\ have\ no\ same\ birthday\right)$. So when *n* is small, we have $P(n) > P(n-1)$. As *n* increases, gradually the negative impact of $p\left(first\ n-1\ people\ have\ no\ same\ birthday\right)$ will catch up and at a certain point we will have $P(n+1) < P(n)$. So we need to find such an *n* that satisfies $P(n) > P(n-1)$ and $P(n) > P(n+1)$.

$$P(n-1) = \frac{365}{365} \times \frac{364}{365} \times \cdots \times \frac{365-(n-3)}{365} \times \frac{n-2}{365}$$

$$P(n) = \frac{365}{365} \times \frac{364}{365} \times \cdots \times \frac{365-(n-2)}{365} \times \frac{n-1}{365}$$

$$P(n+1) = \frac{365}{365} \times \frac{364}{365} \times \cdots \times \frac{365-(n-2)}{365} \times \frac{365-(n-1)}{365} \times \frac{n}{365}$$

Hence,
$$\left. \begin{array}{l} P(n) > P(n-1) \Rightarrow \dfrac{365-(n-2)}{365} \times \dfrac{n-1}{365} > \dfrac{n-2}{365} \\ P(n) > P(n+1) \Rightarrow \dfrac{n-1}{365} > \dfrac{365-(n-1)}{365} \times \dfrac{n}{365} \end{array} \right\} \Rightarrow \left. \begin{array}{l} n^2 - 3n - 363 < 0 \\ n^2 - n - 365 > 0 \end{array} \right\} \Rightarrow n = 20$$

You should be the 20th person in line.

---

[14] Hint: If you are the *n*-th person in line, to get the free ticket, the first (*n*-1) people in line must not have the same birthday and you must have the same birthday as one of them.

Dice order

We throw 3 dice one by one. What is the probability that we obtain 3 points in strictly increasing order?[15]

Solution: To have 3 points in strictly increasing order, first all three points must be different numbers. Conditioned on three different numbers, the probability of strictly increasing order is simply $1/3! = 1/6$ (one specific sequence out of all possible permutations). So we have

P = P(different numbers in all three throws) × P(increasing order|3 different numbers)

$$= (1 \times \tfrac{5}{6} \times \tfrac{4}{6}) \times \tfrac{1}{6} = 5/54$$

Monty Hall problem

Monty Hall problem is a probability puzzle based on an old American show *Let's Make a Deal*. The problem is named after the show's host. Suppose you're on the show now, and you're given the choice of 3 doors. Behind one door is a car; behind the other two, goats. You don't know ahead of time what is behind each of the doors.

You pick one of the doors and announce it. As soon as you pick the door, Monty opens one of the other two doors that he knows has a goat behind it. Then he gives you the option to either keep your original choice or switch to the third door. Should you switch? What is the probability of winning a car if you switch?

Solution: If you don't switch, whether you win or not is independent of Monty's action of showing you a goat, so your probability of winning is 1/3. What if you switch? Many would argue that since there are only two doors left after Monty shows a door with goat, the probability of winning is 1/2. But is this argument correct?

If you look at the problem from a different perspective, the answer becomes clear. Using a switching strategy, you win the car if and only if you originally pick a door with a goat, which has a probability of 2/3 (You pick a door with a goat, Monty shows a door with another goat, so the one you switch to must have a car behind it). If you originally picked the door with the car, which has a probability of 1/3, you will lose by switching. So your probability of winning by switching is actually 2/3.

---

[15] Hint: To obtain 3 points in strictly increasing order, the 3 points must be different. For 3 different points in a sequence, strictly increasing order is one of the possible permutations.

Amoeba population

There is a one amoeba in a pond. After every minute the amoeba may die, stay the same, split into two or split into three with equal probability. All its offspring, if it has any, will behave the same (and independent of other amoebas). What is the probability the amoeba population will die out?

Solution: This is just another standard conditional probability problem once you realize we need to derive the probability conditioned on what happens to the amoeba one minute later. Let $P(E)$ be the probability that the amoeba population will die out and apply the law of total probability conditioned on what happens to the amoeba one minute later:

$$P(E) = P(E \mid F_1)P(F_1) + P(E \mid F_2)P(F_2) + \cdots + P(E \mid F_n)P(F_n).$$

For the original amoeba, as stated in the question, there are four possible mutually exclusive events each with probability 1/4. Let's denote F_1 as the event the amoeba dies; F_2 as the event that it stays the same; F_3 as the event that it splits into two; F_4 as the event that it splits into three. For event F_1, $P(E \mid F_1) = 1$ since no amoeba is left. $P(E \mid F_2) = P(E)$ since the state is the same as the beginning. For F_3, there are two amoebas; either behaves the same as the original one. The total amoeba population will die only if both amoebas die out. Since they are independent, the probability that they both will die out is $P(E)^2$. Similarly we have $P(F_4) = P(E)^3$. Plug in all the numbers, the equation becomes $P(E) = 1/4 \times 1 + 1/4 \times P(E) + 1/4 \times P(E)^2 + 1/4 \times P(E)^3$. Solve this equation with the restriction $0 < P(E) < 1$, and we will get $P(E) = \sqrt{2} - 1 \approx 0.414$ (The other two roots of the equation are 1 and $-\sqrt{2} - 1$).

Candies in a jar

You are taking out candies one by one from a jar that has 10 red candies, 20 blue candies, and 30 green candies in it. What is the probability that there are at least 1 blue candy and 1 green candy left in the jar when you have taken out all the red candies?[16]

Solution: At first look, this problem appears to be a combinatorial one. However, a conditional probability approach gives a much more intuitive answer. Let T_r, T_b and T_g

---

[16] Hint: If there are at least 1 blue candy and 1 green candy left, the last red candy must have been removed before the last blue candy and the last green candy in the sequence of 60 candies. What is the probability that the blue candy is the last one in the 60-candy sequence? Conditioned on that, what is the probability that the last green candy is the last one in the 30-candy sequence (10 red, 20 green)? What if the green candy is the last one in the 60-candy sequence?

be the number that the last red, blue, and green candies are taken out respectively. To have at least 1 blue candy and 1 green candy left when all the red candies are taken out, we need to have $T_r < T_b$ and $T_r < T_g$. In other words, we want to derive $P(T_r < T_b \cap T_r < T_g)$. There are two mutually exclusive events that satisfy $T_r < T_b$ and $T_r < T_g : T_r < T_b < T_g$ and $T_r < T_g < T_b$.

$$\therefore \ P(T_r < T_b \cap T_r < T_g) = P(T_r < T_b < T_g) + P(T_r < T_g < T_b)$$

$T_r < T_b < T_g$ means that the last candy is green ($T_g = 60$). Since each of the 60 candies are equally likely to be the last candy and among them 30 are green ones, we have $P(T_g = 60) = \dfrac{30}{60}$. Conditioned on $T_g = 60$, we need $P(T_r < T_b | T_g = 60)$. Among the 30 red and blue candies, each candy is again equally likely to be the last candy and there are 20 blue candies, so $P(T_r < T_b | T_g = 60) = \dfrac{20}{30}$ and $P(T_r < T_b < T_g) = \dfrac{30}{60} \times \dfrac{20}{30}$. Similarly, we have $P(T_r < T_g < T_b) = \dfrac{20}{60} \times \dfrac{30}{40}$.

Hence,

$$P(T_r < T_b \cap T_r < T_g) = P(T_r < T_b < T_g) + P(T_r < T_g < T_b) = \frac{30}{60} \times \frac{20}{30} + \frac{20}{60} \times \frac{30}{40} = \frac{7}{12}.$$

Coin toss game

Two players, A and B, alternatively toss a fair coin (A tosses the coin first, then B tosses the coin, then A, then B...). The sequence of heads and tails is recorded. If there is a head followed by a tail (HT subsequence), the game ends and the person who tosses the tail wins. What is the probability that A wins the game?[17]

Solution: Let $P(A)$ be the probability that A wins; then the probability that B wins is $P(B) = 1 - P(A)$. Let's condition $P(A)$ on A's first toss, which has $1/2$ probability of H (heads) and $1/2$ probability of T (tails).

$$P(A) = 1/2 P(A | H) + 1/2 P(A | T)$$

If A's first toss is T, then B essentially becomes the first to toss (An H is required for the HT subsequence). So we have $P(A | T) = P(B) = 1 - P(A)$.

If A's first toss ends in H, let's further condition on B's first toss. B has $1/2$ probability of getting T, in that case A loses. For the $1/2$ probability that B gets H, B essentially

---

[17] Hint: condition on the result of A's first toss and use symmetry.

becomes the first one to toss an H. In that case, A has $(1 - P(A|H))$ probability of winning. So $P(A|H) = 1/2 \times 0 + 1/2(1 - P(A|H)) \Rightarrow P(A|H) = 1/3$

Combining all the available information, we have

$$P(A) = 1/2 \times 1/3 + 1/2(1 - P(A)) \Rightarrow P(A) = 4/9.$$

Sanity check: we can see that $P(A) < 1/2$, which is reasonable since A cannot win in his first toss, yet B has 1/4 probability to win in her first toss.

Russian roulette series

Let's play a traditional version of Russian roulette. A single bullet is put into a 6-chamber revolver. The barrel is randomly spun so that each chamber is equally likely to be under the hammer. Two players take turns to pull the trigger—with the gun unfortunately pointing at one's own head—without further spinning until the gun goes off and the person who gets killed loses. If you, one of the players, can choose to go first or second, how will you choose? And what is your probability of loss?

Solution: Many people have the wrong impression that the first person has higher probability of loss. After all, the first player has a 1/6 chance of getting killed in the first round before the second player starts. Unfortunately, this is one of the few times that intuition is wrong. Once the barrel is spun, the position of the bullet is fixed. If you go first, you lose if and only if the bullet is in chamber 1, 3 and 5. So the probability that you lose is the same as the second player, 1/2. In that sense, whether to go first or second does not matter.

Now, let's change the rule slightly. We will spin the barrel again after every trigger pull. Will you choose to be the first or the second player? And what is your probability of loss?

Solution: The difference is that each run now becomes independent. Assume that the first player's probability of losing is p, then the second player's probability of losing is $1 - p$. Let's condition the probability on the first person's first trigger pull. He has 1/6 probability of losing in this run. Otherwise, he essentially becomes the second player in the game with new (conditional) probability of losing $1 - p$. That happens with probability 5/6. That gives us $p = 1 \times 1/6 + (1 - p) \times 5/6 \Rightarrow p = 6/11$. So you should choose to be the second player and have 5/11 probability of losing.

If instead of one bullet, two bullets are randomly put in the chamber. Your opponent played the first and he was alive after the first trigger pull. You are given the option whether to spin the barrel. Should you spin the barrel?

Solution: if you spin the barrel, the probability that you will lose in this round is 2/6. If you don't spin the barrel, there are only 5 chambers left and your probability of losing in this round (conditioned on that your opponent survived) is 2/5. So you should spin the barrel.

What if the two bullets are randomly put in two consecutive positions? If your opponent survived his first round, should you spin the barrel?

Solution: Now we have to condition our probability on the fact that the positions of the two bullets are consecutive. As shown in Figure 4.3, let's label the empty chambers as 1, 2, 3 and 4; label the ones with bullets 5 and 6. Since your opponent survived the first round, the possible position he encountered is 1, 2, 3 or 4 with equal probability. With 1/4 chance, the next one is a bullet (the position was 4). So if you don't spin, the chance of survival is 3/4. If you spin the barrel, each position has equal probability of being chosen, and your chance of survival is only 2/3. So you should not spin the barrel.

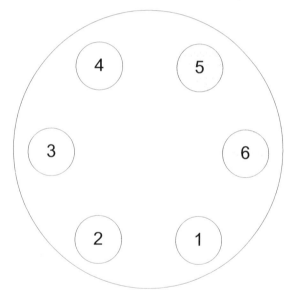

Figure 4.3 Russian roulette with two consecutive bullets.

Aces

Fifty-two cards are randomly distributed to 4 players with each player getting 13 cards. What is the probability that each of them will have an ace?

Solution: The problem can be answered using standard counting methods. To distribute 52 cards to 4 players with 13 cards each has $\dfrac{52!}{13!13!13!13!}$ permutations. If each player needs to have one ace, we can distribute the aces first, which has 4! ways. Then we distribute the rest 48 cards to 4 players with 12 cards each, which has $\dfrac{48!}{12!12!12!12!}$ permutations. So the probability that each of them will have an Ace is

$$4! \times \frac{48!}{12!12!12!12!} \div \frac{52!}{13!13!13!13!} = \frac{52}{52} \times \frac{39}{51} \times \frac{26}{50} \times \frac{13}{49}.$$

The logic becomes clearer if we use a conditional probability approach. Let's begin with any one of the four aces; it has probability $52/52 = 1$ of belonging to a pile. The second ace can be any of the remaining 51 cards, among which 39 belong to a pile different from the first ace. So the probability that the second ace is not in the pile of the first ace is $39/51$. Now there are 50 cards left, among which 26 belong to the other two piles. So the conditional probability that the third ace is in one of the other 2 piles given the first two aces are already in different piles is $26/50$. Similarly, the conditional probability that the fourth ace is in the pile different from the first three aces given that the first three aces are in different piles is $13/49$. So the probability that each pile has an ace is

$$1 \times \frac{39}{51} \times \frac{26}{50} \times \frac{13}{49}.$$

Gambler's ruin problem

A gambler starts with an initial fortune of i dollars. On each successive game, the gambler wins \$1 with probability p, $0 < p < 1$, or loses \$1 with probability $q = 1 - p$. He will stop if he either accumulates N dollars or loses all his money. What is the probability that he will end up with N dollars?

Solution: This is a classic textbook probability problem called the Gambler's Ruin Problem. Interestingly, it is still widely used in quantitative interviews.

From any initial state i (the dollars the gambler has), $0 \le i \le N$, let P_i be the probability that the gambler's fortune will reach N instead of 0. The next state is either $i+1$ with probability p or $i-1$ with probability q. So we have

$$P_i = pP_{i+1} + qP_{i-1} \Rightarrow P_{i+1} - P_i = \frac{q}{p}(P_i - P_{i-1}) = \left(\frac{q}{p}\right)^2 (P_{i-1} - P_{i-2}) = \cdots = \left(\frac{q}{p}\right)^i (P_1 - P_0)$$

We also have the boundary probabilities $P_0 = 0$ and $P_N = 1$.

So starting from P_2, we can successively evaluate P_i as an expression of P_1:

$$P_1 = pP_2 + qP_0 \Rightarrow P_2 = \frac{1}{p}P_1 = \left[1 + \frac{q}{p}\right]P_1$$

$$P_3 = \left[1 + \frac{q}{p} + \left(\frac{q}{p}\right)^2\right]P_1$$

...

$$P_i = \left[1 + \frac{q}{p} + \cdots + \left(\frac{q}{p}\right)^{i-1}\right]P_1$$

Extending this expression to P_N, we have

$$P_N = 1 = \left[1 + \frac{q}{p} + \cdots + \left(\frac{q}{p}\right)^{N-1}\right]P_1 = \begin{cases} \dfrac{1-(q/p)^N}{1-q/p}P_1, & \text{if } q/p \neq 1 \\ NP_1, & \text{if } q/p = 1 \end{cases}$$

$$\Rightarrow P_1 = \begin{cases} \dfrac{1-q/p}{1-(q/p)^N}, & \text{if } q/p \neq 1 \\ 1/N, & \text{if } q/p = 1 \end{cases} \Rightarrow P_i = \begin{cases} \dfrac{1-(q/p)^i}{1-(q/p)^N}P_1, & \text{if } p \neq 1/2 \\ i/N, & \text{if } p = 1/2 \end{cases}$$

Basketball scores

A basketball player is taking 100 free throws. She scores one point if the ball passes through the hoop and zero point if she misses. She has scored on her first throw and missed on her second. For each of the following throw the probability of her scoring is the fraction of throws she has made so far. For example, if she has scored 23 points after the 40th throw, the probability that she will score in the 41th throw is 23/40. After 100 throws (including the first and the second), what is the probability that she scores exactly 50 baskets?[18]

Solution: Let (n,k), $1 \leq k \leq n$, be the event that the player scores k baskets after n throws and $P_{n,k} = P((n,k))$. The solution is surprisingly simple if we use an induction approach starting with $n = 3$. The third throw has 1/2 probability of scoring. So we have $P_{3,1} = 1/2$ and $P_{3,2} = 1/2$. For the case when $n = 4$, let's apply the law of total probability

---

[18] Hint: Again, do not let the number 100 scares you. Start with smallest n, solve the problem; try to find a pattern by increasing n; and prove the pattern using induction.

$$\begin{cases} P_{4,1} = P\big((4,1)\,|\,(3,1)\big) \times P_{3,1} + P\big((4,1)\,|\,(3,2)\big) \times P_{3,2} = \dfrac{2}{3} \times \dfrac{1}{2} + 0 \times \dfrac{1}{2} = \dfrac{1}{3} \\[2mm] P_{4,2} = P\big((4,2)\,|\,(3,1)\big) \times P_{3,1} + P\big((4,2)\,|\,(3,2)\big) \times P_{3,2} = \dfrac{1}{3} \times \dfrac{1}{2} + \dfrac{1}{3} \times \dfrac{1}{2} = \dfrac{1}{3} \\[2mm] P_{4,3} = P\big((4,3)\,|\,(3,1)\big) \times P_{3,1} + P\big((4,3)\,|\,(3,2)\big) \times P_{3,2} = 0 \times \dfrac{1}{2} + \dfrac{2}{3} \times \dfrac{1}{2} = \dfrac{1}{3} \end{cases}$$

The results indicate that $P_{n,k} = \dfrac{1}{n-1}$, $\forall k = 1, 2, \cdots, n-1$, and give the hint that the law of total probability can be used in the induction step.

Induction step: given that $P_{n,k} = \dfrac{1}{n-1}$, $\forall k = 1, 2, \cdots, n-1$, we need to prove

$P_{n+1,k} = \dfrac{1}{(n+1)-1} = \dfrac{1}{n}$, $\forall k = 1, 2, \cdots, n$. To show it, simply apply the law of total probability:

$$P_{n+1,k} = P\big(miss\,|\,(n,k)\big) P_{n,k} + P\big(score\,|\,(n,k-1)\big) P_{n,k-1}$$
$$= \left(1 - \frac{k}{n}\right) \frac{1}{n-1} + \frac{k-1}{n}\frac{1}{n-1} = \frac{1}{n}$$

The equation is also applicable to the $P_{n+1,1}$ and $P_{n+1,n}$, although in these cases $\dfrac{k-1}{n} = 0$

and $\left(1 - \dfrac{k}{n}\right) = 0$, respectively. So we have $P_{n,k} = \dfrac{1}{n-1}$, $\forall k = 1, 2, \cdots, n-1$ and $\forall n \geq 2$.

Hence, $P_{100,50} = 1/99$.

Cars on road

If the probability of observing at least one car on a highway during any 20-minute time interval is 609/625, then what is the probability of observing at least one car during any 5-minute time interval? Assume that the probability of seeing a car at any moment is uniform (constant) for the entire 20 minutes.

Solution: We can break down the 20-minute interval into a sequence of 4 non-overlapping 5-minute intervals. Because of constant default probability (of observing a car), the probability of observing a car in any 5-minute interval is constant. Let's denote the probability to be p, then the probability that in any 5-minute interval we do not observe a car is $1 - p$.

The probability that we do not observe any car in all four of such independent 5-minute intervals is $(1-p)^4 = 1 - 609/625 = 16/625$, which gives $p = 3/5$.

4.4 Discrete and Continuous Distributions

In this section, we review a variety of distribution functions for random variables that are widely used in quantitative modeling. Although it may not be necessary to memorize the properties of these distributions, having an intuitive understanding of the distributions and having the ability to quickly derive important properties are valuable skills in practice. As usual, let's begin with the theories:

Common function of random variables

Table 4.1 summarizes how the basic properties of discrete and continuous random variables are defined or calculated. These are the basics you should commit to memory.

Random variable (X)	Discrete	Continuous[19]
Cumulative distribution function/cdf	$F(a) = P\{X \le a\}$	$F(a) = \int_{-\infty}^{a} f(x)dx$
Probability mass function /pmf Probability density function /pdf	pmf: $p(x) = P\{X = x\}$	pdf: $f(x) = \dfrac{d}{dx}F(x)$
Expected value/ $E[X]$	$\displaystyle\sum_{x:p(x)>0} xp(x)$	$\displaystyle\int_{-\infty}^{\infty} xf(x)dx$
Expected value of g(X)/ $E[g(X)]$	$\displaystyle\sum_{x:p(x)>0} g(x)p(x)$	$\displaystyle\int_{-\infty}^{\infty} g(x)f(x)dx$
Variance of X/ $var(X)$	$E[(X-E[X])^2] = E[X^2] - (E[X])^2$	
Standard deviation of X/ $std(X)$	$\sqrt{var(X)}$	

Table 4.1 Basic properties of discrete and continuous random variables

Discrete random variables

Table 4.2 includes some of the most widely-used discrete distributions. Discrete uniform random variable represents the occurrence of a value between number a and b when all values in the set $\{a, a+1, \cdots, b\}$ have equal probability. Binomial random variable represents the number of successes in a sequence of n experiments when each trial is

---

[19] For continuous random variables, $P(X = x) = 0$, $\forall x \in (-\infty, \infty)$, so $P\{X \le x\} = P\{X < x\}$.

independently a success with probability p. Poisson random variable represents the number of events occurring in a fixed period of time with the expected number of occurrences λt when events occur with a known average rate λ and are independent of the time since the last event. Geometric random variable represents the trial number (n) to get the first success when each trial is independently a success with probability p. Negative Binomial random variable represents the trial number to get to the r-th success when each trial is independently a success with probability p.

Name	Probability mass function (pmf)	$E[X]$	$\text{var}(X)$
Uniform	$P(x)=\dfrac{1}{b-a+1},\quad x=a,a+1,\cdots,b$	$\dfrac{b+a}{2}$	$\dfrac{(b-a+1)^2-1}{12}$
Binomial	$P(x)=\dbinom{n}{x}p^x(1-p)^{n-x},\quad x=0,1,\cdots,n$	np	$np(1-p)$
Poisson	$P(x)=\dfrac{e^{-\lambda t}(\lambda t)^x}{x!},\quad x=0,1,\cdots^{20}$	λt	λt
Geometric	$P(x)=(1-p)^{x-1}p,\; x=1,2,\cdots$	$\dfrac{1}{p}$	$\dfrac{1-p}{p^2}$
Negative Binomial	$P(x)=\dbinom{x-1}{r-1}p^r(1-p)^{x-r},\; x=r,r+1,\cdots$	$\dfrac{r}{p}$	$\dfrac{r(1-p)}{p^2}$

Table 4.2 Probability mass function, expected value and variance of discrete random variables

Continuous random variables

Table 4.3 includes some of the commonly encountered continuous distributions. Uniform distribution describes a random variable uniformly distributed over the interval $[a,b]$. Because of the central limit theorem, normal distribution/Gaussian distribution is by far the most popular continuous distribution. Exponential distribution models the arrival time of an event if it has a constant arrival rate λ. Gamma distribution with parameters (α, λ) often arises, in practice, as the distribution of the amount of time one has to wait until a total of n events occur. Beta distributions are used to model events

---

[20] Here we use the product of arrival rate λ and time t to define the parameter (expected value) since it is the definition used in many Poisson process studies.

that are constrained within a defined interval. By adjusting the shape parameters α and β, it can model different shapes of probability density functions.[21]

Name	Probability density function (pdf)	$E[X]$	var(X)
Uniform	$\dfrac{1}{b-a}, \quad a \leq x \leq b$	$\dfrac{b+a}{2}$	$\dfrac{(b-a)^2}{12}$
Normal	$\dfrac{1}{\sqrt{2\pi}\sigma}e^{\frac{-(x-\mu)^2}{2\sigma^2}}, \quad x \in (-\infty, \infty)$	μ	σ^2
Exponential	$\lambda e^{-\lambda x}, \quad x \geq 0$	$1/\lambda$	$1/\lambda^2$
Gamma	$\dfrac{\lambda e^{-\lambda x}(\lambda x)^{\alpha-1}}{\Gamma(\alpha)}, \quad x \geq 0, \ \Gamma(a) = \int_0^\infty e^{-y}y^{a-1}$	α/λ	α/λ^2
Beta	$\dfrac{\Gamma(\alpha+\beta)}{\Gamma(\alpha)\Gamma(\beta)}x^{\alpha-1}(1-x)^{\beta-1}, \quad 0 < x < 1$	$\dfrac{\alpha}{\alpha+\beta}$	$\dfrac{\alpha\beta}{(\alpha+\beta+1)(\alpha+\beta)^2}$

Table 4.3 Probability density function, expected value and variance of continuous random variables

Meeting probability

Two bankers each arrive at the station at some random time between 5:00 am and 6:00 am (arrival time for either banker is uniformly distributed). They stay exactly five minutes and then leave. What is the probability they will meet on a given day?

Solution: Assume banker A arrives X minutes after 5:00 am and B arrives Y minutes after 5:00 am. X and Y are independent uniform distribution between 0 and 60. Since both only stay exactly five minutes, as shown in Figure 4.4, A and B meet if and only if $|X-Y| \leq 5$.

So the probability that A and B will meet is simply the area of the shadowed region divided by the area of the square (the rest of the region can be combined to a square with size length 55): $\dfrac{60\times60-2\times(1/2\times55\times55)}{60\times60} = \dfrac{(60+55)\times(60-55)}{60\times60} = \dfrac{23}{144}$.

---

[21] For example, beta distribution is widely used in modeling loss given default in risk management. If you are familiar with Bayesian statistics, you will also recognize it as a popular conjugate prior function.

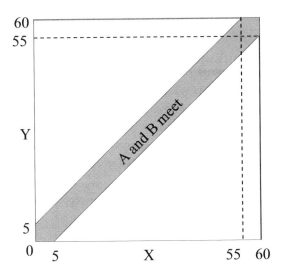

Figure 4.4 Distributions of Banker *A*'s and Banker *B*'s arrival times

Probability of triangle

A stick is cut twice randomly (each cut point follows a uniform distribution on the stick), what is the probability that the 3 segments can form a triangle?[22]

Solution: Without loss of generality, let's assume that the length of the stick is 1. Let's also label the point of the first cut as x and the second cut as y.

If $x < y$, then the three segments are x, y-x and 1-y. The conditions to form a triangle are

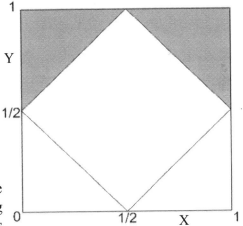

$$x + (y - x) > 1 - y \Rightarrow y > 1/2$$
$$x + (1 - y) > y - x \Rightarrow y < 1/2 + x$$
$$(y - x) + (1 - y) > x \Rightarrow x < 1/2$$

The feasible area is shown in Figure 4.5. The case for $x < y$ is the left gray triangle. Using symmetry, we can see that the case for $x > y$ is the right gray triangle.

Figure 4.5 Distribution of cuts X and Y

---

[22] Hint: Let the first cut point be x, the second one be y, use the figure to show the distribution of x and y.

The total shadowed area represents the region where 3 segments can form a triangle, which is 1/4 of the square. So the probability is 1/4.

Property of Poisson process

You are waiting for a bus at a bus station. The buses arrive at the station according to a Poisson process with an average arrival time of 10 minutes ($\lambda = 0.1 / \min$). If the buses have been running for a long time and you arrive at the bus station at a random time, what is your expected waiting time? On average, how many minutes ago did the last bus leave?

Solution: Considering the importance of jump-diffusion processes in derivative pricing and the role of Poisson processes in studying jump processes, let's elaborate more on exponential random variables and the Poison process. Exponential distribution is widely used to model the time interval between independent events that happen at a constant average rate (arrival rate) λ: $f(t) = \begin{cases} \lambda e^{-\lambda t} & (t \geq 0) \\ 0 & (t < 0) \end{cases}$. The expected arrival time is $1/\lambda$ and the variance is $1/\lambda^2$. Using integration, we can calculate the cdf of an exponential distribution to be $F(t) = P(\tau \leq t) = 1 - e^{-rt}$ and $P(\tau > t) = e^{-rt}$, where τ is the random variable for arrival time. One unique property of exponential distribution is memorylessness: $P\{\tau > s + t \mid \tau > s\} = P(\tau > t)$.[23] That means if we have waited for s time units, the extra waiting time has the same distribution as the waiting time when we start at time 0.

When the arrivals of a series of events each independently follow an exponential distribution with arrival rate λ, the number of arrivals between time 0 and t can be modeled as a Poisson process $P(N(t) = x) = \dfrac{e^{-\lambda t} \lambda t^x}{x!}$, $x = 0, 1, \cdots$ [24] The expected number of arrivals is λt and the variance is also λt. Because of the memoryless nature of exponential distribution, the number of arrivals between time s and t is also a Poisson process $P(N(t - s) = x) = \dfrac{e^{-\lambda(t-s)} \left(\lambda(t-s)\right)^x}{x!}$.

Taking advantage of the memoryless property of exponential distribution, we know that the expected waiting time is $1/\lambda = 10 \min$. If you look back in time, the memoryless property stills applies. So on average, the last bus arrived 10 minutes ago as well.

---

[23] $P\{\tau > s + t \mid \tau > s\} = e^{-\lambda(s+t)} / e^{-\lambda s} = e^{-\lambda t} = P(x > t)$

[24] More rigorously, $N(t)$ is defined as a right-continuous function.

This is another example that your intuition may misguide you. You may be wondering that if the last bus on average arrived 10 minutes ago and the next bus on average will arrive 10 minutes later, shouldn't the average arrival time be 20 minutes instead of 10? The explanation to the apparent discrepancy is that when you arrive at a random time, you are more likely to arrive in a long time interval between two bus arrivals than in a short one. For example, if one interval between two bus arrivals is 30 minutes and another is 5 minutes, you are more likely to arrive at a time during that 30-minute interval rather than 5-minute interval. In fact, if you arrive at a random time, the expected residual life (the time for the next bus to arrive) is $\dfrac{E[X^2]}{2E[X]}$ for a general distribution.[25]

Moments of normal distribution

If X follows standard normal distribution ($X \sim N(0, 1)$), what is $E[X^n]$ for $n = 1, 2, 3$ and 4?

Solution: The first to fourth moments of the standard normal distribution are essentially the mean, the variance, the skewness and the kurtosis. So you probably have remembered that the answers are 0, 1, 0 (no skewness), and 3, respectively.

Standard normal distribution has pdf $f(x) = \dfrac{1}{\sqrt{2\pi}} e^{-x^2/2}$. Using simple symmetry we have $E[x^n] = \displaystyle\int_{-\infty}^{\infty} x^n \dfrac{1}{\sqrt{2\pi}} e^{-x^2/2} dx = 0$ when n is odd. For $n = 2$, integration by parts are often used. To solve $E[X^n]$ for any integer n, an approach using **moment generating functions** may be a better choice. Moment generating functions are defined as

$$M(t) = E[e^{tX}] = \begin{cases} \displaystyle\sum_x e^{tx} p(x), & \text{if } x \text{ is discrete} \\ \displaystyle\int_{-\infty}^{\infty} e^{tx} f(x) dx, & \text{if } x \text{ is continuous} \end{cases}$$

Sequentially taking derivative of $M(t)$, we get one frequently-used property of $M(t)$:

$$M'(t) = \frac{d}{dt} E[e^{tX}] = E[Xe^{tX}] \Rightarrow M'(0) = E[X],$$

$$M''(t) = \frac{d}{dt} E[Xe^{tX}] = E[X^2 e^{tX}] \Rightarrow M''(0) = E[X^2],$$

---

[25] The residual life is explained in Chapter 3 of "***Discrete Stochastic Process***" by Robert G. Gallager.

and $M^n(0) = E[X^n]$, $\forall n \geq 1$ in general.

We can use this property to solve $E[X^n]$ for $X \sim N(0, 1)$. For standard normal distribution $M(t) = E[e^{tX}] = \int_{-\infty}^{\infty} e^{tx} \frac{1}{\sqrt{2\pi}} e^{-x^2/2} dx = e^{t^2/2} \int_{-\infty}^{\infty} \frac{1}{\sqrt{2\pi}} e^{-(x-t)^2/2} dx = e^{t^2/2}$.

($\frac{1}{\sqrt{2\pi}} e^{-(x-t)^2/2}$ is the pdf of normal distribution $X \sim N(t, 1)$, so $\int_{-\infty}^{\infty} f(x)dx = 1$).

Taking derivatives, we have

$$M'(t) = te^{t^2/2} \Rightarrow M'(0) = 0, \ M''(t) = e^{t^2/2} + t^2 e^{t^2/2} \Rightarrow M''(0) = e^0 = 1,$$

$$M^3(t) = te^{t^2/2} + 2te^{t^2/2} + t^3 e^{t^2/2} = 3te^{t^2/2} + t^3 e^{t^2/2} \Rightarrow M^3(0) = 0,$$

and $M^4(t) = 3e^{t^2/2} + 3t^2 e^{t^2/2} + 3t^2 e^{t^2/2} + 3t^4 e^{t^2/2} \Rightarrow M^4(0) = 3e^0 = 3$.

4.5 Expected Value, Variance & Covariance

Expected value, variance and covariance are indispensable in estimating returns and risks of any investments. Naturally, they are a popular test subject in interviews as well. The basic knowledge includes the following:

If $E[x_i]$ is finite for all $i = 1, \cdots, n$, then $E[X_1 + \cdots + X_n] = E[X_1] + \cdots + E[X_n]$. The relationship holds whether the x_i's are independent of each other or not.

If X and Y are independent, then $E[g(X)h(Y)] = E[g(x)]E[h(Y)]$.

Covariance: $Cov(X,Y) = E[(X - E[X])(Y - E[Y])] = E[XY] - E[X]E[Y]$.

Correlation: $\rho(X,Y) = \dfrac{Cov(X,Y)}{\sqrt{Var(X)Var(Y)}}$

If X and Y are independent, $Cov(X,Y) = 0$ and $\rho(X,Y) = 0$.[26]

General rules of variance and covariance:

$$Cov(\sum_{i=1}^{n} a_i X_i, \sum_{j=1}^{m} b_j Y_j) = \sum_{i=1}^{n} \sum_{j=1}^{m} a_i b_j Cov(X_i, Y_j)$$

$$Var(\sum_{i=1}^{n} X_i) = \sum_{i=1}^{n} Var(X_i) + 2 \sum \sum_{i<j} Cov(X_i, X_j)$$

---

[26] The reverse is not true. $\rho(X,Y) = 0$ only means X and Y are uncorrelated; they may well be dependent.

Conditional expectation and variance

For discrete distribution: $E[g(X)|Y=y] = \sum_x g(x)p_{X|Y}(x|y) = \sum_x g(x)p(X=x|Y=y)$

For continuous distribution: $E[g(X)|Y=y] = \int_{-\infty}^{\infty} g(x)f_{X|Y}(x|y)dx$

Law of total expectation:

$$E[X] = E[E[X|Y]] = \begin{cases} \sum_y E[X|Y=y]p(Y=y), & \text{for discrete } Y \\ \int_{-\infty}^{\infty} E[X|Y=y]f_Y(y)dy, & \text{for continuous } Y \end{cases}$$

Connecting noodles

You have 100 noodles in your soup bowl. Being blindfolded, you are told to take two ends of some noodles (each end on any noodle has the same probability of being chosen) in your bowl and connect them. You continue until there are no free ends. The number of loops formed by the noodles this way is stochastic. Calculate the expected number of circles.

Solution: Again do not be frightened by the large number 100. If you have no clue how to start, let's begin with the simplest case where $n=1$. Surely you have only one choice (to connect both ends of the noodle), so $E[f(1)]=1$. How about 2 noodles? Now you have 4 ends (2×2) and you can connect any two of them. There are $\binom{4}{2} = \dfrac{4 \times 3}{2} = 6$ combinations. Among them, 2 combinations will connect both ends of the same noodle together and yield 1 circle and 1 noodle. The other 4 choices will yield a single noodle. So the expected number of circles is

$$E[f(2)] = 2/6 \times (1 + E[f(1)]) + 4/6 \times E[f(1)] = 1/3 + E[f(1)] = 1/3 + 1.$$

We now move on to 3 noodles with $\binom{6}{2} = \dfrac{6 \times 5}{2} = 15$ choices. Among them, 3 choices will yield 1 circle and 2 noodles; the other 12 choices will yield 2 noodles only, so

$$E[f(3)] = 3/15 \times (1 + E[f(2)]) + 12/15 \times E[f(2)] = 1/5 + E[f(2)] = 1/5 + 1/3 + 1.$$

See the pattern? For any n noodles, we will have $E[f(n)] = 1 + 1/3 + 1/5 + \cdots + 1/(2n-1)$, which can be easily proved by induction. Plug 100 in, we will have the answer.

Actually after the 2-noodle case, you probably have found the key to this question. If you start with n noodles, among $\binom{2n}{2} = n(2n-1)$ possible combinations, we have $\dfrac{n}{n(2n-1)} = \dfrac{1}{2n-1}$ probability to yield 1 circle and $n-1$ noodles and $\dfrac{2n-2}{2n-1}$ probability to yield $n-1$ noodles only, so $E[f(n)] = E[f(n-1)] + \dfrac{1}{2n-1}$. Working backward, you can get the final solution as well.

Optimal hedge ratio

You just bought one share of stock A and want to hedge it by shorting stock B. How many shares of B should you short to minimize the variance of the hedged position? Assume that the variance of stock A's return is σ_A^2; the variance of B's return is σ_B^2; their correlation coefficient is ρ.

Solution: Suppose that we short h shares of B, the variance of the portfolio return is
$$\operatorname{var}(r_A - hr_B) = \sigma_A^2 - 2\rho h \sigma_A \sigma_B + h^2 \sigma_B^2$$

The best hedge ratio should minimize $\operatorname{var}(r_A - hr_B)$. Take the first order partial derivative with respect to h and set it to zero: $\dfrac{\partial \operatorname{var}}{\partial h} = -2\rho\sigma_A\sigma_B + 2h\sigma_B^2 = 0 \Rightarrow h = \rho\dfrac{\sigma_A}{\sigma_B}$.

To confirm it's the minimum, we can also check the second-order partial derivative:

$\dfrac{\partial^2 \operatorname{var}}{\partial h^2} = 2\sigma_B^2 > 0$. So Indeed when $h = \rho\dfrac{\sigma_A}{\sigma_B}$, the hedge portfolio has the minimum variance.

Dice game

Suppose that you roll a dice. For each roll, you are paid the face value. If a roll gives 4, 5 or 6, you can roll the dice again. Once you get 1, 2 or 3, the game stops. What is the expected payoff of this game?

Solution: This is an example of the law of total expectation. Clearly your payoff will be different depending on the outcome of first roll. Let $E[X]$ be your expected payoff and Y be the outcome of your first throw. You have 1/2 chance to get $Y \in \{1,2,3\}$, in which case the expected value is the expected face value 2, so $E[X \mid Y \in \{1,2,3\}] = 2$; you have

1/2 chance to get $Y \in \{4, 5, 6\}$, in which case you get expected face value 5 and extra throw(s). The extra throw(s) essentially means you start the game again and have an extra expected value $E[X]$. So we have $E[X \mid Y \in (4, 5, 6)] = 5 + E[X]$. Apply the law of total expectation, we have $E[X] = E[E[X \mid Y]] = \frac{1}{2} \times 2 + \frac{1}{2} \times (5 + E[X]) \Rightarrow E[X] = 7.$[27]

Card game

What is the expected number of cards that need to be turned over in a regular 52-card deck in order to see the first ace?

Solution: There are 4 aces and 48 other cards. Let's label them as card $1, 2, \cdots, 48$. Let

$$X_i = \begin{cases} 1, & \text{if card } i \text{ is turned over before 4 aces} \\ 0, & \text{otherwise} \end{cases}$$

The total number of cards that need to be turned over in order to see the first ace is $X = 1 + \sum_{i=1}^{48} X_i$, so we have $E[X] = 1 + \sum_{i=1}^{48} E[X_i]$. As shown in the following sequence, each card i is equally likely to be in one of the five regions separated by 4 aces:

1 *A* 2 *A* 3 *A* 4 *A* 5

So the probability that card i appears before all 4 aces is $1/5$, and we have $E[X_i] = 1/5$.

Therefore, $E[X] = 1 + \sum_{i=1}^{48} E[X_i] = 1 + 48/5 = 10.6$.

This is just a special case for random ordering of m ordinary cards and n special cards. The expected position of the first special card is $1 + \sum_{i=1}^{m} E[X_i] = 1 + \dfrac{m}{n+1}$.

Sum of random variables

Assume that X_1, X_2, $\cdots$, and X_n are independent and identically-distributed (IID) random variables with uniform distribution between 0 and 1. What is the probability that $S_n = X_1 + X_2 + \cdots + X_n \leq 1$?[28]

---

[27] You will also see that the problem can be solved using Wald's equality in Chapter 5.
[28] Hint: start with the simplest case where n =1, 2, and 3. Try to find a general formula and prove it using induction.

Solution: This problem is a rather difficult one. The general principle to start with the simplest cases and try to find a pattern will again help you approach the problem; even though it may not give you the final answer. When $n=1$, $P(S_1 \leq 1)$ is 1. As shown in Figure 4.6, when $n=2$, the probability that $X_1 + X_2 \leq 1$ is just the area under $X_1 + X_2 \leq 1$ within the square with side length 1 (a triangle). So $P(S_2 \leq 1) = 1/2$. When $n=3$, the probability becomes the tetrahedron ABCD under the plane $X_1 + X_2 + X_3 \leq 1$ within the cube with side length 1. The volume of tetrahedron ABCD is $1/6$.[29] So $P(S_3 \leq 1) = 1/6$. Now we can guess that the solution is $1/n!$. To prove it, let's again resort to induction. Assume $P(S_n \leq 1) = 1/n!$. We need to prove that $P(S_{n+1} \leq 1) = 1/(n+1)!$.

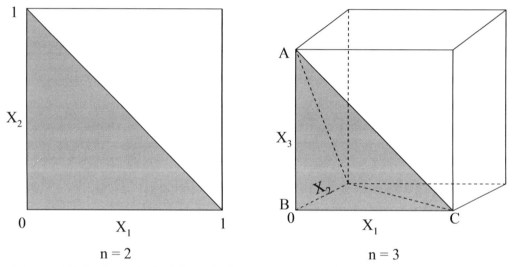

$$n = 2 \qquad\qquad n = 3$$

Figure 4.6 Probability that $S_n \leq 1$ when n = 2 or n = 3.

Here we can use probability by conditioning. Condition on the value of X_{n+1}, we have

$$P(S_{n+1} \leq 1) = \int_0^1 f(X_{n+1}) P(S_n \leq 1 - X_{n+1}) dX_{n+1},$$ where $f(X_{n+1})$ is the probability density function of X_{n+1}, so $f(X_{n+1}) = 1$. But how do we calculate $P(S_n \leq 1 - X_{n+1})$? The cases of $n=2$ and $n=3$ have provided us with some clue. For $S_n \leq 1 - X_{n+1}$ instead of $S_n \leq 1$, we essentially need to shrink every dimension of the *n*-dimensional simplex[30] from 1 to

---

[29] You can derive it by integration: $\int_0^1 A(z) dz = \int_0^1 1/2 z^2 dz = 1/6$, where $A(z)$ is the cross-sectional area.

[30] An *n*-Simplex is the *n*-dimensional analog of a triangle.

$1 - X_{n+1}$. So its volume should be $\dfrac{(1 - X_{n+1})^n}{n!}$ instead of $\dfrac{1}{n!}$. Plugging in these results,

we have $P(S_{n+1} \le 1) = \displaystyle\int_0^1 \dfrac{(1 - X_{n+1})^n}{n!} \, dX_{n+1} = \dfrac{1}{n!} \left[-\dfrac{(1 - X_{n+1})^{n+1}}{n+1} \right]_0^1 = \dfrac{1}{n!} \times \dfrac{1}{n+1} = \dfrac{1}{(n+1)!}$.

So the general result is true for $n + 1$ as well and we have $P(S_n \le 1) = 1/n!$.

Coupon collection

There are N distinct types of coupons in cereal boxes and each type, independent of prior selections, is equally likely to be in a box.

A. If a child wants to collect a complete set of coupons with at least one of each type, how many coupons (boxes) on average are needed to make such a complete set?

B. If the child has collected n coupons, what is the expected number of distinct coupon types?[31]

Solution: For part A, let X_i, $i = 1, 2, \cdots, N$, be the number of additional coupons needed to obtain the i-th type after $(i - 1)$ distinct types have been collected. So the total number of coupons needed is $X = X_1 + X_2 + \cdots + X_N = \displaystyle\sum_{i=1}^N X_i$.

For any i, $i - 1$ distinct types of coupons have already been collected. It follows that a new coupon will be of a different type with probability $1 - (i - 1)/N = (N - i + 1)/N$. Essentially to obtain the i-th distinct type, the random variable X_i follows a geometric distribution with $p = (N - i + 1)/N$ and $E[X_i] = N/(N - i + 1)$. For example, if $i = 1$, we simply have $X_i = E[X_i] = 1$.

$$\therefore E[X] = \sum_{i=1}^N E[X_i] = \sum_{i=1}^N \frac{N}{N - i + 1} = N \left(\frac{1}{N} + \frac{1}{N-1} + \cdots + \frac{1}{1} \right).$$

---

[31] Hint: For part A, let X_i be the number of extra coupons collected to get the i-th distinct coupon after $i - 1$ types of distinct coupons have been collected. Then the total expected number of coupons to collect all distinct types is $E[X] = \displaystyle\sum_{i=1}^N E[X_i]$. For part B, which is the expected probability (P) that the i-th coupon type is not in the n coupons?

For part B, let Y be the number of distinct types of coupons in the set of n coupons. We introduce indicator **random variables** $I_i, i = 1, 2, \cdots, N$, where

$$\begin{cases} I_i = 1, & \text{if at least one coupon of the } i\text{-th type is in the set of } n \text{ coupons} \\ I_i = 0, & \text{otherwise} \end{cases}$$

So we have $Y = I_1 + I_2 + \cdots + I_N = \sum_{i=1}^{N} I_i$

For each collected coupon, the probability that it is not the i-th coupon type is $\dfrac{N-1}{N}$. Since all n coupons are independent, the probability that none of the n coupons is the i-th coupon type is $P(I_i = 0) = \left(\dfrac{N-1}{N} \right)^n$ and we have $E[I_i] = P(I_i = 1) = 1 - \left(\dfrac{N-1}{N} \right)^n$.

$$\therefore E[Y] = \sum_{i=1}^{N} E[I_i] = N - N \left(\frac{N-1}{N} \right)^n .^{32}$$

Joint default probability

If there is a 50% probability that bond A will default next year and a 30% probability that bond B will default. What is the range of probability that at least one bond defaults and what is the range of their correlation?

Solution: The range of probability that at least one bond defaults is easy to find. To have the largest probability, we can assume whenever A defaults, B does not default; whenever B defaults, A does not default. So the maximum probability that at least one bond defaults is $50\% + 30\% = 80\%$. (The result only applies if $P(A) + P(B) \le 1$). For the minimum, we can assume whenever A defaults, B also defaults. So the minimum probability that at least one bond defaults is 50%.

To calculate the corresponding correlation, let I_A and I_B be the indicator for the event that bond A/B defaults next year and ρ_{AB} be their correlation. Then we have $E[I_A] = 0.5$, $E[I_B] = 0.3$, $\text{var}(I_A) = p_A \times (1 - p_A) = 0.25$, $\text{var}(I_B) = 0.21$.

---

[32] A similar question: if you randomly put 18 balls into 10 boxes, what is the expected number of empty boxes?

$$P(A \text{ or } B \text{ defaults}) = E[I_A] + E[I_B] - E[I_A I_B]$$
$$= E[I_A] + E[I_B] - \left(E[I_A] E[I_B] - \text{cov}(I_A, I_B) \right)$$
$$= 0.5 + 0.3 - \left(0.5 \times 0.3 - \rho_{AB} \sigma_A \sigma_B \right)$$
$$= 0.65 - \sqrt{0.21} / 2 \rho_{AB}$$

For the maximum probability, we have $0.65 - \sqrt{0.21} / 2 \rho_{AB} = 0.8 \Rightarrow \rho_{AB} = -\sqrt{3/7}$.

For the minimum probability, we have $0.65 - \sqrt{0.21} / 2 \rho_{AB} = 0.5 \Rightarrow \rho_{AB} = \sqrt{3/7}$.

In this problem, do not start with $P(A \text{ or } B \text{ defaults}) = 0.65 - \sqrt{0.21} / 2 \rho_{AB}$ and try to set $\rho_{AB} = \pm 1$ to calculate the maximum and minimum probability since the correlation cannot be ± 1. The range of correlation is restricted to $\left[-\sqrt{3/7}, \sqrt{3/7} \right]$.

4.6 Order Statistics

Let X be a random variable with cumulative distribution function $F_X(x)$. We can derive the distribution function for the minimum $Y_n = \min(X_1, X_2, \cdots, X_n)$ and for the maximum $Z_n = \max(X_1, X_2, \cdots, X_n)$ of n IID random variables with cdf $F_X(x)$ as

$$P(Y_n \geq x) = (P(X \geq x))^n \Rightarrow 1 - F_{Y_n}(x) = (1 - F_X(x))^n \Rightarrow f_{Y_n}(x) = n f_X(x)(1 - F_X(x))^{n-1}$$
$$P(Z_n \leq x) = (P(X \leq x))^n \Rightarrow F_{Z_n}(x) = (F_X(x))^n \Rightarrow f_{Z_n}(x) = n f_X(x)(F_X(x))^{n-1}$$

Expected value of max and min

Let $X_1, X_2, \cdots, X_n$ be IID random variables with uniform distribution between 0 and 1. What are the cumulative distribution function, the probability density function and expected value of $Z_n = \max(X_1, X_2, \cdots, X_n)$? What are the cumulative distribution function, the probability density function and expected value of $Y_n = \min(X_1, X_2, \cdots, X_n)$?

Solution: This is a direct test of textbook knowledge. For uniform distribution on $[0,1]$, $F_X(x) = x$ and $f_X(x) = 1$. Applying $F_X(x)$ and $f_X(x)$ to $Z_n = \max(X_1, X_2, \cdots, X_n)$ we have

$$P(Z_n \leq x) = (P(X \leq x))^n \Rightarrow F_{Z_n}(x) = (F_X(x))^n = x^n$$
$$\Rightarrow f_{Z_n}(x) = n f_X(x)(F_X(x))^{n-1} = n x^{n-1}$$

and $E[Z_n] = \int_0^1 x f_{Z_n}(x)dx = \int_0^1 nx^n dx = \frac{n}{n+1}\left[x^{n+1}\right]_0^1 = \frac{n}{n+1}$.

Applying $F_X(x)$ and $f_X(x)$ to $Y_n = \min(X_1, X_2, \cdots, X_n)$ we have

$$P(Y_n \geq x) = (P(X \geq x))^n \Rightarrow F_{Y_n}(x) = 1 - (1 - F_X(x))^n = 1 - (1-x)^n$$

$$\Rightarrow f_{Y_n}(x) = nf_X(x)(1 - F_X(x))^{n-1} = n(1-x)^{n-1}$$

and $E[Y_n] = \int_0^1 nx(1-x)^{n-1}dx = \int_0^1 n(1-y)y^{n-1}dy = \left[y^n\right]_0^1 - \frac{n}{n+1}\left[y^{n+1}\right]_0^1 = \frac{1}{n+1}$.

Correlation of max and min

Let X_1 and X_2 be IID random variables with uniform distribution between 0 and 1, $Y = \min(X_1, X_2)$ and $Z = \max(X_1, X_2)$. What is the probability of $Y \geq y$ given that $Z \leq z$ for any $y, z \in [0, 1]$? What is the correlation of Y and Z?

Solution: This problem is another demonstration that a figure is worth a thousand words. As shown in Figure 4.7, the probability that $Z \leq z$ is simply the square with side length z. So $P(Z \leq z) = z^2$. Since $Z = \max(X_1, X_2)$ and $Y = \min(X_1, X_2)$, we must have $Y \leq Z$ for any pair of X_1 and X_2. So if $y > z$, $P(Y \geq y \mid Z \leq z) = 0$. For $y \leq z$, that X_1 and X_2 satisfies $Y \geq y$ and $Z \leq z$ is the square with vertices $(y, y), (z, y), (z, z)$, and (y, z), which has an area $(z - y)^2$. So $P(Y \geq y \cap Z \leq z) = (z - y)^2$. Hence

$$P(Y \geq y \mid Z \leq z) = \begin{cases} (z-y)^2 / z^2, & \text{if } 0 \leq z \leq 1 \text{ and } 0 \leq y \leq z \\ 0, & \text{otherwise} \end{cases}.$$

Now let's move on to calculate the correlation of Y and Z.

$$\text{corr}(Y, Z) = \frac{\text{cov}(Y, Z)}{\text{std}(Y) \times \text{std}(Z)} = \frac{E[YZ] - E[Y]E[Z]}{\sqrt{E[Y^2] - E[Y]^2} \times \sqrt{E[Z^2] - E[Z]^2}}$$

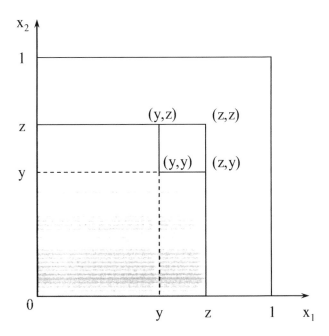

Figure 4.7 Distribution of X_1, X_2, their maximum and minimum.

Using previous problem's conclusions, we have $E[Y] = \dfrac{1}{2+1} = \dfrac{1}{3}$, $E[Z] = \dfrac{2}{2+1} = \dfrac{2}{3}$. From the pdfs of Y and Z, $f_{Y_n}(x) = n(1-x)^{n-1} = 2(1-x)$ and $f_Z(z) = nz^{n-1} = 2z$, we can also get $E[Y_n^2] = \int_0^1 2(1-y)y^2 dy = \dfrac{2}{3} - \dfrac{2}{4} = \dfrac{1}{6}$ and $E[Z_n^2] = \int_0^1 2z^3 dz = \dfrac{2}{4}$, which give us the variances: $\mathrm{var}(Y) = E[Y^2] - E[Y]^2 = \dfrac{1}{6} - \left(\dfrac{1}{3}\right)^2 = \dfrac{1}{18}$ and $\mathrm{var}(Z) = \dfrac{2}{4} - \left(\dfrac{2}{3}\right)^2 = \dfrac{1}{18}$.[33]

To calculate $E[YZ]$, we can use $E[YZ] = \int_0^1 \int_0^z yz f(y,z) dy dz$. To solve this equation, we need $f(y,z)$. Let's again go back to Figure 4.7. From the figure we can see that when $0 \le z \le 1$ and $0 \le y \le z$, $F(y,z)$ is the shadowed area with probability

$$F(y,z) = P(Y \le y \cap Z \le z) = P(Z \le z) - P(Y \ge y \cap Z \le z) = z^2 - (z-y)^2 = 2zy - y^2$$

$$\therefore f(y,z) = \frac{\partial}{\partial y \partial z} F(y,z) = 2 \text{ and } E[YZ] = \int_0^1 \int_0^z 2yz dy dz = \int_0^1 z[y^2]_0^z dz = \int_0^1 z^3 dz = \frac{1}{4}.$$

---

[33] You may have noticed that $\mathrm{var}(Y) = \mathrm{var}(Z)$ and wonder whether it is a coincidence for $n = 2$. It is actually true for all integer n. You may want to think about why that is true without resorting to calculation. Hint: $\mathrm{var}(x) = \mathrm{var}(1-x)$ for any random variable x.

An alternative and simpler approach to calculate $E[YZ]$ is again to take advantage of symmetry. Notice that no matter $x_1 \leq x_2$ or $x_1 > x_2$, we always have $yz = x_1 x_2$ ($z = \max(x_1, x_2)$ and $y = \min(x_1, x_2)$).

$$\therefore E[YZ] = \int_0^1 \int_0^1 x_1 x_2 dx_1 dx_2 = E[X_1]E[X_2] = \frac{1}{2} \times \frac{1}{2} = \frac{1}{4}.$$

Hence $\text{cov}(Y,Z) = E[YZ] - E[Y]E[Z] = \dfrac{1}{36}$ and $\text{corr}(Y,Z) = \dfrac{\text{cov}(Y,Z)}{\sqrt{\text{var}(Y)} \times \sqrt{\text{var}(Z)}} = \dfrac{1}{2}.$

Sanity check: That Y and Z have positive autocorrelation make sense since when Y becomes large, Z tends to become large as well ($Z \geq Y$).

Random ants

500 ants are randomly put on a 1-foot string (independent uniform distribution for each ant between 0 and 1). Each ant randomly moves toward one end of the string (equal probability to the left or right) at constant speed of 1 foot/minute until it falls off at one end of the string. Also assume that the size of the ant is infinitely small. When two ants collide head-on, they both immediately change directions and keep on moving at 1 foot/min. What is the expected time for all ants to fall off the string?[34]

Solution: This problem is often perceived to be a difficult one. The following components contribute to the complexity of the problem: The ants are randomly located; each ant can go either direction; an ant needs to change direction when it meets another ant. To solve the problem, let's tackle these components.

When two ants collide head-on, both immediately change directions. What does it mean? The following diagram illustrates the key point:

Before collision: $\xrightarrow{\ A\ }\xleftarrow{\ B\ }$; After collision: $\xleftarrow{\ \ A\ \ }\xrightarrow{\ \ B\ \ }$; switch label: $\xleftarrow{\ \ B\ \ }\xrightarrow{\ \ A\ \ }$

When an ant A collides with another ant B, both switch direction. But if we exchange the ants' labels, it's like that the collision never happens. A continues to move to the right and B moves to the left. Since the labels are randomly assigned anyway, collisions make no difference to the result. So we can assume that when two ants meet, each just keeps on going in its original direction. What about the random direction that each ant chooses? Once the collision is removed, we can use symmetry to argue that it makes no difference which direction that an ant goes either. That means if an ant is put at the x-th foot, the

---

[34] Hint: If we switch the label of two ants that collide with each other, it's like that the collision never happened.

expected value for it to fall off is just x min. If it goes in the other direction, simply set x to $1-x$. So the original problem is equivalent to the following:

What is the expected value of the maximum of 500 IID random variables with uniform distribution between 0 and 1?

Clearly the answer is $\dfrac{499}{500}$ min, which is the expected time for all ants to fall off the string.

Chapter 5 Stochastic Process and Stochastic Calculus

In this chapter, we cover a few topics—Markov chain, random walk and martingale, dynamic programming—that are often not included in introductory probability courses. Unlike basic probability theory, these tools may not be considered to be standard requirements for quantitative researchers/analysts. But a good understanding of these topics can simplify your answers to many interview problems and give you an edge in the interview process. Besides, once you learn the basics, you'll find many interview problems turning into fun-to-solve math puzzles.

5.1 Markov Chain

A Markov chain is a sequence of random variables $X_0, X_1, \cdots, X_n, \cdots$ with the Markov property that given the present state, the future states and the past states are independent:

$$P\{X_{n+1} = j \mid X_n = i, X_{n-1} = i_{n-1}, \cdots, X_0 = i_0\} = p_{ij} = P\{X_{n+1} = j \mid X_n = i\} \text{ for all } n, i_0, \cdots,$$

$i_{n-1}, i,$ and j, where $i, j \in \{1, 2, \cdots, M\}$ represent the state space $S = \{s_1, s_2, ..., s_M\}$ of X.

In other words, once the current state is known, past history has no bearing on the future. For a homogenous Markov chain, the transition probability from state i to state j does not depend on n.[1] A Markov chain with M states can be completely described by an $M \times M$ transition matrix P and the initial probabilities $P(X_0)$.

Transition matrix: $P = \{p_{ij}\} = \begin{bmatrix} p_{11} & p_{12} & \cdots & p_{1M} \\ p_{21} & p_{22} & \cdots & p_{2M} \\ \vdots & \vdots & \vdots & \vdots \\ p_{M1} & p_{M2} & \cdots & p_{MM} \end{bmatrix}$, where p_{ij} is the transition probability from state i to state j.

Initial probabilities: $P(X_0) = \left(P(X_0 = 1), P(X_0 = 2), \cdots, P(X_0 = M) \right)$, $\sum_{i=1}^{M} P(X_0 = i) = 1$.

The probability of a path: $P(X_1 = i_1, X_2 = i_2 \cdots, X_n = i_n \mid X_0 = i_0) = p_{i_0 i_1} p_{i_1 i_2} \cdots p_{i_{n-1} i_n}$

Transition graph: A transition graph is often used to express the transition matrix graphically. The transition graph is more intuitive than the matrix, and it emphasizes

---

[1] In this chapter, we only consider finite-state homogenous Markov chains (i.e., transition probabilities do not change over time).

possible and impossible transitions. Figure 5.1 shows the transition graph and the transition matrix of a Markov chain with four states:

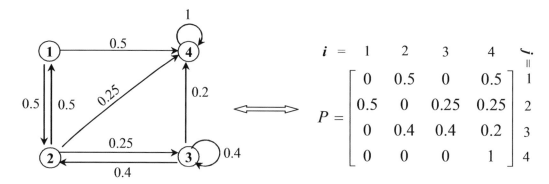

Figure 5.1 Transition graph and transition matrix of the Play

Classification of states

State j is **accessible** from state i if there is a directed path in the transition graph from i to j ($\exists n$ such that $P_{ij}^{(n)} > 0$). Let $T_{ij} = \min(n : X_n = j \mid X_0 = i)$, then $P(T_{ij} < \infty) > 0$) if and only if state j is accessible from state i. States i and j **communicate** if i is accessible from j and j is accessible from i. In Figure 5.1, state 3 and 1 communicate. State 4 is accessible form state 1, but they do not communicate since state 1 is not accessible from state 4.

We say that state i is **recurrent** if for every state j that is accessible from i, i is also accessible from j ($\forall j$, $P(T_{ij} < \infty) > 0 \Rightarrow P(T_{ij} < \infty) = 1$). A state is called **transient** if it is not recurrent ($\exists j$, $P(T_{ij} < \infty) > 0$ and $P(T_{ij} < \infty) < 1$). In Figure 5.1, only state 4 is recurrent. States 1, 2 and 3 are all transient since 4 is accessible from 1/2/3, but 1/2/3 are not accessible from 4.

Absorbing Markov chains: A state i is called absorbing if it is impossible to leave this state ($p_{ii} = 1, p_{ij} = 0, \forall j \neq i$). A Markov chain is absorbing if it has at least one absorbing state and if from every state it is possible to go to an absorbing state. In Figure 5.1, state 4 is an absorbing state. The corresponding Markov chain is an absorbing Markov chain.

Equations for absorption probability: The probability to reach a specific absorbing state s, $a_1, \cdots, a_M$, are unique solutions to equations $a_s = 1$, $a_i = 0$ for all absorbing state(s) $i \neq s$, and $a_i = \sum_{j=1}^{M} a_j p_{ij}$ for all transient states i. These equations can be easily derived using the law of total probability by conditioning the absorption probabilities on the next state.

Equations for the expected time to absorption: The expected times to absorption, $\mu_1, \cdots, \mu_M$, are unique solutions to the equations $\mu_i = 0$ for all absorbing state(s) i and $\mu_i = 1 + \sum_{j=1}^{m} p_{ij}\mu_j$ for all transient states i. These equations can be easily derived using the law of total expectation by conditioning the expected times to absorption on the next state. The number 1 is added since it takes one step to reach the next state.

Gambler's ruin problem

Player M has \$1 and player N has \$2. Each game gives the winner \$1 from the other. As a better player, M wins 2/3 of the games. They play until one of them is bankrupt. What is the probability that M wins?

Solution: The most difficult part of Markov chain problems often lies in how to choose the right state space and define the transition probabilities P_{ij}'s, $\forall i,\ j$. This problem has fairly straightforward states. You can define the state space as the combination of the money that player M has (\$$m$) and the money that player N has (\$$n$): $\{(m,n)\} = \{(3,0),(2,1),(1,2),(0,3)\}$. (Neither m nor n can be negative since the whole game stops when one of them goes bankrupt.) Since the sum of the dollars of both players is always \$3, we can actually simplify the state space using only m: $\{m\} = \{0,1,2,3\}$.

The transition graph and the corresponding transition matrix are shown in Figure 5.2.

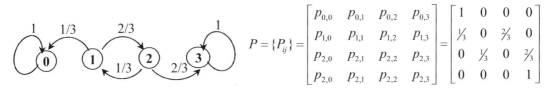

$$P = \{P_{ij}\} = \begin{bmatrix} P_{0,0} & P_{0,1} & P_{0,2} & P_{0,3} \\ P_{1,0} & P_{1,1} & P_{1,2} & P_{1,3} \\ P_{2,0} & P_{2,1} & P_{2,2} & P_{2,3} \\ P_{2,0} & P_{2,1} & P_{2,2} & P_{2,3} \end{bmatrix} = \begin{bmatrix} 1 & 0 & 0 & 0 \\ \frac{1}{3} & 0 & \frac{2}{3} & 0 \\ 0 & \frac{1}{3} & 0 & \frac{2}{3} \\ 0 & 0 & 0 & 1 \end{bmatrix}$$

Figure 5.2 Transition matrix and transition graph for Gambler's ruin problem

The initial state is $X_0 = 1$ (M has \$1 at the beginning). At state 1, the next state is 0 (M loses a game) with probability 1/3 and 2 (M wins a game) with probability 2/3. So $p_{1,0} = 1/3$ and $p_{1,2} = 2/3$. Similarly we can get $p_{2,1} = 1/3$ and $p_{2,3} = 2/3$. Both state 3 (M wins the whole game) and state 0 (M loses the whole game) are absorbing states.

To calculate the probability that M reaches absorbing state 3, we can apply absorption probability equations:

$a_3 = 1, a_0 = 0$, and $a_1 = \sum_{j=0}^{3} p_{1,j} a_j$, $a_2 = \sum_{j=0}^{3} p_{2,j} a_j$

Plugging in the transition probabilities using either the transition graph or transition matrix, we have $\left. \begin{array}{l} a_1 = 1/3 \times 0 + 2/3 \times a_2 \\ a_2 = 1/3 \times a_1 + 2/3 \times 1 \end{array} \right\} \Rightarrow \left\{ \begin{array}{l} a_1 = 4/7 \\ a_2 = 6/7 \end{array} \right.$

So, starting from \$1, player M has $4/7$ probability of winning.

Dice question

Two players bet on roll(s) of the total of two standard six-face dice. Player A bets that a sum of 12 will occur first. Player B bets that two consecutive 7s will occur first. The players keep rolling the dice and record the sums until one player wins. What is the probability that A will win?

Solution: Many of the simple Markov chain problems can be solved using pure conditional probability argument. It is not surprising considering that Markov chain is defined as conditional probability:

$$P\{X_{n+1} = j \mid X_n = i, X_{n-1} = i_{n-1}, \cdots, X_0 = i_0\} = p_{ij} = P\{X_{n+1} = j \mid X_n = i\}.$$

So let's first solve the problem using conditional probability arguments. Let $P(A)$ be the probability that A wins. Conditioning $P(A)$ on the first throw's sum F, which has three possible outcomes $F = 12$, $F = 7$ and $F \notin \{7,12\}$, we have

$$P(A) = P(A \mid F = 12) P(F = 12) + P(A \mid F = 7) P(F = 7) + P(A \mid F \notin \{7,12\}) P(F \notin \{7,12\})$$

Then we tackle each component on the right hand side. Using simple permutation, we can easily see that $P(F = 12) = 1/36$, $P(F = 7) = 6/36$, $P(F \notin \{7,12\}) = 29/36$. Also it is obvious that $P(A \mid F = 12) = 1$ and $P(A \mid F \notin \{7,12\}) = P(A)$. (The game essentially starts over again.) To calculate $P(A \mid F = 7)$, we need to further condition on the second throw's total, which again has three possible outcomes: $E = 12$, $E = 7$, and $E \notin \{7,12\}$.

$$\begin{aligned} P(A \mid F = 7) &= P(A \mid F = 7, E = 12) P(E = 12 \mid F = 7) + P(A \mid F = 7, E = 7) P(E = 7 \mid F = 7) \\ &\quad + P(A \mid F = 7, E \notin \{7,12\}) P(E \notin \{7,12\} \mid F = 7) \\ &= P(A \mid F = 7, E = 12) \times 1/36 + P(A \mid F = 7, E = 7) \times 6/36 \\ &\quad + P(A \mid F = 7, E \notin \{7,12\}) \times 29/36 \\ &= 1 \times 1/36 + 0 \times 6/36 + P(A) \times 29/36 = 1/36 + 29/36 P(A) \end{aligned}$$

Here the second equation relies on the independence between the second and the first rolls. If $F = 7$ and $E = 12$, A wins; if $F = 7$ and $E = 7$, A loses; if $F = 7$ and

$E \notin \{7,12\}$, the game essentially starts over again. Now we have all the necessarily information for $P(A)$. Plugging it into the original equation, we have

$$P(A) = P(A \mid F = 12)P(F = 12) + P(A \mid F = 7)P(F = 7) + P(A \mid F \notin \{7,12\})P(F \notin \{7,12\})$$
$$= 1 \times 1/36 + 6/36 \times (1/36 + 29/36 P(A)) + 29/36 P(A)$$

Solving the equation, we get $P(A) = 7/13$.

This approach, although logically solid, is not intuitively appealing. Now let's try a Markov chain approach. Again the key part is to choose the right state space and define the transition probabilities. It is apparent that we have two absorbing states, 12 (*A* wins) and 7-7 (*B* wins), at least two transient states, *S* (starting state) and 7 (one 7 occurs, yet no 12 or 7-7 occurred). Do we need any other states? Theoretically, you can have other states. In fact, you can use all combination of the outcomes of one roll and two consecutive rolls as states to construct a transition matrix and you will get the same final result. Nevertheless, we want to consolidate as many equivalent states as possible. As we just discussed in the conditional probability approach, if no 12 has occurred and the most recent roll did not yield 7, we essentially go back to the initial starting state *S*. So all we need are states *S*, 7, 7-7 and 12. The transition graph and probability to reach state 12 are shown in Figure 5.3.

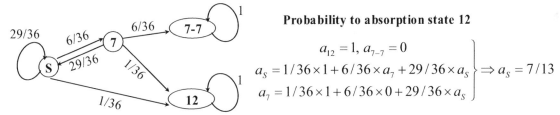

Probability to absorption state 12

$$a_{12} = 1,\ a_{7-7} = 0$$
$$\left. \begin{array}{l} a_S = 1/36 \times 1 + 6/36 \times a_7 + 29/36 \times a_S \\ a_7 = 1/36 \times 1 + 6/36 \times 0 + 29/36 \times a_S \end{array} \right\} \Rightarrow a_S = 7/13$$

Figure 5.3 Transition graph and probability to absorption for dice rolls

Here the transition probability is again derived from conditional probability arguments. Yet the transition graph makes the process crystal clear.

Coin triplets

Part A. If you keep on tossing a fair coin, what is the expected number of tosses such that you can have *HHH* (heads heads heads) in a row? What is the expected number of tosses to have *THH* (tails heads heads) in a row?

Solution: The most difficult part of Markov chain is, again, to choose the right state space. For the *HHH* sequence, the state space is straightforward. We only need four states: *S* (for the starting state when no coin is tossed or whenever a *T* turns up before *HHH*), *H*, *HH*, and *HHH*. The transition graph is

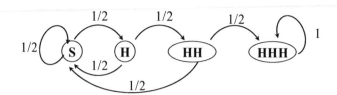

At state S, after a coin toss, the state will stay at S when the toss gives a T. If the toss gives an H, the state becomes H. At state H, it has 1/2 probability goes back to state S if the next toss is T; otherwise, it goes to state HH. At state HH, it also has 1/2 probability goes back to state S if the next toss is T; otherwise, it reaches the absorbing state HHH.

So we have the following transition probabilities: $P_{S,S} = \frac{1}{2}$, $P_{S,H} = \frac{1}{2}$, $P_{H,S} = \frac{1}{2}$, $P_{H,HH} = \frac{1}{2}$, $P_{HH,S} = \frac{1}{2}$, $P_{HH,HHH} = \frac{1}{2}$, and $P_{HHH,HHH} = 1$.

We are interested in the expected number of tosses to get HHH, which is the expected time to absorption starting from state S. Applying the standard equations for the expected time to absorption, we have

$$\left. \begin{aligned} \mu_S &= 1 + \tfrac{1}{2}\mu_S + \tfrac{1}{2}\mu_H \\ \mu_H &= 1 + \tfrac{1}{2}\mu_S + \tfrac{1}{2}\mu_{HH} \\ \mu_{HH} &= 1 + \tfrac{1}{2}\mu_S + \tfrac{1}{2}\mu_{HHH} \\ \mu_{HHH} &= 0 \end{aligned} \right\} \Rightarrow \left\{ \begin{aligned} \mu_S &= 14 \\ \mu_H &= 12 \\ \mu_{HH} &= 8 \\ \mu_{HHH} &= 0 \end{aligned} \right.$$

So from the starting state, the expected number of tosses to get HHH is 14.

Similarly for expected time to reach THH, we can construct the following transition graph and estimate the corresponding expected time to absorption:

$$\left. \begin{aligned} \mu_S &= 1 + \tfrac{1}{2}\mu_S + \tfrac{1}{2}\mu_T \\ \mu_T &= 1 + \tfrac{1}{2}\mu_T + \tfrac{1}{2}\mu_{TH} \\ \mu_{TH} &= 1 + \tfrac{1}{2}\mu_T + \tfrac{1}{2}\mu_{THH} \\ \mu_{THH} &= 0 \end{aligned} \right\} \Rightarrow \left\{ \begin{aligned} \mu_S &= 8 \\ \mu_T &= 4 \\ \mu_{TH} &= 2 \\ \mu_{THH} &= 0 \end{aligned} \right.$$

So from the starting state S, the expected number of tosses to get THH is 8.

Part B. Keep flipping a fair coin until either HHH or THH occurs in the sequence. What is the probability that you get an HHH subsequence before THH?[2]

---

[2] Hint: This problem does not require the drawing of a Markov chain. Just think about the relationship between an HHH pattern and a THH pattern. How can we get an HHH sequence before a THH sequence?

Solution: Let's try a standard Markov chain approach. Again the focus is on choosing the right state space. In this case, we begin with starting state *S*. We only need ordered subsequences of either *HHH* or *THH*. After one coin is flipped, we have either state *T* or *H*. After two flips, we have states *TH* and *HH*. We do not need *TT* (which is equivalent to T for this problem) or *HT* (which is also equivalent to *T* as well). For three coin sequences, we only need *THH* and *HHH* states, which are both absorbing states. Using these states, we can build the following transition graph:

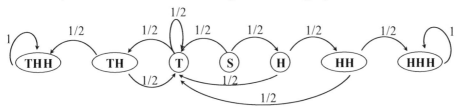

Figure 5.4 Transition graph of coin tosses to reach *HHH* or *THH*

We want to get the probability to reach absorbing state *HHH* from the starting state S. Applying the equations for absorption probability, we have

$$
\left.
\begin{aligned}
&a_{HHH} = 1, \; a_{THH} = 0 \\
&a_S = \tfrac{1}{2}a_T + \tfrac{1}{2}a_H \\
&a_T = \tfrac{1}{2}a_T + \tfrac{1}{2}a_{TH}, \; a_H = \tfrac{1}{2}a_T + \tfrac{1}{2}a_{HH} \\
&a_{TH} = \tfrac{1}{2}a_T + \tfrac{1}{2}a_{THH}, a_{HH} = \tfrac{1}{2}a_T + \tfrac{1}{2}a_{HHH}
\end{aligned}
\right\}
\Rightarrow
\left\{
\begin{aligned}
&a_T = 0, a_{TH} = 0 \\
&a_S = \tfrac{1}{8} \\
&a_H = \tfrac{1}{4} \\
&a_{HH} = \tfrac{1}{2}
\end{aligned}
\right.
$$

So the probability that we end up with the *HHH* pattern is 1/8.

This problem actually has a special feature that renders the calculation unnecessary. You may have noticed that $a_T = 0$. Once a tail occurs, we will always get *THH* before *HHH*.

The reason is that the last two coins in *THH* is *HH*, which is the first two coins in sequence *HHH*. In fact, the only way that the sequence reaches state *HHH* before *THH* is that we get three consecutive *H*s in the beginning. Otherwise, we always have a *T* before the first *HH* sequence and always end in *THH* first. So if we don't start the coin flipping sequence with *HHH*, which has a probability of 1/8, we will always have *THH* before *HHH*.

Part C. (Difficult) Let's add more fun to the triplet game. Instead of fixed triplets for the two players, the new game allows both to choose their own triplets. Player 1 chooses a triplet first and announces it; then player 2 chooses a different triplet. The players again toss the coins until one of the two triplet sequences appears. The player whose chosen triplet appears first wins the game.

If both player 1 and player 2 are perfectly rational and both want to maximize their probability of winning, would you go first (as player 1)? If you go second, what is your probability of winning?[3]

Solution: A common misconception is that there is always a best sequence that beats other sequences. This misconception is often founded on a wrong assumption that these sequences are transitive: if sequence *A* has a higher probability occurring before sequence *B* and sequence *B* has a higher probability occurring before sequence *C*, then sequence *A* has a higher probability occurring before sequence *C*. In reality, such transitivity does not exist for this game. No matter what sequence player 1 chooses, player 2 can always choose another sequence with more than 1/2 probability of winning. The key, as we have indicated in Part B, is to choose the last two coins of the sequence as the first two coins of player 1's sequence. We can compile the following table for each pair of sequences:

2's winning Probability		Player 1							
		HHH	THH	HTH	HHT	TTH	THT	HTT	TTT
	HHH	/	1/8	2/5	1/2	3/10	5/12	2/5	1/2
	THH	**7/8**	/	1/2	**3/4**	1/3	1/2	1/2	3/5
	HTH	3/5	1/2	/	1/3	3/8	1/2	1/2	7/12
Player 2	HHT	1/2	1/4	**2/3**	/	1/2	5/8	**2/3**	7/10
	TTH	7/10	**2/3**	5/8	1/2	/	**2/3**	1/4	1/2
	THT	7/12	1/2	1/2	3/8	1/3	/	1/2	3/5
	HTT	3/5	1/2	1/2	1/3	**3/4**	1/2	/	**7/8**
	TTT	1/2	2/5	5/12	3/10	1/2	2/5	1/8	/

Table 5.1 Player 2's winning probability with different coin sequence pairs

As shown in Table 5.1 (you can confirm the results yourself), no matter what player 1's choices are, player 2 can always choose a sequence to have better odds of winning. The best sequences that player 2 can choose in response to 1's choices are highlighted in bold. In order to maximize his odds of winning, player 1 should choose among HTH, HTT, THH and THT. Even in these cases, player 2 has 2/3 probability of winning.

---

[3] This problem is a difficult one. Interested reader may find the following paper helpful: "Waiting Time and Expected Waiting Time-Paradoxical Situations" by V. C. Hombas, *The American Statistician*, Vol. 51, No. 2 (May, 1997), pp. 130-133. In this section, we will only discuss the intuition.

Color balls

A box contains n balls of n different colors. Each time, you randomly select a pair of balls, repaint the first to match the second, and put the pair back into the box. What is the expected number of steps until all balls in the box are of the same color? (Very difficult)

Solution: Let N_n be the number of steps needed to make all balls the same color, and let F_i, $i = 1, 2, \cdots, n$, be the event that all balls have color i in the end. Applying the law of total expectation, we have

$$E[N_n] = E[N_n \mid F_1]P[F_1] + E[N_n \mid F_2]P[F_2] + \cdots + E[N_n \mid F_n]P[F_n].$$

Since all the colors are symmetric (i.e., they should have equivalent properties), we have $P[F_1] = P[F_2] = \cdots = P[F_n] = 1/n$ and $E[N_n] = E[N_n \mid F_1] = E[N_n \mid F_2] = E[N_n \mid F_n]$. That means we can assume that all the balls have color 1 in the end and use $E[N_n \mid F_1]$ to represent $E[N_n]$.

So how do we calculate $E[N_n \mid F_1]$? Not surprisingly, use a Markov chain. Since we only consider event F_1, color 1 is different from other colors and colors $2, \cdots, n$ become equivalent. In other words, any pairs of balls that have no color 1 ball involved are equivalent and any pairs with a color 1 ball and a ball of another color are equivalent if the order is the same as well. So we only need to use the number of balls that have color 1 as the states. Figure 5.5 shows the transition graph.

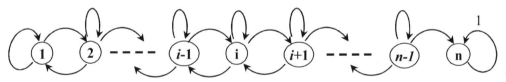

Figure 5.5 Transition graph for all n balls to become color 1

State n is the only absorbing state. Notice that there is no state 0, otherwise it will never reach F_1. In fact, all the transition probability is conditioned on F_1 as well, which makes the transition probability $p_{i,i+1} \mid F_1$ higher than the unconditional probability $p_{i,i+1}$ and $p_{i,i-1} \mid F_1$ lower than $p_{i,i-1}$. For example, $p_{1,0} \mid F_1 = 0$ and $p_{1,0} = 1/n$. (Without conditioning, each ball is likely to be the second ball, so color 1 has $1/n$ probability of being the second ball.) Using the conditional transition probability, the problem essentially becomes expected time to absorption with system equations:

$$E[N_i \mid F_1] = 1 + E[N_{i-1} \mid F_1] \times P_{i,i-1} \mid F_1 + E[N_i \mid F_1] \times P_{i,i} \mid F_1 + E[N_{i+1} \mid F_1] \times P_{i,i+1} \mid F_1.$$

To calculate $P_{i,i-1} | F_1$, let's rewrite the probability as $P(x_{k+1} = i-1 | x_k = i, F_1)$, $\forall k = 0, 1, ...$, to make the derivation step clearer:

$$P(x_{k+1} = i-1 | x_k = i, F_1) = \frac{P(x_k = i, x_{k+1} = i-1, F_1)}{P(x_k = i, F_1)}$$

$$= \frac{P(F_1 | x_{k+1} = i-1, x_k = i) \times P(x_{k+1} = i-1 | x_k = i) \times P(x_k = i)}{P(F_1 | x_k = i) \times P(x_k = i)}$$

$$= \frac{P(F_1 | x_{k+1} = i-1) \times P(x_{k+1} = i-1 | x_k = i)}{P(F_1 | x_k = i)}$$

$$= \frac{\dfrac{i-1}{n} \times \dfrac{i(n-i)}{n(n-1)}}{i/n} = \frac{(n-i) \times (i-1)}{n(n-1)}$$

The first equation is simply the definition of conditional probability; the second equation is the application of Bayes' theorem; the third equation applies the Markov property. To derive $P(F_1 | x_k = i) = i/n$, we again need to use symmetry. We have shown that if all the balls have different colors, then we have $P[F_1] = P[F_2] = \cdots = P[F_n] = 1/n$. What is the probability of ending in a given color, labeled as c, if i of the balls are of color c? It is simply i/n. To see that, we can label the color of each of the i balls of color c as c_j, $j = 1, \cdots, i$ (even though they are in fact the same color). Now it's obvious that all balls will end with color c_j with probability $1/n$. The probability for c is the sum of probabilities of c_j's, which gives the result i/n.

Similarly we have $P(F_1 | x_{k+1} = i-1) = (i-1)/n$. For $P(x_{k+1} = i-1 | x_k = i)$, we use a basic counting method. There are $n(n-1)$ possible permutations to choose 2 balls out of n balls. In order for one color 1 ball to change color, the second ball must be color 1, which has i choices; the first ball needs to be another color, which has $(n-i)$ choices. So $P(x_{k+1} = i-1 | x_k = i) = \dfrac{i(n-i)}{n(n-1)}$.

Applying the same principles, we can get

$$P(x_{k+1} = i | x_k = i, F_1) = \frac{(n-i) \times 2i}{n(n-1)}, \quad P(x_{k+1} = i+1 | x_k = i, F_1) = \frac{(n-i) \times (i+1)}{n(n-1)}.$$

Plugging into $E[N_i | F_1]$ and simplifying $E[N_i | F_1]$ as Z_i, we have

$$(n-i) \times 2i \times Z_i = n(n-1) + (n-i)(i+1)Z_{i+1} + (n-i)(i-1)Z_{i-1}.$$

Using these recursive system equations and the boundary condition $Z_n = 0$, we can get $Z_1 = (n-1)^2$.[4]

5.2 Martingale and Random walk

Random walk: The process $\{S_n; n \geq 1\}$ is called a random walk if $\{X_i; i \geq 1\}$ are IID (identical and independently distributed) random variables and $S_n = X_1 + \cdots X_n$, where $n = 1, 2, \cdots$ The term comes from the fact that we can think of S_n as the position at time n for a walker who makes successive random steps $X_1, X_2, \cdots$

If X_i takes values 1 and -1 with probabilities p and $1 - p$ respectively, S_n is called a **simple random walk** with parameter p. Furthermore, if $p = \frac{1}{2}$, the process S_n is a **symmetric random walk**. For symmetric random walk, it's easy to show that $E[S_n] = 0$ and $\text{var}(S_n) = E[S_n^2] - E[S_n]^2 = E[S_n^2] = n$.[5]

Symmetric random walk is the process that is most often tested in quantitative interviews. The interview questions on random walk often revolve around finding the first n for which S_n reaches a defined threshold α, or the probability that S_n reaches α for any given value of n.

Martingale: a martingale $\{Z_n; n \geq 1\}$ is a stochastic process with the properties that $E[|Z_n|] < \infty$ for all n and $E[Z_{n+1} | Z_n = z_n, Z_{n-1} = z_{n-1}, \cdots, Z_1 = z_1] = z_n$. The property of a martingale can be extended to $E[Z_m; m > n | Z_n = z_n, Z_{n-1} = z_{n-1}, \cdots, Z_1 = z_1] = z_n$, which means the conditional expected value of future Z_m is the current value Z_n.[6]

A symmetric random walk is a martingale. From the definition of the symmetric random walk we have $S_{n+1} = \begin{cases} S_n + 1 & \text{with probability } 1/2 \\ S_n - 1 & \text{with probability } 1/2 \end{cases}$, so $E[S_{n+1} | S_n = s_n, \cdots, S_1 = s_1] = s_n$.

Since $E[S_{n+1}^2 - (n+1)] = \frac{1}{2}[(S_n+1)^2 + (S_n-1)^2] - (n+1) = S_n^2 - n$, $S_n^2 - n$ is a martingale as well.

---

[4] Even this step is not straightforward. You need to plug in the i's and try a few cases starting with $i = n-1$. The pattern will emerge and you can see that all the terms containing $Z_{n-1}, Z_{n-2}, \cdots, Z_2$ cancel out.

[5] Induction again can be used for its proof. $Var(S_1) = Var(Z_1) = 1$. Induction step: If $Var(S_n) = n$, then we have $Var(S_{n+1}) = Var(S_n + x_{n+1}) = Var(S_n) + Var(x_{n+1}) = n+1$ since x_{n+1} is independent of S_n.

[6] Do not confuse a martingale process with a Markov process. A martingale does not need to be a Markov process; a Markov process does not need to be a martingale process, either.

Stopping rule: For an experiment with a set of IID random variables $X_1, X_2, \cdots$, a stopping rule for $\{X_i; i \geq 1\}$ is a positive integer-value random variable N (stopping time) such that for each $n > 1$, the event $\{N \leq n\}$ is independent of $X_{n+1}, X_{n+2}, \cdots$. Basically it says that whether to stop at n depends only on $X_1, X_2, \cdots, X_n$ (i.e., no look ahead).

Wald's Equality: Let N be a stopping rule for IID random variables $X_1, X_2, \cdots$ and let $S_N = X_1 + X_2 + \cdots + X_N$, then $E[S_N] = E[X]E[N]$.

Since it is an important—yet relatively little known—theorem, let's briefly review its proof. Let I_n be the indicator function of the event $\{N \geq n\}$. So S_N can be written as

$$S_N = \sum_{n=1}^{\infty} X_n I_n, \text{ where } I_n = 1 \text{ if } N \geq n \text{ and } I_n = 0 \text{ if } N \leq n-1.$$

From the definition of stopping rules, we know that I_n is independent of X_n, $X_{n+1}, \cdots$ (it only depends on $X_1, X_2, \cdots, X_{n-1}$). So $E[X_n I_n] = E[X_n]E[I_n] = E[X]E[I_n]$ and

$$E[S_N] = E\left[\sum_{n=1}^{\infty} X_n I_n\right] = \sum_{n=1}^{\infty} E[X_n I_n] = \sum_{n=1}^{\infty} E[X]E[I_n] = E[X]\sum_{n=1}^{\infty} E[I_n] = E[X]E[N].\,[7]$$

A martingale stopped at a stopping time is a martingale.

Drunk man

A drunk man is at the 17th meter of a 100-meter-long bridge. He has a 50% probability of staggering forward or backward one meter each step. What is the probability that he will make it to the end of the bridge (the 100th meter) before the beginning (the 0th meter)? What is the expected number of steps he takes to reach either the beginning or the end of the bridge?

Solution: The probability part of the problem—often appearing in different disguises—is among the most popular martingale problems asked by quantitative interviewers. Interestingly, few people use a clear-cut martingale argument. Most candidates either use Markov chain with two absorbing states or treat it as a special version of the gambler's ruin problem with $p = 1/2$. These approaches yield the correct results in the end, yet a martingale argument is not only simpler but also illustrates the insight behind the problem.

---

[7] For detailed proof and applications of Wald's Equality, please refer to the book ***Discrete Stochastic Processes*** by Robert G. Gallager.

Let's set the current position (the 17th meter) to 0; then the problem becomes a symmetric random walk that stops at either 83 or -17. We also know that both S_n and $S_n^2 - n$ are martingales. Since a martingale stopped at a stopping time is a martingale, S_N and $S_N^2 - N$ (where $S_N = X_1 + X_2 + \cdots + X_N$ with N being the stopping time) are martingales as well. Let p_α be the probability that it stops at $\alpha = 83$, p_β be the probability it stops at $-\beta = -17$ ($p_\beta = 1 - p_\alpha$), and N be the stopping time. Then we have

$$\left. \begin{array}{l} E[S_N] = p_\alpha \times 83 - (1 - p_\alpha) \times 17 = S_0 = 0 \\ E[S_N^2 - N] = E[p_\alpha \times 83^2 + (1 - p_\alpha) \times 17^2] - E[N] = S_0^2 - 0 = 0 \end{array} \right\} \Rightarrow \left\{ \begin{array}{l} p_\alpha = 0.17 \\ E[N] = 1441 \end{array} \right.$$

Hence, the probability that he will make it to the end of the bridge (the 100th meter) before reaching the beginning is 0.17, and the expected number of steps he takes to reach either the beginning or the end of the bridge is 1441.

We can easily extend the solution to a general case: a symmetric random walk starting from 0 that stops at either α ($\alpha > 0$) or $-\beta$ ($\beta > 0$). The probability that it stops at α instead of $-\beta$ is $p_\alpha = \beta / (\alpha + \beta)$. The expected stopping time to reach either α or $-\beta$ is $E[N] = \alpha\beta$.

Dice game

Suppose that you roll a dice. For each roll, you are paid the face value. If a roll gives 4, 5 or 6, you can roll the dice again. If you get 1, 2 or 3, the game stops. What is the expected payoff of this game?

Solution: In Chapter 4, we used the law of total expectation to solve the problem. A simpler approach—requiring more knowledge—is to apply Wald's Equality since the problem has clear stopping rules. For each roll, the process has 1/2 probability of stopping. So the stopping time N follows a geometric distribution with $p = 1/2$ and we have $E[N] = 1/p = 2$. For each roll, the expected face value is $E[X] = 7/2$. The total expected payoff is $E[S_N] = E[X]E[N] = 7/2 \times 2 = 7$.

Ticket line

At a theater ticket office, $2n$ people are waiting to buy tickets. n of them have only \$5 bills and the other n people have only \$10 bills. The ticket seller has no change to start with. If each person buys one $5 ticket, what is the probability that all people will be able to buy their tickets without having to change positions?

Solution: This problem is often considered to be a difficult one. Although many can correctly formulate the problem, few can solve the problem using the reflection principle.[8] This problem is one of the many cases where a broad knowledge makes a difference.

Assign +1 to the n people with $5 bills and -1 to the n people with $10 bills. Consider the process as a walk. Let (a,b) represent that after a steps, the walk ends at b. So we start at $(0,0)$ and reaches $(2n,0)$ after $2n$ steps. For these $2n$ steps, we need to choose n steps as +1, so there are $\binom{2n}{n} = \dfrac{2n!}{n!n!}$ possible paths. We are interested in the paths that have the property $b \geq 0$, $\forall 0 < a < 2n$ steps. It's easier to calculate the number of complement paths that reach $b = -1$, $\exists 0 < a < 2n$. As shown in Figure 5.6, if we reflect the path across the line $y = -1$ after a path first reaches -1, for every path that reaches $(2n,0)$ at step $2n$, we have one corresponding reflected path that reaches $(2n,-2)$ at step $2n$. For a path to reach $(2n,-2)$, there are $(n-1)$ steps of +1 and $(n+1)$ steps of -1. So there are $\binom{2n}{n-1} = \dfrac{2n!}{(n-1)!(n+1)!}$ such paths. The number of paths that have the property $b = -1$, $\exists 0 < a < 2n$, given that the path reaches $(2n,0)$ is also $\binom{2n}{n-1}$ and the number of paths that have the property $b \geq 0$, $\forall 0 < a < 2n$ is

$$\binom{2n}{n} - \binom{2n}{n-1} = \binom{2n}{n} - \frac{n}{n+1}\binom{2n}{n} = \frac{1}{n+1}\binom{2n}{n}.$$

Hence, the probability that all people will be able to buy their tickets without having to change positions is $1/(n+1)$.

---

[8] Consider a random walk starting at a, $S_0 = a$, and reaching b in n steps: $S_n = b$. Denote $N_n(a,b)$ as the number of possible paths from $(0,a)$ to (n,b) and $N_n^0(a,b)$ as the number possible paths from $(0,a)$ to (n,b) that at some step k ($k > 0$,), $S_k = 0$; in other words, $N_n^0(a,b)$ are the paths that contain $(k,0)$, $\exists 0 < k < n$. **The reflection principle** says that if a, $b > 0$, then $N_n^0(a,b) = N_n(-a,b)$. The proof is intuitive: for each path $(0,a)$ to $(k,0)$, there is a one-to-one corresponding path from $(0,-a)$ to $(k,0)$.

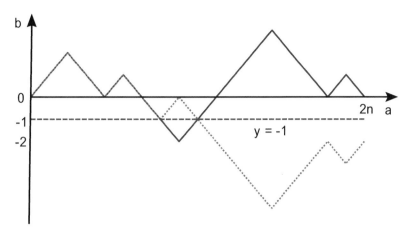

Figure 5.6 Reflected paths: the dashed line is the reflection of the solid line after it reaches -1

Coin sequence

Assume that you have a fair coin. What is the expected number of coin tosses to get n heads in a row?

Solution: Let $E[f(n)]$ be the expected number of coin tosses to get n heads in a row. In the Markov chain section, we discussed the case where $n = 3$ (to get the pattern *HHH*). For any integer n, we can consider an induction approach. Using the Markov chain approach, we can easy get that $E[f(1)] = 2$, $E[f(2)] = 6$ and $E[f(3)] = 14$. A natural guess for the general formula is that $E[f(n)] = 2^{n+1} - 2$. As always, let's prove the formula using induction. We have shown the formula is true for $n = 1, 2, 3$. So we only need to prove that if $E[f(n)] = 2^{n+1} - 2$, $E[f(n+1)] = 2^{n+2} - 2$. The following diagram shows how to prove that the equation holds for $E[f(n+1)]$:

The state before $(n+1)$ heads in a row (denoted as $(n+1)H$) must be n heads in a row (denoted as nH). It takes an expected $E[f(n)] = 2^{n+1} - 2$ tosses to reach nH. Conditioned on state nH, there is a 1/2 probability it will go to $(n+1)H$ (the new toss yields H) and the process stops. There is also a 1/2 probability that it will go to the starting state 0 (the new toss yields T) and we need another expected $E[f(n+1)]$ tosses to reach $(n+1)H$. So we have

$$E[f(n+1)] = E[F(n)] + \tfrac{1}{2} \times 1 + \tfrac{1}{2} \times E[f(n+1)]$$
$$\Rightarrow E[f(n+1)] = 2 \times E[F(n)] + 2 = 2^{n+2} - 2$$

General Martingale approach: Let's use $HH \cdots H_n$ to explain a general approach for the expected time to get any coin sequence by exploring the stopping times of martingales.[9] Imagine a gambler has \$1 to bet on a sequence of n heads ($HH \cdots H_n$) in a fair game with the following rule: Bets are placed on up to n consecutive games (tosses) and each time the gambler bets all his money (unless he goes bankrupt). For example, if H appears at the first game, he will have \$2 and he will put all \$2 into the second game. He stops playing either when he loses a game or when he wins n games in a roll, in which case he collects \$$2^n$ (with probability $1/2^n$). Now let's imagine, instead of one gambler, before each toss a new gambler joins the game and bets on the same sequence of n heads with a bankroll of \$1 as well. After the i-th game, i gamblers have participated in the game and the total amount of money they have put in the game should be \$$i$. Since each game is fair, the expected value of their total bankroll is \$$i$ as well. In other words, if we denote x_i as the amount of money all the participating gamblers have after the i-th game, then $(x_i - i)$ is a martingale.

Now, let's add a stopping rule: the whole game will stop if one of the gamblers becomes the first to get n heads in a roll. A martingale stopped at a stopping time is a martingale. So we still have $E[(x_i - i)] = 0$. If the sequence stops after the i-th toss ($i \geq n$), the $(i-n+1)$-th player is the (first) player who gets n heads in a roll with payoff 2^n. So all the $(i-n)$ players before him went bankrupt; the $(i-n+2)$-th player gets $(n-1)$ heads in a roll with payoff 2^{n-1}; ...; the i-th player gets one head with payoff 2. So the total payoff is fixed and $x_i = 2^n + 2^{n-1} + \cdots + 2^1 = 2^{n+1} - 2$.

Hence, $E[(x_i - i)] = 2^{n+1} - 2 - E[i] = 0 \Rightarrow E[i] = 2^{n+1} - 2$.

This approach can be applied to any coin sequences—as well as dice sequences or any sequences with arbitrary number of elements. For example, let's consider the sequence HHTTHH. We can again use a stopped martingale process for sequence HHTTHH. The gamblers join the game one by one before each toss to bet on the same sequence HHTTHH until one gambler becomes the first to get the sequence HHTTHH. If the sequence stops after the i-th toss, the $(i-5)th$ gambler gets the HHTTHH with payoff

---

[9] If you prefer more details about the approach, please refer to "A Martingale Approach to the Study of Occurrence of Sequence Patterns in Repeated Experiments" by Shuo-Yen Robert Li, *The Annals of Probability,* Vol. 8, No. 6 (Dec., 1980), pp. 1171-1176.

2^6. All the $(i-6)$ players before him went bankrupt; the $(i-4)th$ player loses in the second toss (HT); the $(i-3)th$ player and the $(i-2)th$ player lose in the first toss (T); the $(i-1)th$ player gets sequence HH with payoff 2^2 and the i-th player gets H with payoff 2.

Hence, $E[(x_i - i)] = 2^6 + 2^2 + 2^1 - E[i] = 0 \Rightarrow E[i] = 70$.

5.3 Dynamic Programming

Dynamic Programming refers to a collection of general methods developed to solve sequential, or multi-stage, decision problems.[10] It is an extremely versatile tool with applications in fields such as finance, supply chain management and airline scheduling. Although theoretically simple, mastering dynamic programming algorithms requires extensive mathematical prerequisites and rigorous logic. As a result, it is often perceived to be one of the most difficult graduate level courses.

Fortunately, the dynamic programming problems you are likely to encounter in interviews—although you often may not recognize them as such—are rudimentary problems. So in this section we will focus on the basic logic used in dynamic programming and apply it to several interview problems. Hopefully the solutions to these examples will convey the gist and the power of dynamic programming.

A discrete-time dynamic programming model includes two inherent components:

1. The underlying discrete-time dynamic system

A dynamic programming problem can always be divided into stages with a decision required at each stage. Each stage has a number of states associated with it. The decision at one stage transforms the current state into a state in the next stage (at some stages and states, the decision may be trivial if there is only one choice).

Assume that the problem has $N+1$ stages (time periods). Following the convention, we label these stages as 0, 1, $\cdots, N-1$, N. At any stage k, $0 \le k \le N-1$, the state transition can be expressed as $x_{k+1} = f(x_k, u_k, w_k)$, where x_k is the state of system at stage k;[11] u_k is the decision selected at stage k; w_k is a random parameter (also called disturbance).

---

[10] This section barely scratches the surface of dynamic programming. For up-to-date dynamic programming topics, I'd recommend the book ***Dynamic Programming and Optimal Control*** by Professor Dimitri P. Bertsekas.

[11] In general, x_k can incorporate all past relevant information. In our discussion, we only consider the present information by assuming Markov property.

Basically the state of next stage x_{k+1} is determined as a function of the current state x_k, current decision u_k (the choice we make at stage k from the available options) and the random variable w_k (the probability distribution of w_k often depends on x_k and u_k).

2. A cost (or profit) function that is additive over time.

Except for the last stage (N), which has a cost/profit $g_N(x_N)$ depending only on x_N, the costs at all other stages $g_k(x_k, u_k, w_k)$ can depend on x_k, u_k, and w_k. So the total cost/profit is $g_N(x_N) + \sum_{k=i}^{N-1} g_k(x_k, u_k, w_k)\}$.

The goal of optimization is to select strategies/policies for the decision sequences $\pi^* = \{u_0^*, \cdots, u_{N-1}^*\}$ that minimize expected cost (or maximize expected profit):

$$J_{\pi^*}(x_0) = \min_{\pi} E\{g_N(x_N) + \sum_{k=0}^{N-1} g_k(x_k, u_k, w_k)\} .$$

Dynamic programming (DP) algorithm

The dynamic programming algorithm relies on an idea called the **Principle of Optimality**: If $\pi^* = \{u_0^*, \cdots, u_{N-1}^*\}$ is the optimal policy for the original dynamic programming problem, then the tail policy $\pi_i^* = \{u_i^*, \cdots, u_{N-1}^*\}$ must be optimal for the tail subproblem $E\{g_N(x_N) + \sum_{k=i}^{N-1} g_k(x_k, u_k, w_k)\}$.

DP algorithm: To solve the basic problem $J_{\pi^*}(x_0) = \min_{\pi} E\{g_N(x_N) + \sum_{k=0}^{N-1} g_k(x_k, u_k, w_k)\}$, start with $J_N(x_N) = g_N(x_N)$, and go backwards minimizing cost-to-go function $J_k(x_k)$:
$J_k(x_k) = \min_{u_k \in U_k(x_k)} E_{w_k} \{g_k(x_k, u_k, w_k) + J_{k+1}(f(x_k, u_k, w_k))\}$, $k = 0, \cdots, N-1$. Then the $J_0(x_0)$ generated from this algorithm is the expected optimal cost.

Although the algorithm looks complicated, the intuition is straightforward. For dynamic programming problems, we should start with optimal policy for every possible state of the final stage (which has the highest amount of information and least amount of uncertainty) first and then work backward towards earlier stages by applying the tail policies and cost-to-go functions until you reach the initial stage.

Now let's use several examples to show how the DP algorithm is applied.

Dice game

You can roll a 6-side dice up to 3 times. After the first or the second roll, if you get a number x, you can decide either to get x dollars or to choose to continue rolling. But once you decide to continue, you forgo the number you just rolled. If you get to the third roll, you'll just get x dollars if the third number is x and the game stops. What is the game worth and what is your strategy?

Solution: This is a simple dynamic programming strategy game. As all dynamic programming questions, the key is to start with the final stage and work backwards. For this question, it is the stage where you have forgone the first two rolls. It becomes a simple dice game with one roll. Face values 1, 2, 3, 4, 5, and 6 each have a 1/6 probability and your expected payoff is $3.5.

Now let's go back one step. Imagine that you are at the point after the second roll, for which you can choose either to have a third roll with an expected payoff of $3.5 or keep the current face value. Surely you will keep the face value if it is larger than 3.5; in other words, when you get 4, 5 or 6, you stop rolling. When you get 1, 2 or 3, you keep rolling. So your expected payoff before the second roll is $3/6 \times 3.5 + 1/6 \times (4 + 5 + 6) = \$4.25$.

Now let's go back one step further. Imagine that you are at the point after the first roll, for which you can choose either to have a second roll with expected payoff $4.25 (when face value is 1, 2, 3 or 4) or keep the current face value. Surely you will keep the face value if it is larger than 4.25; In other words, when you get 5 or 6, you stop rolling. So your expected payoff before the first roll is $4/6 \times 4.25 + 1/6 \times (5 + 6) = \$14/3$.

This backward approach—called tail policy in dynamic programming—gives us the strategy and also the expected value of the game at the initial stage, $14/3.

World series

The Boston Red Sox and the Colorado Rockies are playing in the World Series finals. In case you are not familiar with the World Series, there are a maximum of 7 games and the first team that wins 4 games claims the championship. You have $100 dollars to place a double-or-nothing bet on the Red Sox.

Unfortunately, you can only bet on each individual game, not the series as a whole. How much should you bet on each game so that if the Red Sox wins the whole series, you win exactly $100, and if Red Sox loses, you lose exactly $100?

Solution: Let (i, j) represents the state that the Red Sox has won i games and the Rockies has won j games, and let $f(i, j)$ be our net payoff, which can be negative when we lose money, at state (i, j). From the rules of the game, we know that there may be between 4 and 7 games in total. We need to decide on a strategy so that whenever the series is over, our final net payoff is either +100—when Red Sox wins the championship—or −100—when Red Sox loses. In other words, the state space of the final stage includes $\{(4,0), (4,1), (4,2), (4,3)\}$ with payoff $f(i,j)=100$ and $\{(0,4), (1,4), (2,4), (3,4)\}$ with payoff $f(i,j)=-100$. As all dynamic programming questions, the key is to start with the final stage and work backwards—even though in this case the number of stages is not fixed. For each state (i, j), if we bet \$$y$ on the Red Sox for the next game, we will have $(f(i, j)+y)$ if the Red Sox wins and the state goes to $(i+1, j)$, or $(f(i,j)-y)$ if the Red Sox loses and the state goes to $(i, j+1)$. So clearly we have

$$\left. \begin{array}{l} f(i+1,\ j) = f(i,\ j)+y \\ f(i,\ j+1) = f(i,\ j)-y \end{array} \right\} \Rightarrow \left\{ \begin{array}{l} f(i,\ j) = \big(f(i+1,\ j)+f(i,\ j+1)\big)/2 \\ y = \big(f(i+1,\ j)-f(i,\ j+1)\big)/2 \end{array} \right. .$$

For example, we have $f(3, 3) = \dfrac{f(4,\ 3)+f(3,\ 4)}{2} = \dfrac{100-100}{2} = 0$. Let's set up a table with the columns representing i and the rows representing j. Now we have all the information to fill in $f(4,0)$, $f(4,1)$, $f(4,3)$, $f(4,2)$, $f(0,4)$, $f(1,4)$, $f(2,4)$, $f(3,4)$, as well as $f(3,3)$. Similarly we can also fill in all $f(i,j)$ for the states where $i=3$ or $j=3$ as shown in Figure 5.7. Going further backward, we can fill in the net payoffs at every possible state. Using equation $y = \big(f(i+1,\ j)-f(i,\ j+1)\big)/2$, we can also calculate the bet we need to place at each state, which is essentially our strategy.

If you are not accustomed to the table format, Figure 5.8 redraws it as a binomial tree, a format you should be familiar with. If you consider that the boundary conditions are $f(4,0)$, $f(4,1)$, $f(4,3)$, $f(4,2)$, $f(0,4)$, $f(1,4)$, $f(2,4)$, and $f(3,4)$, the underlying asset either increases by 1 or decrease by 1 after each step, and there is no interest, then the problem becomes a simple binomial tree problem and the bet we place each time is the delta in dynamic hedging. In fact, both European options and American options can be solved numerically using dynamic programming approaches.

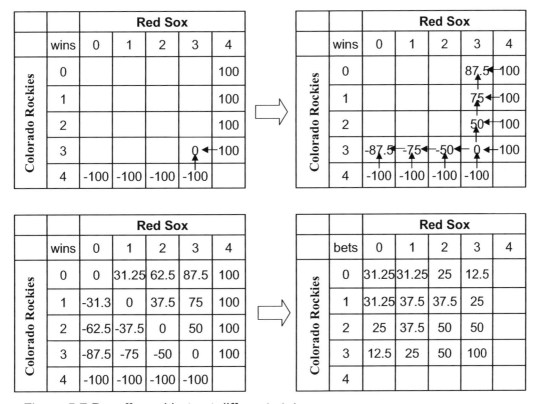

Figure 5.7 Payoffs and bets at different states

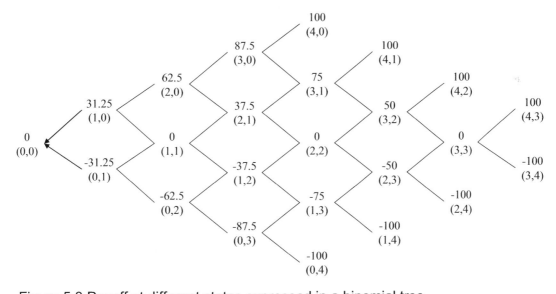

Figure 5.8 Payoff at different states expressed in a binomial tree

Dynamic dice game

A casino comes up with a fancy dice game. It allows you to roll a dice as many times as you want unless a 6 appears. After each roll, if 1 appears, you will win $1; if 2 appears, you will win $2; …; if 5 appears, you win $5; but if 6 appears all the moneys you have won in the game is lost and the game stops. After each roll, if the dice number is 1-5, you can decide whether to keep the money or keep on rolling. How much are you willing to pay to play the game (if you are risk neutral)?[12]

Solution: Assuming that we have accumulated n dollars, the decision to have another roll or not depends on the expected profit versus expected loss. If we decide to have an extra roll, our expected payoff will become

$$\frac{1}{6}(n+1)+\frac{1}{6}(n+2)+\frac{1}{6}(n+3)+\frac{1}{6}(n+4)+\frac{1}{6}(n+5)+\frac{1}{6}\times 0=\frac{5}{6}n+2.5.$$

We have another roll if the expected payoff $\frac{5}{6}n+2.5>n$, which means that we should keep rolling if the money is no more than $14. Considering that we will stop rolling when $n\geq 15$, the maximum payoff of the game is $19 (the dice rolls a 5 after reaching the state $n=14$). We then have the following: $f(19)=19$, $f(18)=18$, $f(17)=17$, $f(16)=16$, and $f(15)=15$. When $n\leq 14$, we will keep on rolling, so $E[f(n)\,|\,n\leq 14]=\frac{1}{6}\sum_{i=1}^{5}E[f(n+i)]$. Using this equation, we can calculate the value for $E[f(n)]$ recursively for all $n=14,13,\cdots,0$. The results are summarized in Table 5.2. Since $E[f(0)]=6.15$, we are willing to pay at most $6.15 for the game.

n	19	18	17	16	15	14	13	12	11	10
E[*f(n)*]	19.00	18.00	17.00	16.00	15.00	14.17	13.36	12.59	11.85	11.16
n	9	8	7	6	5	4	3	2	1	0
E[*f(n)*]	10.52	9.91	9.34	8.80	8.29	7.81	7.36	6.93	6.53	6.15

Table 5.2 Expected payoff of the game when the player has accumulated n dollars

---

[12] Hint: If you decide to have another roll, the expected amount you have after the roll should be higher than the amount before the roll. As the number of dollars increases, you risk losing more money if a 6 appears. So when the amount of dollar reaches a certain number, you should stop rolling.

Dynamic card game

A casino offers yet another card game with the standard 52 cards (26 red, 26 black). The cards are thoroughly shuffled and the dealer draws cards one by one. (Drawn cards are not returned to the deck.) You can ask the dealer to stop at any time you like. For each red card drawn, you win \$1; for each black card drawn, you lose \$1. What is the optimal stopping rule in terms of maximizing expected payoff and how much are you willing to pay for this game?

Solution: It is another problem perceived to be difficult by many interviewees. Yet it is a simple dynamic programming problem. Let (b, r) represent the number of black and red cards left in the deck, respectively. By symmetry, we have

red cards drawn − black cards drawn = black cards left − red cards left = b − r

At each (b, r), we face the decision whether to stop or keep on playing. If we ask the dealer to stop at (b, r), the payoff is $b-r$. If we keep on going, there is $\dfrac{b}{b+r}$ probability that the next card will be black—in which case the state changes to $(b-1, r)$—and $\dfrac{r}{b+r}$ probability that the next card will be red—in which case the state changes to $(b, r-1)$. We will stop if and only if the expected payoff of drawing more cards is less than $b-r$. That also gives us the system equation:

$$E[f(b,r)] = \max\left(b-r, \frac{b}{b+r}E[f(b-1,r)] + \frac{r}{b+r}[f(b,r-1)] \right).^{13}$$

As shown in Figure 5.9 (next page), using the boundary conditions $f(0, r) = 0$, $f(b, 0) = b$, $\forall b, r = 0, 1, \cdots, 26$, and the system equation for $E[f(b, r)]$, we can recursively calculate $E[f(b, r)]$ for all pairs of b and r.

The expected payoff at the beginning of the game is $E[f(26, 26)] = \$2.62$.

---

[13] You probably have recognized this system equation as the one for American options. Essentially you decide whether you want to exercise the option at state (b, r).

Number of Black Cards Left

f(b,r)	0	1	2	3	4	5	6	7	8	9	10	11	12	13	14	15	16	17	18	19	20	21	22	23	24	25	26
0	0	1	2	3	4	5	6	7	8	9	10	11	12	13	14	15	16	17	18	19	20	21	22	23	24	25	26
1	0	0.50	1	2	3	4	5	6	7	8	9	10	11	12	13	14	15	16	17	18	19	20	21	22	23	24	25
2	0	0.33	0.67	1.20	2	3	4	5	6	7	8	9	10	11	12	13	14	15	16	17	18	19	20	21	22	23	24
3	0	0.25	0.50	0.85	1.34	2	3	4	5	6	7	8	9	10	11	12	13	14	15	16	17	18	19	20	21	22	23
4	0	0.20	0.40	0.66	1.00	1.44	2.07	3	4	5	6	7	8	9	10	11	12	13	14	15	16	17	18	19	20	21	22
5	0	0.17	0.33	0.54	0.79	1.12	1.55	2.15	3	4	5	6	7	8	9	10	11	12	13	14	15	16	17	18	19	20	21
6	0	0.14	0.29	0.45	0.66	0.91	1.23	1.66	2.23	3	4	5	6	7	8	9	10	11	12	13	14	15	16	17	18	19	20
7	0	0.13	0.25	0.39	0.56	0.76	1.01	1.34	1.75	2.30	3	4	5	6	7	8	9	10	11	12	13	14	15	16	17	18	19
8	0	0.11	0.22	0.35	0.49	0.66	0.86	1.11	1.43	1.84	2.36	3.05	4	5	6	7	8	9	10	11	12	13	14	15	16	17	18
9	0	0.10	0.20	0.31	0.43	0.58	0.75	0.95	1.21	1.52	1.92	2.43	3.10	4	5	6	7	8	9	10	11	12	13	14	15	16	17
10	0	0.09	0.18	0.28	0.39	0.52	0.66	0.83	1.04	1.30	1.61	2.00	2.50	3.15	4	5	6	7	8	9	10	11	12	13	14	15	16
11	0	0.08	0.17	0.26	0.35	0.46	0.59	0.74	0.91	1.12	1.38	1.69	2.08	2.57	3.20	4	5	6	7	8	9	10	11	12	13	14	15
12	0	0.08	0.15	0.24	0.32	0.42	0.54	0.66	0.81	0.99	1.20	1.46	1.77	2.15	2.63	3.24	4	5	6	7	8	9	10	11	12	13	14
13	0	0.07	0.14	0.22	0.30	0.39	0.49	0.60	0.73	0.89	1.06	1.28	1.53	1.84	2.22	2.70	3.28	4.03	5	6	7	8	9	10	11	12	13
14	0	0.07	0.13	0.20	0.28	0.36	0.45	0.55	0.67	0.80	0.95	1.13	1.35	1.60	1.91	2.29	2.75	3.33	4.06	5	6	7	8	9	10	11	12
15	0	0.06	0.13	0.19	0.26	0.33	0.42	0.51	0.61	0.73	0.86	1.02	1.20	1.42	1.67	1.98	2.36	2.81	3.38	4.09	5	6	7	8	9	10	11
16	0	0.06	0.12	0.18	0.24	0.31	0.39	0.47	0.57	0.67	0.79	0.93	1.08	1.27	1.48	1.74	2.05	2.42	2.87	3.43	4.13	5	6	7	8	9	10
17	0	0.06	0.11	0.17	0.23	0.29	0.36	0.44	0.53	0.62	0.73	0.85	0.99	1.15	1.33	1.55	1.81	2.11	2.48	2.93	3.48	4.16	5	6	7	8	9
18	0	0.05	0.11	0.16	0.22	0.28	0.34	0.41	0.49	0.58	0.67	0.78	0.90	1.04	1.21	1.39	1.61	1.87	2.17	2.54	2.99	3.53	4.19	5	6	7	8
19	0	0.05	0.10	0.15	0.20	0.26	0.32	0.39	0.46	0.54	0.63	0.73	0.84	0.96	1.10	1.26	1.45	1.67	1.93	2.24	2.60	3.04	3.57	4.22	5.01	6	7
20	0	0.05	0.10	0.14	0.19	0.25	0.31	0.37	0.43	0.51	0.59	0.68	0.78	0.89	1.01	1.16	1.32	1.51	1.73	1.99	2.30	2.66	3.09	3.62	4.25	5.03	6
21	0	0.05	0.09	0.14	0.19	0.24	0.29	0.35	0.41	0.48	0.55	0.63	0.72	0.83	0.94	1.07	1.21	1.38	1.57	1.79	2.05	2.35	2.72	3.15	3.66	4.28	5.05
22	0	0.04	0.09	0.13	0.18	0.23	0.28	0.33	0.39	0.45	0.52	0.60	0.68	0.77	0.87	0.99	1.12	1.26	1.43	1.62	1.85	2.11	2.41	2.77	3.20	3.71	4.32
23	0	0.04	0.08	0.13	0.17	0.22	0.26	0.32	0.37	0.43	0.49	0.56	0.64	0.72	0.82	0.92	1.04	1.17	1.32	1.48	1.68	1.90	2.16	2.47	2.82	3.25	3.75
24	0	0.04	0.08	0.12	0.16	0.21	0.25	0.30	0.35	0.41	0.47	0.53	0.60	0.68	0.77	0.86	0.97	1.08	1.22	1.37	1.54	1.73	1.96	2.22	2.52	2.88	3.30
25	0	0.04	0.08	0.12	0.16	0.20	0.24	0.29	0.34	0.39	0.45	0.51	0.57	0.64	0.72	0.81	0.90	1.01	1.13	1.26	1.42	1.59	1.78	2.01	2.27	2.57	2.93
26	0	0.04	0.07	0.11	0.15	0.19	0.23	0.28	0.32	0.37	0.43	0.48	0.54	0.61	0.68	0.76	0.85	0.95	1.06	1.18	1.31	1.46	1.64	1.83	2.06	2.32	**2.62**

Number of Red Cards Left

Figure 5.9 Expected payoffs at different states (b, r)

5.4 Brownian Motion and Stochastic Calculus

In this section, we briefly go over some problems for stochastic calculus, the counterpart of stochastic processes in continuous space. Since the basic definitions and theorems of Brownian motion and stochastic calculus are directly used as interview problems, we'll simply integrate them into the problems instead of starting with an overview of definitions and theorems.

Brownian motion

A. Define and enumerate some properties of a Brownian motion?[1]

Solution: This is the most basic Brownian motion question. Interestingly, part of the definition, such as $W(0) = 0$, and some properties are so obvious that we often fail to recite all the details.

A continuous stochastic process $W(t)$, $t \geq 0$, is a Brownian motion if

- $W(0) = 0$;

- The increments of the process $W(t_1) - W(0)$, $W(t_2) - W(t_1)$, $\cdots$, $W(t_n) - W(t_{n-1})$, $\forall 0 \leq t_1 \leq t_2 \leq \cdots \leq t_n$ are independent;

- Each of these increments is normally distributed with distribution $W(t_{i+1}) - W(t_i) \sim N(0, t_{i+1} - t_i)$.

Some of the important properties of Brownian motion are the following: continuous (no jumps); $E[W(t)] = 0$; $E[W(t)^2] = t$; $W(t) \sim N(0, t)$; martingale property $E[W(t+s) | W(t)] = W(t)$; $\text{cov}(W(s), W(t)) = s$, $\forall 0 < s < t$; and Markov property (in continuous space).

There are two other important martingales related to Brownian motion that are valuable tools in many applications.

- $Y(t) = W(t)^2 - t$ is a martingale.

- $Z(t) = \exp\left\{\lambda W(t) - \frac{1}{2}\lambda^2 t\right\}$, where λ is any constant and $W(t)$ is a Brownian motion, is a martingale. (Exponential martingale).

---

[1] A Brownian motion is often denoted as B_t. Alternatively it is denoted as $W(t)$ since it is a Wiener process. In this section, we use both notations interchangeably so that you get familiar with both.

We'll show a proof of the first martingale using Ito's lemma in the next section. A sketch for the exponential martingale is the following:[2]

$$E\left[Z(t+s)\right] = E\left[\exp\left\{\lambda\left(W(t)+W(s)\right)-\tfrac{1}{2}\lambda^2(t+s)\right\}\right]$$
$$= \exp\left\{\lambda W(t)-\tfrac{1}{2}\lambda^2 t\right\}\exp\left\{-\tfrac{1}{2}\lambda^2 s\right\}E\left[\exp\left\{\lambda W(s)\right\}\right]$$
$$= Z_t\exp\left\{-\tfrac{1}{2}\lambda^2 s\right\}\exp\left\{\tfrac{1}{2}\lambda^2 s\right\} = Z_t$$

B. What is the correlation of a Brownian motion and its square?

Solution: The solution to this problem is surprisingly simple. At time t, $B_t \sim N(0,t)$, by symmetry, $E[B_t]=0$ and $E[B_t^3]=0$. Applying the equation for covariance $Cov(X,Y) = E[XY]-E[X]E[Y]$, we have $Cov(B_t, B_t^2) = E[B_t^3]-E[B_t]E[B_t^2]=0-0=0$. So the correlation of a Brownian motion and its square is 0, too.

C. Let B_t be a Brownian motion. What is the probability that $B_1 > 0$ and $B_2 < 0$?

Solution: A standard solution takes advantage of the fact that $B_1 \sim N(0,1)$, and $B_2 - B_1$ is independent of B_1, which is again a normal distribution: $B_2 - B_1 \sim N(0,1)$. If $B_1 = x > 0$, then for $B_2 < 0$, we must have $B_2 - B_1 < -x$.

$$P(B_1 > 0, B_2 < 0) = P(B_1 > 0, B_2 - B_1 < -B_1)$$
$$= \int_0^\infty \frac{1}{\sqrt{2\pi}}e^{-x^2/2}dx\int_{-\infty}^{-x}\frac{1}{\sqrt{2\pi}}e^{-y^2/2}dy = \int_0^\infty\int_{-\infty}^{-x}\frac{1}{2\pi}e^{-(x^2+y^2)/2}dxdy$$
$$= \int_0^\infty\int_{3/2\pi}^{7/4\pi}\frac{1}{2\pi}e^{-r^2/2}rdrd\theta = \frac{7/4\pi-3/2\pi}{2\pi}\left[-e^{-r^2/2}\right]_0^\infty = \frac{1}{8}$$

But do we really need the integration step? If we fully take advantage of the facts that B_1 and $B_2 - B_1$ are two IID $N(0,1)$, the answer is no. Using conditional probability and independence, we can reformulate the equation as

$$P(B_1 > 0, B_2 < 0) = P(B_1 > 0)P(B_2 - B_1 < 0)P(|B_2 - B_1| > |B_1|)$$
$$= 1/2\times1/2\times1/2 = 1/8$$

---

[2] $W(s) \sim N(0,s)$. So $E\left[\exp\left\{\lambda W(s)\right\}\right]$ is the moment generating function of normal random variable $N(0,s)$.

This approach is better demonstrated in Figure 5.10. When we have $B_1 > 0$ and $B_2 - B_1 < -B_1$, which accounts for 1/8 of the density volume. (All 8 regions separated by $x = 0$, $y = 0$, $y = x$, and $y = -x$ have the same density volume by symmetry.)

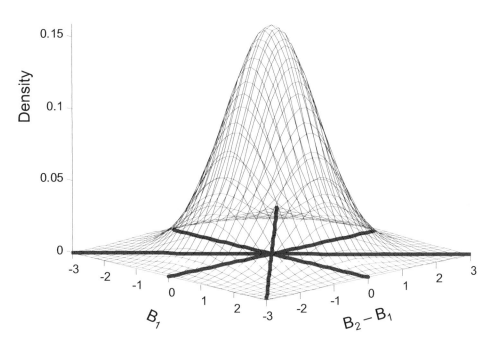

Figure 5.10 Probability density graph of (B_1, B_2-B_1)

Stopping time/ first passage time

A. What is the mean of the stopping time for a Brownian motion to reach either -1 or 1?

Solution: As we have discussed, $B_t^2 - t$ is martingale. It can be proved by applying Ito's lemma:

$$d(B_t^2 - t) = \frac{\partial(B_t^2 - t)}{\partial B_t} dB_t + \frac{\partial(B_t^2 - t)}{\partial t} dt + \frac{1}{2} \frac{\partial^2(B_t^2 - t)}{\partial B_t^2} dt = 2B_t dB_t - dt + dt = 2B_t dB_t.$$

So $d(B_t^2 - t)$ has no drift term and is a martingale. Let $T = \min\{t; B_t = 1 \text{ or } -1\}$. At continuous time and space, the following property still applies: A martingale stopped at a stopping time is a martingale! So $B_T^2 - T$ is a martingale and $E\left[B_T^2 - T\right] = B_0^2 - 0 = 0$. The probability that B_t hits 1 or -1 is 1, so $B_T^2 = 1 \Rightarrow E[T] = E\left[B_T^2\right] = 1$.

B. Let $W(t)$ be a standard Wiener process and τ_x ($x > 0$) be the first passage time to level x ($\tau_x = \min\{t; W(t) = x\}$). What is the probability density function of τ_x and the expected value of τ_x?

Solution: This is a textbook problem that is elegantly solved using the reflection principle, so we will simply summarize the explanation. For any Wiener process paths that reach x before t ($\tau_x \leq t$), they have equal probability ending above x or below x at time t, $P(\tau_x \leq t, W(t) \geq x) = P(\tau_x \leq t, W(t) \leq x)$. The explanation lies in the reflection principle. As shown in Figure 5.11, for each path that reaches x before t and is at a level y above x at time t, we can switch the sign of any move starting from τ_x and the reflected path will end at $2x - y$ that is below x at time t. For a standard Wiener process (Brownian motion), both paths have equal probability.

$$P(\tau_x \leq t) = P(\tau_x \leq t, W(t) \geq x) + P(\tau_x \leq t, W(t) \leq x) = 2P(\tau_x \leq t, W(t) \geq x)$$

$$= 2P(W(t) \geq x) = 2\int_x^\infty \frac{1}{\sqrt{2\pi t}} e^{-w^2/2t} dw$$

Let $v = \dfrac{w}{\sqrt{t}}$, we have $e^{-w^2/2t} = e^{-v^2/2}$ and $dv = \dfrac{dw}{\sqrt{t}}$.

$$\therefore P(\tau_x \leq t) = 2\int_m^\infty \frac{1}{\sqrt{2\pi t}} e^{-w^2/2t} dw = 2\int_{x/\sqrt{t}}^\infty \frac{1}{\sqrt{2\pi}} e^{-v^2/2} dv = 2 - 2N(x/\sqrt{t}).[3]$$

Take the derivative with respect to t, we have

$$f_{\tau_x}(t) = \frac{dP\{\tau_x \leq t\}}{dt} = \frac{dP\{\tau_x \leq t\}}{d(x/\sqrt{t})} \frac{d(x/\sqrt{t})}{dt} = 2N'(x/\sqrt{t}) \times \frac{x}{2} t^{-3/2} \Rightarrow \frac{xe^{-x^2/2t}}{t\sqrt{2\pi t}}, \quad \forall x > 0.$$

From part A, it's easy to show that the expected stopping time to reach either α ($\alpha > 0$) or $-\beta$ ($\beta > 0$) is again $E[N] = \alpha\beta$. The expected first passage time to level x is

---

[3] If we define $M(t) = \max\limits_{0 \leq s \leq t} W(s)$, then $P(\tau_x \leq t)$ if and only if $M(t) \geq x$. Taking the derivative of $P(\tau_x \leq t)$ with respect to x, we can derive the probability density function of $M(t)$.

essentially the expected stopping time to reach either x or $-\infty$ and $E[\tau_x] = x \times \infty = \infty$. Although we have $P(\tau_x \leq \infty) = 2 - 2N(x/\sqrt{\infty}) = 1$, the expected value of τ_x is ∞!

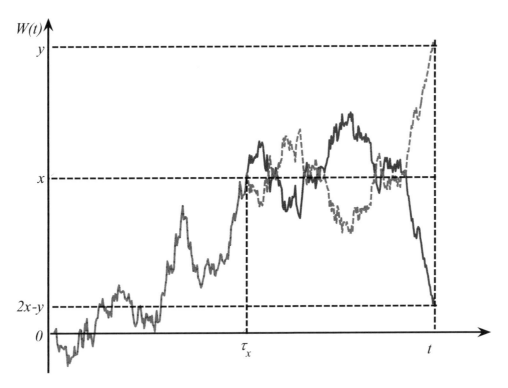

Figure 5.11 Sample path of a standard Weiner process and its reflected path

C. Suppose that X is a Brownian motion with no drift, i.e. $dX(t) = dW(t)$. If X starts at 0, what is the probability that X hits 3 before hitting -5? What if X has drift m, i.e. $dX(t) = mdt + dW(t)$?

Solution: A Brownian motion is a martingale. Let p_3 be the probability that the Brownian motion hits 3 before -5. Since a martingale stopped at a stopping time is a martingale, we have $3P_3 + (-5)(1 - P_3) = 0 \Rightarrow P_3 = 5/8$. Similar to random walk, if we have stopping boundaries ($\alpha > 0$) and $-\beta$ ($\beta > 0$), the probability that it stops at α instead of $-\beta$ is $p_\alpha = \beta/(\alpha + \beta)$. The expected stopping time to reach either α or $-\beta$ is again $E[N] = \alpha\beta$.

When X has drift m, the process is no longer a martingale. Let $P(t, x)$ be the probability that the process hits 3 before hitting -5 when $X = x$ at time t. Although X is no longer a martingale process, it is still a Markov process. So $P(t,x) = P(x)$ is actually independent of t. Applying the Feynman-Kac equation[4], we have

$$mP_x(x) + 1/2P_{xx}(x) = 0 \text{ for } -5 < x < 3.$$

We also have boundary conditions that $P(3) = 1$ and $P(-5) = 0$.

$mP_x(x) + 1/2P_{xx}(x) = 0$ is a homogeneous linear differential equation with two real roots: $r_1 = 0$ and $r_2 = -2m$. So the general solution is $P(x) = c_1 e^{0x} + c_2 e^{-2mx} = c_1 + c_2 e^{-2mx}$. Applying the boundary conditions, we have

$$\begin{cases} c_1 + c_2 e^{-6m} = 1 \\ c_1 + c_2 e^{10m} = 0 \end{cases} \Rightarrow \begin{cases} c_1 = -e^{10m}/(e^{-6m} - e^{10m}) \\ c_2 = 1/(e^{-6m} - e^{10m}) \end{cases} \Rightarrow P(0) = c_1 + c_2 = \frac{e^{10m} - 1}{e^{10m} - e^{-6m}}$$

A different and simpler approach takes advantage of the exponential martingale: $Z(t) = \exp\left\{\lambda W(t) - \frac{1}{2}\lambda^2 t\right\}$. Since $W(t) = X(t) - mt$, $X(t) - mt$ is a Brownian motion as well. Applying the exponential martingale, we have $E\left[\exp\left(\lambda(X - mt) - \frac{1}{2}\lambda^2 t\right)\right] = 1$ for any constant λ. To remove the terms including time t, we can set $\lambda = -2m$ and the equation becomes $E\left[\exp(-2mX)\right] = 1$. Since a martingale stopped at a stopping time is a martingale, we have $P_3 \exp(-2m \times 3) + (1 - P_3)\exp(-2m \times -5) = 1 \Rightarrow \dfrac{e^{10m} - 1}{e^{10m} - e^{-6m}}$.

D. Suppose that X is a generalized Weiner process $dX = dt + dW(t)$, where $W(t)$ is a Brownian motion. What is the probability that X ever reaches -1?

Solution: To solve this problem, we again can use the equation $E\left[\exp(-2mX)\right] = 1$ from the previous problem with $m = 1$. It may not be obvious since we only have one apparent boundary, -1. To apply the stopping time, we also need a corresponding positive boundary. To address this problem, we can simply use $+\infty$ as the positive boundary and the equation becomes

---

[4] Let X be an Ito process given by equation $dX(t) = \beta(t, X)dt + \gamma(t, X)dW$ and $f(x)$ be a function of X. Define function $V(t,x) = E[f(X_T) \mid X_t = x]$, then $V(t,x)$ is a martingale process that satisfies the partial differential equation $\dfrac{\partial V}{\partial t} + \beta(t,x)\dfrac{\partial V}{\partial S} + \dfrac{1}{2}\gamma^2(t,x)\dfrac{\partial^2 V}{\partial S^2} = 0$ and terminal condition $V(T,x) = f(x)$ for all x.

$$P_{-1} \exp(-2 \times -1) + (1 - P_{-1}) \exp(-2 \times +\infty) = P_{-1} e^2 = 1 \Rightarrow P_{-1} = e^{-2}.$$

Ito's lemma

Ito's lemma is the stochastic counterpart of the chain rule in ordinary calculus. Let $X(t)$ be an Ito process satisfying $dX(t) = \beta(t, X)dt + \gamma(t, X)dW(t)$, and $f(X(t), t)$ be a twice-differentiable function of $X(t)$ and t. Then $f(X(t), t)$ is an Ito process satisfying

$$df = \left(\frac{\partial f}{\partial t} + \beta(t, X)\frac{\partial f}{\partial x} + \frac{1}{2}\gamma^2(t, X)\frac{\partial^2 f}{\partial x^2} \right) dt + \gamma(t, X)\frac{\partial f}{\partial x}dW(t).$$

$$\text{Drift rate} = \frac{\partial f}{\partial t} + \beta(t, X)\frac{\partial f}{\partial x} + \frac{1}{2}\gamma^2(t, X)\frac{\partial^2 f}{\partial x^2}$$

A. Let B_t be a Brownian motion and $Z_t = \sqrt{t}B_t$. What is the mean and variance of Z_t? Is Z_t a martingale process?

Solution: As a Brownian motion, $B_t \sim N(0, t)$, which is symmetric about 0. Since $\sqrt{t}$ is a constant at t, $Z_t = \sqrt{t}B_t$ is symmetric about 0 and has mean 0 and variance $t \times \text{var}(B_t) = t^2$. More exactly, $Z_t \sim N(0, t^2)$.

Although Z_t has unconditional expected value 0, it is not a martingale. Applying Ito's lemma to $Z_t = \sqrt{t}B_t$, we have $dZ_t = \frac{\partial Z_t}{\partial B_t}dB_t + \frac{\partial Z_t}{\partial t}dt + \frac{1}{2} \times \frac{\partial^2 Z_t}{\partial B_t^2}dt = \frac{1}{2}t^{-1/2}B_t dt + \sqrt{t}dB_t$.

For all the cases that $B_t \neq 0$, which has probability 1, the drift term $\frac{1}{2}t^{-1/2}B_t dt$ is not zero.[5] Hence, the process $Z_t = \sqrt{t}B_t$ is not a martingale process.

B. Let $W(t)$ be a Brownian motion. Is $W(t)^3$ a martingale process?

---

[5] A generalized Wiener process $dx = a(x, t)dt + b(x, t)dW(t)$ is a martingale process if and only if the drift term has coefficient $a(x, t) = 0$.

Solution: Applying Ito's lemma to $f\left(W(t), t\right) = W(t)^3$, we have $\dfrac{\partial f}{\partial W(t)} = 3W(t)^2$,

$\dfrac{\partial f}{\partial t} = 0$, $\dfrac{\partial^2 f}{\partial W(t)^2} = 6W(t)$, and $df\left(W(t), t\right) = 3W(t)dt + 3W(t)^2 dW(t)$. So again for the cases $W(t) \neq 0$, which has probability 1, the drift term is not zero. Hence, $W(t)^3$ is not a martingale process.

Chapter 6 Finance

It used to be common for candidates with no finance knowledge to get hired into quantitative finance positions. Although this still happens for candidates with specialized knowledge that is in high demand, it's more likely that you are required, or at least expected, to have a basic grasp of topics in finance. So you should expect to answer some finance questions and be judged on your answers.

Besides classic textbooks,[1] there are a few interview books in the market to help you prepare for finance interviews.[2] If you want to get prepared for general finance problems, you may want to read a finance interview book to get a feel for what types of questions are asked. The focus of this chapter is more on the intuitions and mathematics behind derivative pricing instead of basic finance knowledge. Derivative problems are popular choices in quantitative interviews—even for divisions that are not directly related to derivative markets—because these problems are complex enough to test your understanding of quantitative finance.

6.1. Option Pricing

Let's begin with some notations that we will use in the following sections.

T: maturity date; t: the current time; $\tau = T - t$: time to maturity; S: stock price at time t; r: continuous risk-free interest rate; y: continuous dividend yield; σ: annualized asset volatility; c: price of a European call; p: price of a European put; C: price of an American call; P: price of an American put; D: present value, at t, of future dividends; K: strike price; PV: present value at t.

Price direction of options

How do vanilla European/American option prices change when S, K, τ, σ, r, or D changes?

Solution: The payoff of a call is $\max(S - K, 0)$ and the payoff of a put is $\max(K - S, 0)$. A European option can only be exercised at the expiration time, while an American option can be exercised at any time before maturity. Intuitively we can figure out that the price of a European/American call should decrease when the strike price increases

---

[1] For basic finance theory and financial market knowledge, I recommend **Investments** by Zvi Bodie, Alex Kane and Alan J. Marcus. For derivatives, **Options, Futures and Other Derivatives** by John C. Hull is a classic. If you want to gain a deeper understanding of stochastic calculus and derivative pricing, I'd recommend **Stochastic Calculus for Finance** (Volumes I and II) by Steven E. Shreve.
[2] For example, **Vault Guide to Finance Interviews** and **Vault Guide to Advanced and Quantitative Finance Interviews**.

since a call with a higher strike has no higher—and sometimes lower—payoff than a call with a lower strike. Using similar analyses, we summarize the effect of changing market conditions on an option's value in Table 6.1.

The impact of time to maturity on the price of a European call/put is uncertain. If there is a large dividend payoff between two different maturity dates, a European call with shorter maturity that expires before the ex-dividend date may be worth more than a call with longer maturity. For deep in-the-money European puts, the one with shorter maturity is worth more since it can be exercised earlier (time value of the money).

Variable	European call	European put	American call	American Put
Stock price ↑	↑	↓	↑	↓
Strike price ↑	↓	↑	↓	↑
Time to maturity ↑	?	?	↑	↑
Volatility ↑	↑	↑	↑	↑
Risk-free rate ↑	↑	↓	↑	↓
Dividends ↑	↓	↑	↓	↑

Table 6.1 Impact of S, K, τ, σ, r, and D on option prices

↑: increase; ↓: decrease; ?: increase or decrease

It is also worth noting that Table 6.1 assumes that only one factor changes value while all others stay the same, which in practice may not be realistic since some of the factors are related. For example, a large decrease in interest rate often triggers a stock market rally and increases the stock price, which has an opposite effect on option value.

Put-call parity

Put-call parity: $c + K^{-rt} = p + S - D$, where the European call option and the European put option have the same underlying security, the same maturity T and the same strike price K. Since $p \geq 0$, we can also derive boundaries for c, $S - D - Ke^{-rt} \leq c \leq S$, from the put-call parity.

For American options, the equality no longer holds and it becomes two inequalities: $S - D - K \leq C - P \leq S - K^{-rt}$.

Can you write down the put-call parity for European options on non-dividend paying stocks and prove it?

Solution: The put-call parity for European options on non-dividend paying stocks is $c + K^{-r\tau} = p + S$. We can treat the left side of the equation as portfolio *A*—a call and a zero-coupon bond with face value *K*—and the right side as portfolio *B*—a put and the underlying stock, which is a protective put. Portfolio *A* has payoff $\max(S_T - K, 0) + K = \max(S_T, K)$ at maturity *T*; portfolio *B* has payoff $\max(K - S_T, 0) + S_T = \max(S_T, K)$ at *T*. Since both portfolios have the same payoff at *T* and no payoff between *t* and *T*, the no-arbitrage argument[3] dictates that they must have the same value at *t*. Hence, $c + K^{-r\tau} = p + S$.

If we rearrange the put-call parity equation into $c - p = S - K^{-r\tau}$, it will give us different insight. The portfolio on the left side of the equation—long a call and short a put—has the payoff $\max(S_T - K, 0) - \max(K - S_T, 0) = S_T - K$, which is the payoff of a forward with delivery price *K*. A forward with delivery price *K* has present value $S - K^{-r\tau}$. So we again have the put-call parity $c - p = S - K^{-r\tau}$. This expression shows that when the strike price $K = S^{r\tau}$ (forward price), a call has the same value as put; when $K < S^{r\tau}$, a call has higher value; and when $K > S^{r\tau}$, a put has higher value.

American v.s. European options

A. Since American options can be exercised at any time before maturity, they are often more valuable than European options with the same characteristics. But when the stock pays no dividend, the theoretical price for an American call and European call should be the same since it is never optimal to exercise the American call. Why should you never exercise an American call on a non-dividend paying stock before maturity?

Solution: There are a number of solutions to this popular problem. We present three arguments for the conclusion.

Argument 1. If you exercises the call option, you will only get the intrinsic value of the call $S - K$. The price of the American/European call also includes time value, which is positive for a call on a non-dividend paying stock. So the investor is better off selling the option than exercising it before maturity.

In fact, if we rearrange the put-call parity for European options, we have $c = S - K^{-r\tau} + p = (S - K) + (K - K^{-r\tau}) + p$. The value of a European call on a non-dividend paying stock includes three components: the first component is the intrinsic value $S - K$; the second component is the time value of the strike (if you exercise now,

---

[3] A set of transactions is an arbitrage opportunity if the initial investment ≤ 0; payoff ≥ 0; and at least one of the inequalities is strict.

you pay K now instead of K at the maturity date, which is lower in present value); and the third component is the value of the put, which is often considered to be a protection against falling stock price. Clearly the second and the third components are both positive. So the European call should be worth more than its intrinsic value. Considering that the corresponding American call is worth at least as much as the European call, it is worth more than its intrinsic value as well. As a result, it is not optimal to exercise the American call before maturity.

Argument 2. Let's compare two different strategies. In strategy 1, we exercise the call option[4] at time t ($t < T$) and receive cash $S - K$. Alternatively, we can keep the call, short the underlying stock and lend K dollars with interest rate r (the cash proceeds from the short sale, S, is larger than K). At the maturity date T, we exercise the call if it's in the money, close the short position and close the lending. Table 6.2 shows the cash flow of such a strategy:

It clearly shows that at time t, we have the same cash flow as exercising the call, $S - K$. But at time T, we always have positive cash flow as well. So this strategy is clearly better than exercising the call at time t. By keeping the call alive, the extra benefit can be realized at maturity.

Cash flow		T	
	t	$S_T \leq K$	$S_T > K$
Call option	0	0	$S_T - K$
Short Stock	S	$-S_T$	$-S_T$
Lend K at t	$-K$	Ke^{rt}	Ke^{rt}
Total	$S - K$	$Ke^{rt} - S_T > 0$	$Ke^{rt} - K > 0$

Table 6.2 Payoff of an alternative strategy without exercising the call

Argument 3. Let's use a mathematical argument relying on risk-neutral pricing and **Jensen's inequality**—if $f(X)$ is a convex function,[5] then $E[f(X)] \geq f(E[X])$. From Figure 6.1, it's obvious that the payoff (if exercised when $S > K$) of a call option $C(S) = (S - K)^+$ is a convex function of stock price with property

$$C(\lambda S_1 + (1 - \lambda)S_2) \leq \lambda C(S_1) + (1 - \lambda)C(S_2), \ 0 < \lambda < 1.$$

---

[4] We assume $S > K$ in our discussion. Otherwise, the call surely should not be exercised.

[5] A function $f(X)$ is convex if and only if $f(\lambda x + (1 - \lambda)y) \leq \lambda f(x) + (1 - \lambda)f(y), \ 0 < \lambda < 1.$ If $f''(x) > 0, \ \forall x,$ then $f(X)$ is convex.

Let $S_1 = S$ and $S_2 = 0$, then $C(\lambda S) \leq \lambda C(S) + (1-\lambda)C(0) = \lambda C(S)$ since $C(0) = 0$.

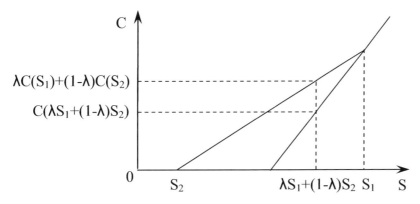

Figure 6.1 Payoff of a European call option

If the option is exercised at time t, the payoff at t is $C(S_t - K)$. If it is not exercised until maturity, the discounted expected payoff (to t) is $\tilde{E}\left[e^{-r\tau}C(S_T)\right]$ under risk-neutral measure. Under risk-neutral probabilities, we also have $\tilde{E}[S_T] = S_t e^{r\tau}$.

So $\tilde{E}\left[e^{-r\tau}C(S_T)\right] = e^{-r\tau}\tilde{E}\left[C(S_T)\right] \geq e^{-r\tau}C\left(\tilde{E}[S_T]\right) = e^{-r\tau}C\left(e^{r\tau}S_t\right)$,

where the inequality is from Jensen's inequality.

Let $S = e^{r\tau}S_t$ and $\lambda = e^{-r\tau}$, we have $C(\lambda S) = C(S_t) \leq e^{-r\tau}C\left(e^{r\tau}s_t\right) \leq e^{-r\tau}\tilde{E}\left[C(S_T)\right]$.

Since the discounted payoff $e^{-r\tau}\tilde{E}\left[C(S_T)\right]$ is no less than $C(S_t)$ for any $t \leq T$ under the risk neutral measure, it is never optimal to exercise the option before expiration.

I should point out that the payoff of a put is also a convex function of the stock price. But it is often optimal to exercise an American put on a non-dividend paying stock. The difference is that $P(0) = K$, so it does not have the property that $P(\lambda S) \leq \lambda P(S)$. In fact, $P(\lambda S) \geq \lambda P(S)$. So the argument for American calls does not apply to American puts.

Similar analysis can also show that early exercise of an American call option for dividend-paying stocks is never optimal except possibly for the time right before an ex-dividend date.

B. A European put option on a non-dividend paying stock with strike price $80 is currently priced at $8 and a put option on the same stock with strike price $90 is priced at $9. Is there an arbitrage opportunity existing in these two options?

Solution: In the last problem, we mentioned that the payoff of a put is a convex function in **stock price**. The price of a put option as a function of the **strike price** is a convex function as well. Since a put option with strike 0 is worthless, we always have $P(0) + \lambda P(K) = \lambda P(K) > P(\lambda K)$.

For this specific problem, we should have $8/9 \times P(90) = 8/9 \times 9 = 8 > P(80)$. Since the put option with strike price $80 is currently price at 8, it is overpriced and we should short it. The overall arbitrage portfolio is to short 9 units of put with $K = \$80$ and long 8 units of put with $K = 90$. At time 0, the initial cash flow is 0. At the maturity date, we have three possible scenarios:

$S_T \geq 90$, payoff $= 0$ (No put is exercised.)

$90 > S_T \geq 80$, payoff $= 8 \times (90 - S_T) > 0$ (Puts with $K = 90$ are exercised.)

$S_T < 80$, payoff $= 8 \times (90 - S_T) - 9 \times (80 - S_T) = S_T > 0$ (All puts are exercised.)

The final payoff ≥ 0 with positive probability that payoff > 0. So it is clearly an arbitrage opportunity.

Black-Scholes-Merton differential equation

Can you write down the Black-Scholes-Merton differential equation and briefly explain how to derive it?

Solution: If the evolution of the stock price is a geometric Brownian motion, $dS = \mu S dt + \sigma S dW(t)$, and the derivative $V = V(S,t)$ is a function of S and t, then applying Ito's lemma yields:

$$dV = \left(\frac{\partial V}{\partial t} + \mu S \frac{\partial V}{\partial S} + \frac{1}{2}\sigma^2 S^2 \frac{\partial^2 V}{\partial S^2}\right)dt + \sigma S \frac{\partial V}{\partial S} dW(t), \text{ where } W(t) \text{ is a Brownian motion.}$$

The Black-Scholes-Merton differential equation is a partial differential equation that should be satisfied by V: $\frac{\partial V}{\partial t} + rS \frac{\partial V}{\partial S} + \frac{1}{2}\sigma^2 S^2 \frac{\partial^2 V}{\partial S^2} = rV$.

To derive the Black-Scholes-Merton differential equation, we build a portfolio with two components: long one unit of the derivative and short $\frac{\partial V}{\partial S}$ unit of the underlying stock.

Then the portfolio has value $\Pi = V - \frac{\partial V}{\partial S} S$ and the change of Π follows equation

$$d\Pi = dV - \frac{\partial V}{\partial S}dS$$

$$= (\frac{\partial V}{\partial t} + \mu S\frac{\partial V}{\partial S} + \frac{1}{2}\sigma^2 S^2\frac{\partial^2 V}{\partial S^2})dt + \sigma S\frac{\partial V}{\partial S}dW(t) - \frac{\partial V}{\partial S}(\mu S dt + \sigma S dW(t))$$

$$= (\frac{\partial V}{\partial t} + \frac{1}{2}\sigma^2 S^2\frac{\partial^2 V}{\partial S^2})dt$$

It is apparent that this portfolio is risk-free since it has no diffusion term. It should have risk-free rate of return as well: $d\Pi = r(V - \frac{\partial V}{\partial S}S)dt$. Combining these results we have

$$(\frac{\partial V}{\partial t} + \frac{1}{2}\sigma^2 S^2\frac{\partial^2 V}{\partial S^2})dt = r(V - \frac{\partial V}{\partial S}S)dt \Rightarrow \frac{\partial V}{\partial t} + rS\frac{\partial V}{\partial S} + \frac{1}{2}\sigma^2 S^2\frac{\partial^2 V}{\partial S^2} = rV,$$

which is the Black-Scholes-Merton differential equation.

The Black-Scholes-Merton differential equation is a special case of the discounted Feynman-Kac theorem. The discounted Feynman-Kac theorem builds the bridge between stochastic differential equations and partial differential equations and applies to all Ito processes in general:

Let X be an Ito process given by equation $dX(t) = \beta(t, X)dt + \gamma(t, X)dW(t)$ and $f(x)$ be a function of X. Define function $V(t, x) = E[e^{-r(T-t)}f(X_T) | X_t = x]$, then $V(t, x)$ is a martingale process that satisfies the partial differential equation

$$\frac{\partial V}{\partial t} + \beta(t, x)\frac{\partial V}{\partial x} + \frac{1}{2}\gamma^2(t, x)\frac{\partial^2 V}{\partial x^2} = rV(t, x)$$

and boundary condition $V(T, x) = f(x)$ for all x.

Under risk-neutral measure, $dS = rSdt + \sigma SdW(t)$. Let $S = X$, $\beta(t, X) = rS$ and $\gamma(t, X) = \sigma S$, then the discounted Feynman-Kac equation becomes the Black-Scholes-Merton differential equation $\frac{\partial V}{\partial t} + rS\frac{\partial V}{\partial S} + \frac{1}{2}\sigma^2 S^2\frac{\partial^2 V}{\partial S^2} = rV$.

Black-Scholes formula

The Black-Scholes formula for European calls and puts with continuous dividend yield y is:

$$c = Se^{-y\tau}N(d_1) - Ke^{-r\tau}N(d_2) \text{ and } p = Ke^{-r\tau}N(-d_2) - Se^{-y\tau}N(-d_1),$$

$$d_1 = \frac{\ln(Se^{-y\tau}/K)+(r+\sigma^2/2)\tau}{\sigma\sqrt{\tau}} = \frac{\ln(S/K)+(r-y+\sigma^2/2)\tau}{\sigma\sqrt{\tau}}$$

where

$$d_2 = \frac{\ln(S/K)+(r-y-\sigma^2/2)\tau}{\sigma\sqrt{\tau}} = d_1 - \sigma\sqrt{\tau}$$

$N(x)$ is the cdf of the standard normal distribution and $N'(x)$ is the pdf of the standard normal distribution: $N(x) = \int_{-\infty}^{x} \frac{1}{\sqrt{2\pi}} e^{-y^2/2} dy$ and $N'(x) = \frac{1}{\sqrt{2\pi}} e^{-x^2/2}$.

If the underlying asset is a futures contract, then yield $y = r$. If the underlying asset is a foreign currency, then yield $y = r_f$, where r_f is the foreign risk-free interest rate.

A. What are the assumptions behind the Black-Scholes formula?

Solution: The original Black-Scholes formula for European calls and puts consists of the equations $c = SN(d_1) - Ke^{-r\tau}N(d_2)$ and $p = Ke^{-r\tau}N(-d_2) - SN(-d_1)$, which require the following assumptions:

1. The stock pays no dividends.

2. The risk-free interest rate is constant and known.

3. The stock price follows a geometric Brownian motion with constant drift μ and volatility σ: $dS = \mu S dt + \sigma S dW(t)$.

4. There are no transaction costs or taxes; the proceeds of short selling can be fully invested.

5. All securities are perfectly divisible.

6. There are no risk-free arbitrage opportunities.

B. How can you derive the Black-Scholes formula for a European call on a non-dividend paying stock using risk-neutral probability measure?

Solution: The Black-Scholes formula for a European call on a non-dividend paying stock is

$$c = SN(d_1) - Ke^{-r\tau}N(d_2), \quad \text{where } d_1 = \frac{\ln(S/K)+(r+\sigma^2/2)\tau}{\sigma\sqrt{\tau}} \text{ and } d_2 = d_1 - \sigma\sqrt{\tau}.$$

Under the risk-neutral probability measure, the drift of stock price becomes the risk-free interest rate $r(t)$: $dS = r(t)Sdt + \sigma SdW(t)$. Risk-neutral measure allows the option to be priced as the discounted value of its expected payoff with the risk-free interest rate:

$$V(t) = E\left[e^{-\int_t^T r(u)du} V(T) \bigg| S(t) \right], \ 0 \le t \le T, \text{ where } V(T) \text{ is the payoff at maturity } T.$$

When r is constant, the formula can be further simplified as $V(t) = e^{-r\tau}E\left[V(T)|S(t)\right]$. Under risk-neutral probabilities, $dS = rSdt + \sigma SdW(t)$. Applying Ito's lemma, we get

$$d\left(\ln(S)\right) = (r - \sigma^2/2)dt + \sigma dW(t) \Rightarrow \ln S_T \sim N\left(\ln S + (r - \sigma^2/2)\tau, \sigma^2\tau\right).$$

So $S_T = Se^{(r-\sigma^2/2)\tau + \sigma\sqrt{\tau}\varepsilon}$, where $\varepsilon \sim N(0, 1)$. For a European option, we have

$$V(T) = \begin{cases} Se^{(r-\sigma^2/2)\tau + \sigma\sqrt{\tau}\varepsilon} - K, & \text{if } Se^{(r-\sigma^2/2)\tau + \sigma\sqrt{\tau}\varepsilon} > K \\ 0, & \text{otherwise} \end{cases}$$

$$Se^{(r-\sigma^2/2)\tau + \sigma\sqrt{\tau}\varepsilon} > K \Rightarrow \varepsilon > \frac{\ln(K/S) - (r - \sigma^2/2)\tau}{\sigma\sqrt{\tau}} = -d_2 \text{ and}$$

$$E[V(T)|S] = E\left[\max(S_T - K, 0)|S\right] = \int_{-d_2}^{\infty} \left(Se^{(r-\sigma^2/2)\tau + \sigma\sqrt{\tau}\varepsilon} - K\right)\frac{1}{\sqrt{2\pi}}e^{-\varepsilon^2/2}d\varepsilon$$

$$= Se^{r\tau}\int_{-d_2}^{\infty}\frac{1}{\sqrt{2\pi}}e^{-\left(\varepsilon - \sqrt{\tau}\sigma\right)^2/2}d\varepsilon - K\int_{-d_2}^{\infty}\frac{1}{\sqrt{2\pi}}e^{-\varepsilon^2/2}d\varepsilon$$

Let $\tilde{\varepsilon} = \varepsilon - \sigma\sqrt{\tau}$, then $d\varepsilon = d\tilde{\varepsilon}$, $\varepsilon = -d_2 \Rightarrow \tilde{\varepsilon} = -d_2 - \sigma\sqrt{\tau} = -d_1$ and we have

$$Se^{r\tau}\int_{-d_2}^{\infty}\frac{1}{\sqrt{2\pi}}e^{-\left(\varepsilon - \sqrt{\tau}\sigma\right)^2/2}d\varepsilon = Se^{r\tau}\int_{-d_1}^{\infty}\frac{1}{\sqrt{2\pi}}e^{-\tilde{\varepsilon}^2/2}d\tilde{\varepsilon} = Se^{r\tau}N(d_1),$$

$$K\int_{-d_2}^{\infty}\frac{1}{\sqrt{2\pi}}e^{-\varepsilon^2/2}d\varepsilon = K\left(1 - N(-d_2)\right) = KN(d_2)$$

$\therefore E[V(T)] = Se^{r\tau}N(d_1) - KN(d_2)$ and $V(t) = e^{-r\tau}E[V(T)] = SN(d_1) - Ke^{-r\tau}N(d_2)$

From the derivation process, it is also obvious that $1 - N(-d_2) = N(d_2)$ is the risk-neutral probability that the call option finishes in the money.

C. How do you derive the Black-Scholes formula for a European call option on a non-dividend paying stock by solving the Black-Scholes-Merton differential equation?

Solution: You can skip this problem if you don't have background in partial differential equations (PDE). One approach to solving the problem is to convert the Black-Scholes-Merton differential equation to a heat equation and then apply the boundary conditions to the heat equation to derive the Black-Scholes formula.

Let $y = \ln S$ ($S = e^y$) and $\tilde{\tau} = T - t$, then $\dfrac{\partial V}{\partial t} = -\dfrac{\partial V}{\partial \tilde{\tau}}$, $\dfrac{\partial V}{\partial S} = \dfrac{\partial V}{\partial y}\dfrac{dy}{dS} = \dfrac{1}{S}\dfrac{\partial V}{\partial y}$ and

$$\dfrac{\partial^2 V}{\partial S^2} = \dfrac{\partial V}{\partial S}\left(\dfrac{\partial V}{\partial S}\right) = \dfrac{\partial V}{\partial S}\left(\dfrac{1}{S}\dfrac{\partial V}{\partial y}\right) = \dfrac{-1}{S^2}\dfrac{\partial V}{\partial y} + \dfrac{1}{S}\dfrac{\partial V}{\partial S}\left(\dfrac{\partial V}{\partial y}\right) = \dfrac{-1}{S^2}\dfrac{\partial V}{\partial y} + \dfrac{1}{S^2}\dfrac{\partial^2 V}{\partial y^2}.$$ [6]

The Black-Scholes-Merton differential equation $\dfrac{\partial V}{\partial t} + rS\dfrac{\partial V}{\partial S} + \dfrac{1}{2}\sigma^2 S^2 \dfrac{\partial^2 V}{\partial S^2} - rV = 0$

can be converted to $-\dfrac{\partial V}{\partial \tilde{\tau}} + \left(r - \dfrac{1}{2}\sigma^2\right)\dfrac{\partial V}{\partial y} + \dfrac{1}{2}\sigma^2 \dfrac{\partial^2 V}{\partial y^2} - rV = 0.$

Let $u = e^{r\tilde{\tau}}V$, the equation becomes $-\dfrac{\partial u}{\partial \tilde{\tau}} + \left(r - \dfrac{1}{2}\sigma^2\right)\dfrac{\partial u}{\partial y} + \dfrac{1}{2}\sigma^2 \dfrac{\partial^2 u}{\partial y^2} = 0.$

Finally, let $x = y + \left(r - \dfrac{1}{2}\sigma^2\right)\tilde{\tau} = \ln S + \left(r - \dfrac{1}{2}\sigma^2\right)\tilde{\tau}$ and $\tau = \tilde{\tau}$, then $\dfrac{\partial u}{\partial y} = \dfrac{\partial u}{\partial x}$ and

$\dfrac{\partial u}{\partial \tilde{\tau}} = \dfrac{\partial u}{\partial \tau} + \left(r - \dfrac{1}{2}\sigma^2\right)\dfrac{\partial u}{\partial x}$, which transforms the equation to

$$-\dfrac{\partial u}{\partial \tau} - \left(r - \dfrac{1}{2}\sigma^2\right)\dfrac{\partial u}{\partial x} + \left(r - \dfrac{1}{2}\sigma^2\right)\dfrac{\partial u}{\partial x} + \dfrac{1}{2}\sigma^2 \dfrac{\partial^2 u}{\partial x^2} = 0 \Rightarrow \dfrac{\partial u}{\partial \tau} = \dfrac{1}{2}\sigma^2 \dfrac{\partial^2 u}{\partial x^2}$$

So the original equation becomes a heat/diffusion equation $\dfrac{\partial u}{\partial \tau} = \dfrac{1}{2}\sigma^2 \dfrac{\partial^2 u}{\partial x^2}$. For heat

equation $\dfrac{\partial u}{\partial \tau} = \dfrac{1}{2}\sigma^2 \dfrac{\partial^2 u}{\partial x^2}$, where $u = u(x, \tau)$ is a function of time τ and space variable x,

with boundary condition $u(x, 0) = u_0(x)$, the solution is

$$u(x, \tau) = \dfrac{1}{\sqrt{2\pi\tau}\sigma}\int_{-\infty}^{\infty} u_0(\psi)\exp\left(-\dfrac{(x - \psi)^2}{2\sigma^2\tau}\right)d\psi.$$ [7]

---

[6] The log is taken to convert the geometric Brownian motion to an arithmetic Brownian motion; $\tau = T - t$ is used to convert the equation from a backward equation to a forward equation with initial condition at $\tau = 0$ (the boundary condition at $t = T \Rightarrow \tau = 0$).

For European calls, the boundary condition is $u_0(S_T) = \max(S_T - K, 0)$.

$S = \exp(x - (r - 0.5\sigma^2)\tau)$. When $x = \psi$ and $\tau = 0$, $S_T = e^\psi$.

$$u(S, \tau) = u(x, \tau) = \frac{1}{\sqrt{2\pi\tau}\sigma} \int_{-\infty}^{\infty} \max(e^\psi - K, 0) \exp\left(-\frac{(x - \psi)^2}{2\sigma^2\tau}\right) d\psi$$

$$= \frac{1}{\sqrt{2\pi\tau}\sigma} \int_{\ln K}^{\infty} (e^\psi - K) \exp\left(-\frac{(x - \psi)^2}{2\sigma^2\tau}\right) d\psi$$

Let $\varepsilon = \dfrac{\psi - x}{\sigma\sqrt{\tau}}$, then $d\varepsilon = \dfrac{d\psi}{\sigma\sqrt{\tau}}$, $e^\psi = e^{x + \varepsilon\sigma\sqrt{\tau}}$, $\exp\left(-\dfrac{(x - \psi)^2}{2\sigma^2\tau}\right) = e^{-\varepsilon^2/2}$ and when

$\psi = \ln K$, $\varepsilon = \dfrac{\ln(K/S) - (r - \sigma^2/2)\tau}{\sigma\sqrt{\tau}} = -d_2$

$$\therefore \ u(S, \tau) = \int_{-d_2}^{\infty} \left(Se^{(r - \sigma^2/2)\tau + \sigma\sqrt{\tau}\varepsilon} - K\right) \frac{1}{\sqrt{2\pi}} e^{-\varepsilon^2/2} d\varepsilon$$

Now, it's clear that the equation for $u(S, \tau)$ is exactly the same as the equation for $E[V(T)|S]$ in question B. Hence, we have $V(S, t) = e^{-r\tau} u(S, \tau) = SN(d_1) - Ke^{-r\tau} N(d_2)$ as well.

D. Assume zero interest rate and a stock with current price at \$1 that pays no dividend. When the price hits level \$H ($H > 1$) for the first time you can exercise the option and receive \$1. What is this option worth to you today?

Solution: First let's use a brute-force approach to solve the problem by assuming that the stock price follows a geometric Brownian motion under risk-neutral measure: $dS = rSdt + \sigma SdW(t)$. Since $r = 0$, $dS = \sigma SdW(t) \Rightarrow d(\ln S) = -\frac{1}{2}\sigma^2 dt + \sigma dW(t)$. When $t = 0$, we have $S_0 = 1 \Rightarrow \ln(S_0) = 0$.

---

[7] The **fundamental solution** to heat equation $\dfrac{\partial u}{\partial \tau} = \dfrac{1}{2} \dfrac{\partial^2 u}{\partial x^2}$ with initial condition $u_0(\psi) = f(\psi)$ is

$u(x, t) = \int_{\psi = -\infty}^{\infty} p(x_t = x | x_0 = \psi) f(\psi) d\psi$, where $p(x_t = x | x_0 = \psi) = \dfrac{1}{\sqrt{2\pi t}} \exp\left\{-(x - \psi)^2/2t\right\}$.

For detailed discussion about heat equation, please refer to *The Mathematics of Financial Derivatives* by Paul Wilmott, Sam Howison, and Jeff Dewynne.

Hence, $\ln S = -\frac{1}{2}\sigma^2 t + \sigma W(t) \Rightarrow \dfrac{\ln S + \frac{1}{2}\sigma^2 t}{\sigma} = W(t)$ is a Brownian motion.

Whenever S reaches \$$H$, the payoff is \$1. Because the interest rate is 0, the discounted payoff is also \$1 under risk-neutral measure. So the value of the option is the probability that S ever reaches \$$H$, which is equivalent to the probability that $\ln S$ ever reaches $\ln H$. Again we can apply the exponential martingale $Z(t) = \exp\left\{\lambda W(t) - \frac{1}{2}\lambda^2 t\right\}$ as we did in Chapter 5: $E\left[Z(t)\right] = E\left[\exp\left\{\lambda \dfrac{\ln S + \frac{1}{2}\sigma^2 t}{\sigma} - \frac{1}{2}\lambda^2 t\right\}\right] = 1.$

To remove the terms including time t, we can set $\lambda = \sigma$ and the equation becomes $E\left[\exp(\ln S)\right] = 1$. The Let P be the probability that $\ln S$ ever reaches $\ln H$ (using $-\infty$ as the negative boundary for stopping time), we have

$$P\exp(\ln H) + (1-P)\exp(-\infty) = P \times H = 1 \Rightarrow P = 1/H.$$

So the probability that S ever reaches \$$H$ is $1/H$ and the price of the option should be \$$1/H$. Notice that S is a martingale under the risk-neutral measure;[8] but $\ln S$ has a negative drift. The reason is that $\ln S$ follows a (symmetrical) normal distribution, but S itself follows a lognormal distribution, which is positively skewed. As $T \to \infty$, although the expected value of S_T is 1, the probability that $S_T \geq 1$ actually approaches 0.

It is simpler to use a no-arbitrage argument to derive the price. In order to pay \$1 when the stock price hits \$$H$, we need to buy $1/H$ shares of the stock (at \$$1/H$). So the option should be worth no more than \$$1/H$. Yet if the option price C is less than \$$1/H$ ($C < 1/H \Rightarrow CH < 1$), we can buy an option by borrowing C shares of the stock. The initial investment is 0. Once the stock price hits \$$H$, we will excise the option and return the stock by buying C shares at price \$$H$, which gives payoff $1 - CH > 0$. That means we have no initial investment, yet we have possible positive future payoff, which is contradictory to the no arbitrage argument. So the price cannot be less than \$$1/H$. Hence, the price is exactly \$$1/H$.

E. Assume a non-dividend paying stock follows a geometric Brownian motion. What is the value of a contract that at maturity T pays the inverse of the stock price observed at the maturity?

---

[8] Once we recognize that S is a martingale under the risk neutral measure, we do not need the assumption that S follows a geometric Brownian motion. S has two boundaries for stopping: 0 and H. The boundary conditions are $f(0) = 0$ and $f(H) = 1$. Using the martingale, the probability that it will ever reaches H is $P \times H + (1-P) \times 0 = S_0 = 1 \Rightarrow P = 1/H.$

Solution: Under risk-neutral measure $dS = rSdt + \sigma SdW(t)$. Apply Ito's lemma to

$$V = \frac{1}{S}: \quad dV = \left(\frac{\partial V}{\partial S} rS + \frac{\partial V}{\partial t} + \frac{1}{2} \frac{\partial^2 V}{\partial S^2} \sigma^2 S^2 \right) dt + \frac{\partial V}{\partial S} \sigma SdW(t)$$

$$= \left(-\frac{1}{S^2} rS + 0 + \frac{1}{2} \frac{2}{S^3} \sigma^2 S^2 \right) dt - \frac{1}{S^2} \sigma SdW(t) = (-r + \sigma^2)Vdt - \sigma VdW(t)$$

So V follows a geometric Brownian motion as well and we can apply Ito's lemma to $\ln V$:

$$d(\ln V) = \left(\frac{V}{V}(-r + \sigma^2) + 0 - \frac{1}{2} \frac{V^2}{V^2} \sigma^2 \right) dt + \frac{V}{V} \sigma dW(t) = \left(-r + \frac{1}{2} \sigma^2 \right) dt - \sigma dW(t).$$

Hence, $\ln(V_T) \sim \ln(V_t) + N\left((-r + \frac{1}{2}\sigma^2)\tau, \sigma^2\tau \right)$ and $E[V_T] = E[e^{\ln V_T}] = \frac{1}{S_t} e^{-r\tau + \sigma^2\tau}$.

Discounting the payoff by $e^{-r\tau}$, we have $V = e^{-r\tau} E[V_T] = \frac{1}{S_t} e^{-2r\tau + \sigma^2\tau}$.

6.2. The Greeks

All Greeks are first-order or second-order partial derivatives of the option price with respect to different underlying factors, which are used to measure the risks—as well as potential returns—of the financial derivative. The following Greeks for a derivative f are routinely used by financial institutions:

Delta: $\Delta = \dfrac{\partial f}{\partial S}$; **Gamma:** $\Gamma = \dfrac{\partial^2 f}{\partial S^2}$; **Theta:** $\Theta = \dfrac{\partial f}{\partial t}$; **Vega:** $\upsilon = \dfrac{\partial f}{\partial \sigma}$; **Rho:** $\rho = \dfrac{\partial f}{\partial r}$

Delta

For a European call with dividend yield y: $\Delta = e^{-y\tau} N(d_1)$

For a European put with dividend yield y: $\Delta = -e^{-y\tau}[1 - N(d_1)]$

A. What is the delta of a European call option on a non-dividend paying stock? How do you derive the delta?

Solution: The delta of a European call on a non-dividend paying stock has a clean expression: $\Delta = N(d_1)$. For the derivation, though, many make the mistake by treating

$N(d_1)$ and $N(d_2)$ as constants in the call pricing formula $c = SN(d_1) - Ke^{-r\tau}N(d_2)$ and simply taking the partial derivative on S to yield $N(d_1)$. The derivation step is actually more complex than that since both $N(d_1)$ and $N(d_2)$ are functions of S through d_1 and d_2. So the correct partial derivative is $\dfrac{\partial c}{\partial S} = N(d_1) + S \times \dfrac{\partial}{\partial S}N(d_1) - Ke^{-r\tau}\dfrac{\partial}{\partial S}N(d_2)$.

Take the partial derivative with respect to S for $N(d_1)$ and $N(d_2)$[9]:

$$\frac{\partial}{\partial S}N(d_1) = N'(d_1)\frac{\partial}{\partial S}d_1 = \frac{1}{\sqrt{2\pi}}e^{-d_1^2/2} \times \frac{1}{S\sigma\sqrt{\tau}} = \frac{1}{S\sigma\sqrt{2\pi\tau}}e^{-d_1^2/2}$$

$$\frac{\partial}{\partial S}N(d_2) = N'(d_2)\frac{\partial}{\partial S}d_2 = \frac{1}{\sqrt{2\pi}}e^{-d_2^2/2} \times \frac{1}{S\sigma\sqrt{\tau}} = \frac{1}{S\sigma\sqrt{2\pi\tau}}e^{-(d_1-\sigma\sqrt{\tau})^2/2}$$

$$= \frac{1}{S\sigma\sqrt{2\pi\tau}}e^{-d_1^2/2}e^{\sigma\sqrt{\tau}d_1}e^{-\sigma^2\tau/2} = \frac{1}{S\sigma\sqrt{2\pi\tau}}e^{-d_1^2/2} \times \frac{S}{K}e^{r\tau}$$

So we have $\dfrac{\partial}{\partial S}N(d_2) = \dfrac{S}{K}e^{r\tau}N(d_1) \Rightarrow S \times \dfrac{\partial}{\partial S}N(d_1) - Ke^{-r\tau}\dfrac{\partial}{\partial S}N(d_2) = 0$. Hence, the last two components of $\dfrac{\partial c}{\partial S}$ cancel out and $\dfrac{\partial c}{\partial S} = N(d_1)$.

B. What is your estimate of the delta of an at-the-money call on a stock without dividend? What will happen to delta as the at-the-money option approaches maturity date?

Solution: For an at-the-money European call, the stock price equals the strike price. $S = K \Rightarrow d_1 = \dfrac{(r + \sigma^2/2)\tau}{\sigma\sqrt{\tau}} = (\dfrac{r}{\sigma} + \dfrac{\sigma}{2})\sqrt{\tau} > 0$ and $\Delta = N(d_1) > 0.5$. As shown in Figure 6.2, all at-the-money call options indeed have $\Delta > 0.5$ and the longer the maturity, the higher the Δ. As $T - t \to 0$, $(\dfrac{r}{\sigma} + \dfrac{\sigma}{2})\sqrt{\tau} \to 0 \Rightarrow N(d_1) = N(0) = 0.5$, which is also shown in Figure 6.2 ($T = 10$ days). The same argument is true for calls on stock with continuous dividend rate y if $r > y$.

Figure 6.2 also shows that when S is large ($S \gg K$), Δ approaches 1. Furthermore, the shorter the maturity, the faster the delta approaches 1. On the other hand, if S is small ($S \ll K$), Δ approaches 0 and the shorter the maturity, the faster the delta approaches 0.

---

[9] $d_2 = d_1 - \sigma\sqrt{\tau} \Rightarrow N'(d_2) = \dfrac{S}{K}e^{(r-y)\tau}N'(d_1)$, $\dfrac{\partial d_2}{\partial S} = \dfrac{\partial d_1}{\partial S}$

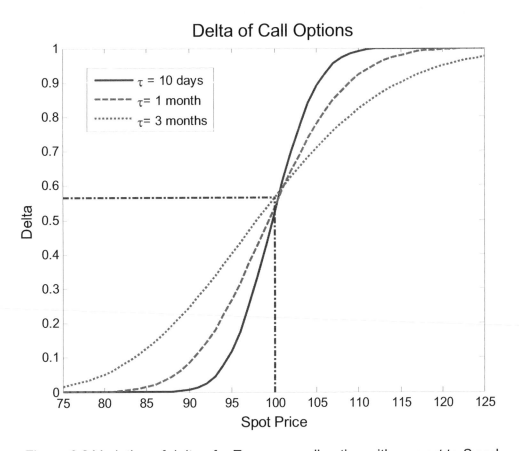

Figure 6.2 Variation of delta of a European call option with respect to S and T. $K = 100$, $r = 0.05$, $\sigma = 0.25$.

C. You just entered a long position for a European call option on GM stock and decide to dynamically hedge the position to eliminate the risk from the fluctuation of GM stock price. How will you hedge the call option? If after your hedge, the price of GM has a sudden increase, how will you rebalance your hedging position?

Solution: Since $d_1 = \dfrac{\ln(S/K) + (r - y + \sigma^2/2)\tau}{\sigma\sqrt{\tau}}$ and $\Delta = e^{-y\tau} N(d_1)$ is a monotonously increasing function of d_1, we have $S\uparrow \Rightarrow d_1\uparrow \Rightarrow \Delta\uparrow$.

One hedging method is delta hedging, for which we short $\Delta = e^{-y\tau} N(d_1)$ shares of stock for each unit of call option to make the portfolio delta-neutral. Since Δ shares of GM stock costs more than one unit of GM option, we also need to invest cash (if the option price exactly follows the Black-Scholes formula, we need to lend $\$Ke^{-r\tau}N(d_2)$ for each unit of option) in the money market. If there is a sudden increase in S, d_1 increases and Δ increases as well. That means we need to short more stock and lend more cash ($Ke^{-r\tau}N(d_2)$ also increases).

The delta hedge only replicates the value and the slope of the option. To hedge the curvature of the option, we will need to hedge gamma as well.

D. Can you estimate the value of an at-the-money call on a non-dividend paying stock? Assume the interest rate is low and the call has short maturity.

Solution: When $S = K$, we have $c = S\left(N(d_1) - e^{-r\tau}N(d_2)\right)$. In a low-interest environment, $r \approx 0$ and $e^{-r\tau} \approx 1$, so $c \approx S\left(N(d_1) - N(d_2)\right)$.

We also have $N(d_1) - N(d_2) = \int_{d_2}^{d_1} \frac{1}{\sqrt{2\pi}} e^{-1/2x^2} dx$,

where $d_2 = (\frac{r}{\sigma} - \frac{\sigma}{2})\sqrt{\tau}$ and $d_1 = (\frac{r}{\sigma} + \frac{\sigma}{2})\sqrt{\tau}$.

For a small r, a typical σ for stocks ($< 40\%$ per year) and a short maturity (< 3 months), both d_2 and d_1 are close to 0. For example, if $r = 0.03$, $\sigma = 0.3$, and $\tau = 1/6$ year, then $d_2 = -0.02$ and $e^{-1/2d_2^2} = 0.98$.

$$\therefore N(d_1) - N(d_2) \approx \frac{1}{\sqrt{2\pi}}(d_1 - d_2) = \frac{\sigma\sqrt{\tau}}{\sqrt{2\pi}} \approx 0.4\sigma\sqrt{T-t} \Rightarrow c \approx 0.4\sigma S\sqrt{\tau}.$$

In practice, this approximation is used by some volatility traders to estimate the implied volatility of an at-the-money option.

(The approximation $e^{-1/2x^2} \approx 1$ causes a small overestimation since $e^{-1/2x^2} < 1$; but the approximation $-e^{-r\tau}K \approx -K$ causes a small underestimation. To some extent, the two opposite effects cancel out and the overall approximation is fairly accurate.)

Gamma

For a European call/put with dividend yield y: $\Gamma = \dfrac{N'(d_1)e^{-y\tau}}{S_0\sigma\sqrt{\tau}}$

What happens to the gamma of an at-the-money European option when it approaches its maturity?

Solution: From the put-call parity, it is obvious that a call and a put with identical characteristics have the same gamma (since $\Gamma = 0$ for both the cash position and the underlying stock). Taking the partial derivative of the Δ of a call option with respect to S, we have $\Gamma = \dfrac{N'(d_1)e^{-y\tau}}{S\sigma\sqrt{\tau}}$, where $N'(d_1) = \dfrac{1}{\sqrt{2\pi}}e^{-1/2d_1^2}$.

So for plain vanilla call and put options, gamma is **always positive**.

Figure 6.3 shows that gamma is high when options are at the money, which is the stock price region that Δ changes rapidly with S. If $S \ll K$ or $S \gg K$ (deep in the money or out of the money), gamma approaches 0 since Δ stays constant at 1 or 0.

The gamma of options with shorter maturities approaches 0 much faster than options with longer maturities as S moves away from K. So for deep in-the-money or deep out-of-the-money options, longer maturity means higher gamma. In contrast, if the stock prices are close to the strike price (at the money) as the maturity nears, the slope of delta for an at-the-money call becomes steeper and steeper. So for options close to the strike price, shorter-term options have higher gammas.

As $\tau \to 0$, an at-the-money call/put has $\Gamma \to \infty$ (Δ becomes a step function). This can be shown from the formula of gamma for a European call/put with no dividend, $\Gamma = \dfrac{N'(d_1)}{S\sigma\sqrt{\tau}}$:

When $S = K$, $d_1 = \lim\limits_{\tau \to 0}(\dfrac{r}{\sigma} + \dfrac{\sigma}{2})\sqrt{\tau} \to 0 \Rightarrow \lim\limits_{\tau \to 0} N'(d_1) \to \dfrac{1}{\sqrt{2\pi}}$. The numerator is $1/\sqrt{2\pi}$;

yet the denominator has a limit $\lim\limits_{\tau \to 0} S\sigma\sqrt{\tau} \to 0$, so $\Gamma \to \infty$. In other words, When $t = T$, delta becomes a step function. This phenomenon makes hedging at-the-money options difficult when $t \to T$ since delta is extremely sensitive to changes in S.

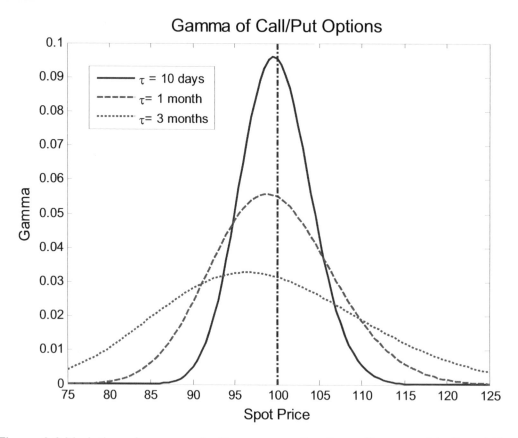

Figure 6.3 Variation of gamma of a European call option with respect to S and T. $K = 100$, $r = 0.05$, $\sigma = 0.25$.

Theta

For a European call option: $\Theta = -\dfrac{SN'(d_1)\sigma e^{-y\tau}}{2\sqrt{\tau}} + ySe^{-y\tau}N(d_1) - rKe^{-r\tau}N(d_2)$

For a European put option: $\Theta = -\dfrac{SN'(d_1)\sigma e^{-y\tau}}{2\sqrt{\tau}} - ySe^{-y\tau}N(-d_1) + rKe^{-r\tau}N(-d_2)$

When there is no dividend, the theta for a European call option is simplified to $\Theta = -\dfrac{SN'(d_1)}{2\sqrt{\tau}} - rKe^{-r\tau}N(d_2)$, which is always negative. As shown in Figure 6.4, when $S \ll K$, $N(d_2) \approx 0$ and $N'(d_1) \approx 0$. Hence, $\Theta \rightarrow 0$. When $S \gg K$, $N(d_2) \approx 1$ and

$N'(d_1) \approx 0$. Hence, $\Theta \rightarrow -rKe^{-r\tau}$. When $S \approx K$, Θ has large negative value and the smaller the τ, the more negative the Θ.

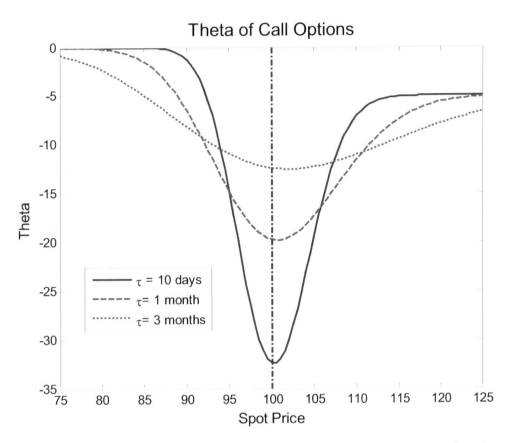

Figure 6.4 Variation of theta of a European call option with respect to S and T. $K = 100$, $\sigma = 0.25$, $r = 0.05$

A. When will a European option have positive theta?

Solution: For American options as well as European calls on non-dividend paying assets, theta is always negative. But for deep in-the-money European puts, their values may increase as t approaches T if all other factors remain the same, so they may have positive theta.

A put option on a non-dividend paying asset has $\Theta = -\dfrac{SN'(d_1)\sigma}{2\sqrt{\tau}} + rKe^{-r\tau}N(-d_2)$. If the put option is deep in-the-money $(S \ll K)$, then $N'(d_1) \approx 0$ and $N(-d_2) \approx 1$. Hence,

$\Theta \approx rKe^{-r\tau} > 0$. That's also the reason why it can be optimal to exercise a deep in-the-money American put before maturity.

For deep in-the-money European call options with high dividend yield, the theta can be positive as well. If a call option with high dividend yield is deep in-the-money ($S \gg K$), $N(d_1) \approx N(d_2) \approx 1$, $N'(d_1) \approx 0$, so the component $ySe^{-y\tau}N(d_1)$ can make Θ positive.

B. You just entered a long position for a call option on GM and hedged the position by shorting GM shares to make the portfolio delta neutral. If there is an immediate increase or decrease in GM's stock price, what will happen to the value of your portfolio? Is it an arbitrage opportunity? Assume that GM does not pay dividends.

Solution: A position in the underlying asset has zero gamma. So the portfolio is delta-neutral and long gamma. Therefore, either an immediate increase or decrease in the GM stock price will increase the portfolio value. The convexity (positive gamma) enhances returns when there is a large move in the stock price in either direction.

Nevertheless, it is not an arbitrage opportunity. It is a trade-off between gamma and theta instead. From the Black-Scholes-Merton differential equation, the portfolio V satisfies the equation $\dfrac{\partial V}{\partial t} + rS\dfrac{\partial V}{\partial S} + \dfrac{1}{2}\sigma^2 S^2 \dfrac{\partial^2 V}{\partial S^2} = \Theta + rS\Delta + \dfrac{1}{2}\sigma^2 S^2 \Gamma = rV$. For a delta-neutral portfolio, we have $\Theta + \dfrac{1}{2}\sigma^2 S^2 \Gamma = rV$. This indicates that gamma and theta often have opposite signs. For example, when an at-the-money call approaches maturity, gamma is large and positive, so theta is large and negative. Our delta neutral portfolio has positive gamma and negative theta. That means if the price does not move, the passage of time will result in a lower portfolio value unless we rebalance. So the portfolio does not provide an arbitrage opportunity.

Vega

For European options: $\upsilon = \dfrac{\partial c}{\partial \sigma} = \dfrac{\partial p}{\partial \sigma} = Se^{-y\tau}\sqrt{\tau}N'(d_1)$

At-the-money options are most sensitive to volatility change, so they have higher vegas than either in-the-money or out-of-the-money options. The vegas of all options decrease as time to expiration becomes shorter ($\sqrt{\tau} \to 0$) since a long-term option is more sensitive to change in volatility.

A. Explain implied volatility and volatility smile. What is the implication of volatility smile for the Black-Scholes pricing model?

Solution: Implied volatility is the volatility that makes the model option price equal to the market option price. Volatility smile describes the relationship between the implied volatility of the options and the strike prices for a given asset. For currency options, implied volatilities tend to be higher for in-the-money and out-of-the-money options than for at-the-money options. For equity, volatility often decreases as the strike price increases (also called volatility skew). The Black-Scholes model assumes that the asset price follows a lognormal distribution with constant volatility. In reality, volatilities are neither constant nor deterministic. In fact, the volatility is a stochastic process itself. Furthermore, there may be jumps in asset prices.

B. You have to price a European call option either with a constant volatility 30% or by drawing volatility from a random distribution with a mean of 30%. Which option would be more expensive?

Solution: Many would simply argue that stochastic volatility makes the stock price more volatile, so the call price is more valuable when the volatility is drawn from a random distribution. Mathematically, the underlying argument is that the price of a European call option is a convex function of volatility and as a result $c(E[\sigma]) \leq E[c(\sigma)]$, where σ is the random variable representing volatility and c is the call option price. Is the underlying argument correct? It's correct in most, but not all, cases. If the call price c is always a convex function of σ, then $\dfrac{\partial^2 c}{\partial \sigma^2} \geq 0$. $\dfrac{\partial c}{\partial \sigma}$ is the Vega of the option. For a European call option,

$$\upsilon = \frac{\partial c}{\partial \sigma} = S\sqrt{\tau}N'(d_1) = \frac{S\sqrt{\tau}}{\sqrt{2\pi}}\exp\left(-d_1^2/2\right).$$

The secondary partial derivative $\dfrac{\partial^2 c}{\partial \sigma^2}$ is called Volga. For a European call option,

$$\frac{\partial^2 c}{\partial \sigma^2} = \frac{S\sqrt{\tau}}{\sqrt{2\pi}}\exp\left(-d_1^2/2\right)\frac{d_1 d_2}{\sigma} = \upsilon\frac{d_1 d_2}{\sigma}.$$

υ is always positive. For most out-of-the-money call options, both d_1 and d_2 are negative; for most in-the-money call options, both d_1 and d_2 are positive. So $d_1 d_2 > 0$ in most cases and c is a convex function of σ when $d_1 d_2 > 0$. But theoretically, we can have conditions that $d_1 > 0$ and $d_2 < 0$ and $\dfrac{\partial^2 c}{\partial \sigma^2} < 0$ when the option is close to being at-the-money. So the function is not always convex. In those cases, the option with constant volatility may have a higher value.

C. The Black-Scholes formula for non-dividend paying stocks assumes that the stock follows a geometric Brownian motion. Now assume that you don't know the stochastic process followed by the stock price, but you have the European call prices for all (continuous) strike prices K. Can you determine the risk-neutral probability density function of the stock price at time T?

Solution: The payoff a European call at its maturity date is $Max(S_T - K, 0)$. Therefore under risk-neutral measure, we have $c = e^{-rt} \int_K^\infty (s-K) f_{S_T}(s) ds$, where $f_{S_T}(s)$ is the probability density function of S_T under the risk-neutral probability measure. Taking the first and second derivatives of c with respect to K,[10] we have

$$\frac{\partial c}{\partial K} = e^{-rt} \frac{\partial}{\partial K} \int_K^\infty (s-K) f_{S_T}(s) ds$$

$$= e^{-rt} \int_K^\infty \frac{\partial(s-K)}{\partial K} f_{S_T}(s) ds - e^{-rt}(K-K) \times 1$$

$$= e^{-rt} \int_K^\infty -f_{S_T}(s) ds$$

and $\dfrac{\partial^2 c}{\partial K^2} = \dfrac{\partial}{\partial K}\left(\dfrac{\partial c}{\partial K}\right) = e^{-rt} \dfrac{\partial}{\partial K} \int_K^\infty -f_{S_T}(s) ds = e^{-rt} f_{S_T}(K)$.

Hence the risk-neutral probability density function is $f_{S_T}(K) = e^{rt} \dfrac{\partial^2 c}{\partial K^2}$.

6.3. Option Portfolios and Exotic Options

In addition to the pricing and properties of vanilla European and American options, you may be expected to be familiar with the construction and payoff of basic option-based trading strategies—covered call, protective put, bull/bear spread, butterfly spread, straddle, etc. Furthermore, if you are applying for a derivatives-related position, you

---

[10] To calculate the derivatives requires the Leibniz integral rule, a formula for differentiating a definite integral whose limits are functions of the differential variable:

$$\frac{\partial}{\partial z} \int_{a(z)}^{b(z)} f(x,z) dx = \int_{a(z)}^{b(z)} \frac{\partial f(x,z)}{\partial z} dx + f(b(z),z)\frac{\partial b}{\partial z} - f(a(z),z)\frac{\partial a}{\partial z}$$

should also have a good understanding of pricing and hedging of some of the common exotic derivatives—binary option, barrier option, Asian option, chooser option, etc.

Bull spread

What are the price boundaries for a bull call spread?

Solution: A bull call spread is a portfolio with two options: long a call c_1 with strike K_1 and short a call c_2 with strike K_2 $(K_1 < K_2)$. The cash flow of a bull spread is summarized in table 6.3.

Cash flow	Time 0	Maturity T		
		$S_T \leq K_1$	$K_1 < S_T < K_2$	$S_T \geq K_2$
Long c_1	$-c_1$	0	$S_T - K_1$	$S_T - K_1$
Short c_2	c_2	0	0	$-(S_T - K_2)$
Total	$c_2 - c_1 < 0$	0	$S_T - K_1$	$K_2 - K_1$

Table 6.3 Cash flows of a bull call spread.

Since $K_1 < K_2$, the initial cash flow is negative. Considering that the final payoff is bounded by $K_2 - K_1$, the price of the spread, $c_1 - c_2$, is bounded by $e^{-rT}(K_2 - K_1)$. Besides, the payoff is also bounded by $\dfrac{K_2 - K_1}{K_2} S_T$, so the price is also bounded by $\dfrac{K_2 - K_1}{K_2} S$.

Straddle

Explain what a straddle is and when you want to purchase a straddle.

Solution: A straddle includes long positions in both a call option and a put option with the same strike price K and maturity date T on the same stock. The payoff of a long straddle is $|S_T - K|$. So a straddle may be used to bet on large stock price moves. In practice, a straddle is also used as a trading strategy for making bets on volatility. If an investor believes that the realized (future) volatility should be much higher than the implied volatility of call and put options, he or she will purchase a straddle. For example, the value of an at-the-money call or put is almost a linear function of volatility. If the investor purchases an at-the-money straddle, both the call and the put options have the price $c \approx p \approx 0.4\sigma_i S\sqrt{\tau}$, where σ_i is the implied volatility. If the realized volatility $\sigma_r > \sigma_i$, both options are undervalued. When the market prices converge to the prices with the realized volatility, both the call and the put will become more valuable.

Although initially a straddle with an at-the-money call and an at-the-money put ($K = S$) has a delta close to 0, as the stock price moves away from the strike price, the delta is no longer close to 0 and the investor is exposed to stock price movements. So a straddle is not a pure bet on stock volatility. For a pure bet on volatility, it is better to use volatility swaps or variance swaps.[11] For example, a variance swap pays $N \times (\sigma_r^2 - K_{var})$, where N is the notional value, σ_r^2 is the realized variance and K_{var} is the strike for the variance.

Binary options

What is the price of a binary (cash-or-nothing digital) European call option on a non-dividend paying stock if the stock price follows a geometric Brownian motion? How would you hedge a cash-or-nothing call option and what's the limitation of your hedging strategy?

Solution: A cash-or-nothing call option with strike price K pays \$1 if the asset price is above the strike price at the maturity date, otherwise it pays nothing. The price of the option is $c_B = e^{-rt}N(d_2)$ if the underlying asset is a non-dividend paying stock. As we have discussed in the derivation of the Black-Scholes formula, $N(d_2)$ is the probability that a vanilla call option finishes in the money under the risk-neutral measure. So its discounted value is $e^{-rt}N(d_2)$.

Theoretically, a cash-or-nothing call option can be hedged using the standard delta hedging strategy. Since $\Delta = \dfrac{\partial c_B}{\partial S} = e^{-rt}N'(d_2)\dfrac{1}{S\sigma\sqrt{\tau}}$, a long position in a cash-or-nothing call option can be hedged by shorting $e^{-rt}N'(d_2)\dfrac{1}{S\sigma\sqrt{\tau}}$ shares (and a risk-free money market position). Such a hedge works well when the difference between S and K is large and τ is not close to 0. But when the option is approaching maturity T ($\tau \to 0$)

---

[11] For detailed discussion about volatility swaps, please refer to the paper "More Than You Ever Wanted to Know about Volatility Swaps" by Kresimir Demeterfi, et al. The paper shows that a variance swap can be approximated by a portfolio of straddles with proper weights inversely proportional to $1/k^2$.

and the stock price S is close to K, Δ is extremely volatile[12] and small changes in the stock price cause very large changes in Δ. In these cases, it is practically impossible to hedge a cash-or-nothing call option by delta hedging.

We can also approximate a digital option using a bull spread with two calls. If call options are available for all strike prices and there are no transaction costs, we can long $1/2\varepsilon$ call options with strike price $K-\varepsilon$ and short $1/2\varepsilon$ call options with strike price $K+\varepsilon$. The payoff of the bull spread is the same as the digital call option if $S_T \leq K-\varepsilon$ (both have payoff 0) or $S_T \geq K+\varepsilon$ (both have payoff \$1). When $K-\varepsilon < S_T < K+\varepsilon$, their payoffs are different. Nevertheless, if we set $\varepsilon \to 0$, such a strategy will exactly replicate the digital call. So it provides another way of hedging a digital call option. This hedging strategy suffers its own drawback. In practice, not all strike prices are traded in the market. Even if all strike prices were traded in the market, the number of options needed for hedging, $1/2\varepsilon$, will be large in order to keep ε small.

Exchange options

How would you price an exchange call option that pays $\max\left(S_{T,1} - S_{T,2}, 0\right)$ at maturity. Assume that S_1 and S_2 are non-dividend paying stocks and both follow geometric Brownian motions with correlation ρ.

Solution: The solution to this problem uses change of numeraire. Numeraire means a unit of measurement. When we express the price of an asset, we usually use the local currency as the numeraire. But for modeling purposes, it is often easier to use a different asset as the numeraire. The only requirement for a numeraire is that it must always be positive.

The payoff of the exchange option depends on both $S_{T,1}$ (price of S_1 at maturity date T) and $S_{T,2}$ (price of S_2 at T), so it appears that we need two geometric Brownian motions:

$$dS_1 = \mu_1 S_1 dt + \sigma_1 S_1 dW_{t,1}$$

$$dS_2 = \mu_2 S_2 dt + \sigma_2 S_2 dW_{t,2}$$

Yet if we use S_1 as the numeraire, we can convert the problem to just one geometric Brownian motion. The final payoff is $\max\left(S_{T,2} - S_{T,1}, 0\right) = S_{T,1} \max\left(\dfrac{S_{T,2}}{S_{T,1}} - 1, 0\right)$. When

---

[12] $S \to K$ and $\tau \to 0 \Rightarrow \ln(S/K) \to 0 \Rightarrow d_2 \to (r/\sigma + 0.5\sigma)\sqrt{\tau} \to 0 \Rightarrow \Delta \to \dfrac{1}{\sqrt{2\pi}} \dfrac{e^{-r\tau}}{S\sigma\sqrt{\tau}} \to \infty.$

S_1 and S_2 are geometrical Browian motions, $f = \dfrac{S_2}{S_1}$ is a geometric Brownian motion as well. One intuitive explanation is that both $\ln S_1$ and $\ln S_2$ follow normal distributions, so $\ln f = \ln S_2 - \ln S_1$ follows a normal distribution as well and f follows a lognormal distribution. More rigorously, we can apply the Ito's lemma to $f = \dfrac{S_2}{S_1}$:

$$\frac{\partial f}{\partial S_1} = \frac{-S_2}{S_1^2}, \frac{\partial f}{\partial S_2} = \frac{1}{S_1}, \frac{\partial^2 f}{\partial S_1^2} = \frac{2S_2}{S_1^3}, \frac{\partial^2 f}{\partial S_2^2} = 0, \frac{\partial^2 f}{\partial S_1 \partial S_2} = \frac{-1}{S_1^2}$$

$$df = \frac{\partial f}{\partial S_1} dS_1 + \frac{\partial f}{\partial S_2} dS_2 + \frac{1}{2}\frac{\partial^2 f}{\partial S_1^2}(dS_1)^2 + \frac{1}{2}\frac{\partial^2 f}{\partial S_2^2}(dS_2)^2 + \frac{\partial^2 f}{\partial S_1 \partial S_2} dS_1 dS_2$$

$$= -\mu_1 \frac{S_2}{S_1} dt - \sigma_1 \frac{S_2}{S_1} dW_{t,1} + \mu_2 \frac{S_2}{S_1} dt + \sigma_2 \frac{S_2}{S_1} dW_{t,2} + \sigma_1^2 \frac{S_2}{S_1} dt - \rho\sigma_1\sigma_2 \frac{S_2}{S_1} dt$$

$$= \left(\mu_2 - \mu_1 + \sigma_1^2 - \rho\sigma_1\sigma_2\right) f dt - \sigma_1 f dW_{t,1} + \sigma_2 f dW_{t,2}$$

$$= \left(\mu_2 - \mu_1 + \sigma_1^2 - \rho\sigma_1\sigma_2\right) f dt + \sqrt{\sigma_1^2 - 2\rho\sigma_1\sigma_2 + \sigma_2^2} \times f dW_{t,3}$$

To make $f = \dfrac{S_2}{S_1}$ a martingale, set $\mu_2 - \mu_1 + \sigma_1^2 - \rho\sigma_1\sigma_2 = 0$ and we have $\tilde{E}\left[\dfrac{S_{T,2}}{S_{T,1}}\right] = \dfrac{S_2}{S_1}$, and $\dfrac{S_{t,2}}{S_{t,1}}$ is a martingale under the new measure. The value of the exchange option using S_1 as the numeraire is $C_s = \tilde{E}\left[\max\left(\dfrac{S_{T,2}}{S_{T,1}} - 1, 0\right)\right]$, which is just the value of a call option with underlying asset price $S = \dfrac{S_2}{S_1}$, strike price $K = 1$, interest rate $r = 0$, and volatility $\sigma_S = \sqrt{\sigma_1^2 - 2\rho\sigma_1\sigma_2 + \sigma_2^2}$. So its value is $C_S = \dfrac{S_2}{S_1} N(d_1) - N(d_2)$, where $d_1 = \dfrac{\ln(S_2/S_1) + 0.5\sigma_S^2\tau}{\sigma_S\sqrt{\tau}}$ and $d_2 = d_1 - \sigma\sqrt{\tau}$. The payoff of the exchange option expressed in local currency is $S_1 C_S = S_2 N(d_1) - S_1 N(d_2)$.

6.4. Other Finance Questions

Besides option pricing problems, a variety of other quantitative finance problems are tested in quantitative interviews as well. Many of these problems tend to be position-specific. For example, if you are applying for a risk management job, prepare to answer questions about VaR; for fixed-income jobs, get ready to answer questions about interest rate models. As I explained in Chapter 1, it always helps if you grasp the basic knowledge before the interview. In this section, we use several examples to show some typical interview problems.

Portfolio optimization

You are constructing a simple portfolio using two stocks A and B. Both have the same expected return of 12%. The standard deviation of A's return is 20% and the standard deviation of B's return is 30%; the correlation of their returns is 50%. How will you allocate your investment between these two stocks to minimize the risk of your portfolio?

Solution: Portfolio optimization has always been a crucial topic for investment management firms. Harry Markowitz's mean-variance portfolio theory is by far the most well-known and well-studied portfolio optimization model. The essence of the mean-variance portfolio theory assumes that investors prefer (1) higher expected returns for a given level of standard deviation/variance and (2) lower standard deviations/variances for a given level of expected return. Portfolios that provide the minimum standard deviation for a given expected return are termed efficient portfolios. The expected return and the variance of a portfolio with N assets can be expressed as

$$\mu_p = w_1\mu_1 + w_2\mu_2 + \cdots + w_N\mu_N = w^T\mu$$

$$\text{var}(r_p) = \sum_{i=1}^{N}\sigma_i^2 w_i^2 + \sum_{i\neq j}\sigma_{ij}w_i w_j = w^T\Sigma w$$

where $w_i, \forall i = 1,\cdots,N$, is the weight of the i-th asset in the portfolio; $\mu_i, \forall i = 1,\cdots,N$, is the expected return of the i-th asset; σ_i^2 is the variance of i-th asset's return; $\sigma_{ij} = \rho_{ij}\sigma_i\sigma_j$ is the covariance of the returns of the i-th and the j-th assets and ρ_{ij} is their correlation; w is an $N \times 1$ column vector of w_i's; μ is an $N \times 1$ column vector of μ_i's; Σ is the covariance matrix of the returns of N assets, an $N \times N$ matrix.

Since the optimal portfolio minimizes the variance of the return for a given level of expected return, the efficient portfolio can be formulated as the following optimization problem:

$$\min_{w} w^{T} \Sigma w$$

$$s.t. \ w^{T}\mu = \mu_{p}, \ w^{T}e = 1$$, where e is an $N \times 1$ vector with all elements equal to 1.[13]

For this specific problem, the expected returns are 12% for both stocks. So μ_{p} is always 12% no matter what w_{A} and w_{B} ($w_{A} + w_{B} = 1$) are. The variance of the portfolio is

$$var(r_{p}) = \sigma_{A}^{2}w_{A}^{2} + \sigma_{B}^{2}w_{B}^{2} + 2\rho_{A,B}\sigma_{A}\sigma_{B}w_{A}w_{B}$$
$$= \sigma_{A}^{2}w_{A}^{2} + \sigma_{B}^{2}(1 - w_{A})^{2} + 2\rho_{A,B}\sigma_{A}\sigma_{B}w_{A}(1 - w_{A})$$

Taking the derivative of $var(r_{p})$ with respect to w_{A} and setting it to zero, we have

$$\frac{\partial \, var(r_{p})}{\partial w_{A}} = 2\sigma_{A}^{2}w_{A} - 2\sigma_{B}^{2}(1 - w_{A}) + 2\rho_{A,B}\sigma_{A}\sigma_{B}(1 - w_{A}) - 2\rho_{A,B}\sigma_{A}\sigma_{B}w_{A} = 0$$

$$\Rightarrow w_{A} = \frac{\sigma_{B}^{2} - \rho_{A,B}\sigma_{A}\sigma_{B}}{\sigma_{A}^{2} - 2\rho_{A,B}\sigma_{A}\sigma_{B} + \sigma_{B}^{2}} = \frac{0.09 - 0.5 \times 0.2 \times 0.3}{0.04 - 2 \times 0.5 \times 0.2 \times 0.3 + 0.09} = \frac{6}{7}.$$

So we should invest 6/7 of the money in stock A and 1/7 in stock B.

Value at risk

Briefly explain what VaR is. What is the potential drawback of using VaR to measure the risk of derivatives?

Solution: Value at Risk (VaR) and stress test—or more general scenario analysis—are two important aspects of risk management. In the *Financial Risk Manager Handbook*,[14] VaR is defined as the following: VAR is the maximum loss over a target horizon such that there is a low, pre-specified probability that the actual loss will be larger.

Given a confidence level $\alpha \in (0, 1)$, the VaR can be implicitly defined as $\alpha = \int_{-VaR}^{\infty} xf(x)dx$, where x is the dollar profit (loss) and $f(x)$ is its probability density function. In practice, α is often set to 95% or 99%. VaR is an extremely popular choice in financial risk management since it summarizes the risk to a single dollar number.

---

[13] The optimal weights have closed form solution $w^{*} = \lambda \Sigma^{-1}e + \gamma \Sigma^{-1}\mu$, where $\lambda = \dfrac{C - \mu_{p}B}{D}$,

$\gamma = \dfrac{\mu_{p}A - B}{D}$, $A = e'\Sigma^{-1}e > 0$, $B = e'\Sigma^{-1}\mu$, $C = \mu'\Sigma^{-1}\mu > 0$, $D = AC - B^{2}$.

[14] *Financial Risk Manager Handbook* by Phillippe Jorion is a comprehensive book covering different aspects of risk management. A classic book for VaR is *Value at Risk*, also by Philippe Jorion.

Mathematically, it is simply the (negative) first or fifth percentile of the profit distribution.

As a percentile-based measure on the profit distribution, VaR does not depend on the shape of the tails before (and after) probability $1-\alpha$, so it does not describe the loss on the left tail. When the profit/loss distribution is far from a normal distribution, as in the cases of many derivatives, the tail portion has a large impact on the risk, and VaR often does not reflect the real risk.[15] For example, let's consider a short position in a credit default swap. The underlying asset is bond A with a $1M notional value. Further assume that A has a 3% default probability and the loss given default is 100% (no recovery). Clearly we are facing the credit risk of bond A. Yet if we use 95% confidence level, $VaR(A) = 0$ since the probability of default is less than 5%.

Furthermore, VaR is not sub-additive and is not a coherent measure of risk, which means that when we combine two positions A and B to form a portfolio C, we do not always have $VaR(C) \leq VaR(A) + VaR(B)$. For example, if we add a short position in a credit default swap on bond B with a $1M notional value. B also has a 3% default probability independent of A and the loss given default is 100%. Again we have $VaR(B) = 0$. When A and B form a portfolio C, the probability that at least one bond will default becomes $1 - (1 - 3\%)(1 - 3\%) \approx 5.9\%$. So $VaR(C) = \$1M > VaR(A) + VaR(B)$. Lack of sub-additivity directly contradicts the intuitive idea that diversification reduces risk. So it is a theoretical drawback of VaR.

(Sub-additivity is one property of a coherent risk measure. A risk measure $\rho(X)$ is considered coherent if the following conditions holds: $\rho(X + Y) \leq \rho(X) + \rho(Y)$; $\rho(aX) = a\rho(X), \forall a > 0$; $\rho(X) \leq \rho(Y)$, if $X \leq Y$; and $\rho(X + k) = \rho(X) - k$ for any constant k. It is defined in *Coherent Measure of Risk* by Artzner, P., et al., Mathematical Finance, 9 (3):203–228. Conditional VaR is a coherent risk measure.)

Duration and convexity

The duration of a bond is defined as $D = -\dfrac{1}{P}\dfrac{dP}{dy}$, where P is the price of the bond and y is yield to maturity. The convexity of a bond is defined as $C = \dfrac{1}{P}\dfrac{d^2P}{dy^2}$. Applying Taylor's expansion, $\dfrac{\Delta P}{P} \approx -D\Delta y + \dfrac{1}{2}C\Delta y^2$. when Δy is small, $\dfrac{\Delta P}{P} \approx -D\Delta y$.

For a fixed-rate bond with coupon rate c and time-to-maturity T:

---

[15] Stress test is often used as a complement to VaR by estimating the tail risk.

$$T\uparrow \Rightarrow D\uparrow \quad c\uparrow \Rightarrow D\downarrow \quad y\uparrow \Rightarrow D\downarrow \qquad T\uparrow \Rightarrow C\uparrow \quad c\uparrow \Rightarrow C\downarrow \quad y\uparrow \Rightarrow C\downarrow.$$

Another important concept is dollar duration: $\$D = -\dfrac{dP}{dy} = P \times D$. Many market

participants use a concept called DV01: $DV01 = -\dfrac{dP}{10,000 \times dy}$, which measures the

price change when the yield changes by one basis point. For some bond derivatives, such as swaps, dollar duration is especially important. A swap may have value $P = 0$, in which case dollar duration is more meaningful than duration.

When n bonds with values P_i, $i = 1, \cdots, n$, and Durations D_i (convexities C_i) form a portfolio, the duration of the portfolio is the value-weighted average of the durations of

the components: $D = \displaystyle\sum_{i=1}^{n} \dfrac{P_i}{P} D_i$ ($C = \displaystyle\sum_{i=1}^{n} \dfrac{P_i}{P} C_i$), where $P = \displaystyle\sum_{i=1}^{n} P_i$. The dollar duration of

the portfolio is simply the sum of the dollar durations of the components: $\$D = \displaystyle\sum_{i=1}^{n} \$D_i$.

What are the price and duration of an inverse floater with face value $100 and annual coupon rate $30\% - 3r$ that matures in 5 years? Assume that the coupons are paid semiannually and the current yield curve is flat at 7.5%.

Solution: The key to solving basic fixed-income problems is cash flow replication. To price a fixed-income security with exotic structures, if we can replicate its cash flow using a portfolio of fundamental bond types such as fixed-rate coupon bonds (including zero-coupon bonds) and floating-rate bonds, no-arbitrage arguments give us the following conclusions:
Price of the exotic security = Price of the replicating portfolio
Dollar duration of the exotic security = Dollar duration of the replicating portfolio

To replicate the described inverse floater, we can use a portfolio constructed by shorting 3 floating rate bonds, which is worth $100 each, and longing 4 fixed-rate bonds with a 7.5% annual coupon rate, which is worth $100 each as well. The coupon rate of a floating-rate bond is adjusted every 0.5 years payable in arrear: the coupon rate paid at $t + 0.5y$ is determined at t. The cash flows of both positions and the whole portfolio are summarized in the following table. It is apparent that the total cash flows of the portfolio are the same as the described inverse floater. So the price of the inverse float is the price of the replicating portfolio: $P_{inverse} = \$100$.

Cash flow	Year 0	Year 0.5	...	Year 4.5	Year 5
Short 3 floating-rate bonds	300	$-150r_0$	...	$-150r_4$	$-300 - 150r_{4.5}$
Long 4 bonds with 7.5% coupon rate	-400	15	...	15	$400 + 15$
Total	-100	$15 - 150r_0$	...	$30 - 300r_0$	$115 - 150r_{4.5}$

The dollar duration of the inverse floater is the same as the dollar duration of the portfolio as well: $\$D_{inverse} = 4 \times \$D_{fixed} - 3 \times \$D_{floating}$. Since the yield curve is flat, $r_0 = 7.5\%$ and the floating-rate bond is always worth $103.75 (after the payment of $3.75, the price of the floating-rate bond is $100) at year 0.5, and the dollar duration[16] is

$$\$D_{floating} = -\frac{d(103.75/(1+y/2))}{dy} = 0.5 \times \frac{103.75}{(1+y/2)^2} = 100 \times \frac{0.5}{1+y/2} = 48.19.$$

The price of a fixed-rate bond is $P = \sum_{t=1}^{2T} \frac{c/2}{(1+y/2)^t} + \frac{100}{(1+y/2)^{2T}}$, where T is the maturity of the bond. So the dollar duration of the fixed-rate bond is

$$\$D_{fixed} = -\frac{dP}{dy} = \frac{1}{1+y/2} \left(\sum_{t=1}^{2T} \frac{t}{2} \frac{c/2}{(1+y/2)^t} + \frac{100T}{(1+y/2)^{2T}} \right) = 410.64.$$

So $\$D_{inverse} = 4 \times \$D_{fixed} - 3 \times \$D_{floating} = 1498$ and the duration of the inverse floater is

$$D_{inverse} = \$D_{inverse} / P_{inverse} = 14.98.$$

Forward and futures

What's the difference between futures and forwards? If the price of the underlying asset is strongly positively correlated with interest rates, and the interest rates are stochastic, which one has higher price: futures or forwards? Why?

Solution: Futures contracts are exchange-traded standardized contracts; forward contracts are over-the-counter agreements so they are more flexible. Futures contracts are marked-to-market daily; forwards contacts are settled at the end of the contract term.

---

[16] The initial duration of a floating rate bond is the same as the duration of a six-month zero coupon bond.

If the interest rate is deterministic, futures and forwards have the same theoretical price: $F = Se^{(r+u-y)\tau}$, where u represents all the storage costs and y represents dividend yield for investment assets, convenience yield for commodities and foreign risk-free interest rate for foreign currencies.

The mark-to-market property of futures makes their values differ from forwards when interest rates vary unpredictably (as they do in the real world). As the life of a futures contract increases, the differences between forward and futures contracts may become significant. If the futures price is positively correlated with the interest rate, the increases of the futures price tend to occur the same time when interest rate is high. Because of the mark-to-market feature, the investor who longs the futures has an immediate profit that can be reinvested at a higher rate. The loss tends to occur when the interest rate is low so that it can be financed at a low rate. So a futures contract is more valuable than the forward when its value is positively correlated with interest rates and the futures price should be higher.

Interest rate models

Explain some of the basic interest rate models and their differences.

Solution: In general, interest rate models can be separated into two categories: short-rate models and forward-rate models. The short-rate models describe the evolution of the instantaneous interest rate $R(t)$ as stochastic processes, and the forward rate models (e.g., the one- or two-factor Heath-Jarrow-Morton model) capture the dynamics of the whole forward rate curve. A different classification separates interest rate models into arbitrage-free models and equilibrium models. Arbitrage-free models take the current term structure—constructed from most liquid bonds—and are arbitrage-free with respect to the current market prices of bonds. Equilibrium models, on the other hand, do not necessarily match the current term structure.

Some of the simplest short-rate models are the Vasicek model, the Cox-Ingersoll-Ross model, the Ho-Lee model, and the Hull-White model.

Equilibrium short-rate models

Vasicek model: $dR(t) = a\big(b - R(t)\big)dt + \sigma\, dW(t)$

When $R(t) > b$, the drift rate is negative; when $R(t) < b$, the drift rate is positive. So the Vasicek model has the desirable property of mean-reverting towards long-term average b. But with constant volatility, the interest rate has positive probability of being negative, which is undesirable.

Cox-Ingersoll-Ross model: $dR(t) = a\big(b - R(t)\big)dt + \sigma\sqrt{R(u)}\, dW(t)$

The Cox-Ingersoll-Ross model keeps the mean-reversion property of the Vasicek model. But the diffusion rate $\sigma\sqrt{R(u)}$ addresses the drawback of Vasicek model by guaranteeing that the short rate is positive.

No-arbitrage short-rate models

Ho-Lee model: $dr = \theta(t)dt + \sigma dz$

The Ho-Lee model is the simplest no-arbitrage short-rate model where $\theta(t)$ is a time-dependent drift. $\theta(t)$ is adjusted to make the model match the current rate curve.

Hull-White model: $dR(t) = a\big(b(t) - R(t)\big)dt + \sigma dW(t)$

The Hull-White model has a structure similar to the Vasicek model. The difference is that $b(t)$ is a time-dependent variable in the Hull-White model to make it fit the current term structure.

Chapter 7 Algorithms and Numerical Methods

Although the percentage of time that a quant spends on programming varies with the job function (e.g., quant analyst/researcher versus quant developer) and firm culture, a typical quant generally devotes part of his or her time to implementing models through programming. Therefore, programming skill test is often an inherent part of the quantitative interview.

To a great extent, the programming problems asked in quantitative interviews are similar to those asked in technology interviews. Not surprisingly, many of these problems are platform- or language-specific. Although C++ and Java still dominate the market, we've seen a growing diversification to other programming languages such as Matlab, SAS, S-Plus, and R. Since there are many existing books and websites dedicated to technology interviews, this chapter will not give a comprehensive review of programming problems. Instead, it discusses some algorithm problems and numerical methods that are favorite topics of quantitative interviews.

7.1. Algorithms

In programming, the analysis of algorithm complexity often uses asymptotic analysis that ignores machine-dependent constants and studies the running time $T(n)$ —the number of primitive operations such as addition, multiplication, and comparison—as the number of inputs $n \to \infty$.[1]

Three of the most important notations in algorithm complexity are big-O notation, Ω notation and Θ notation:

$O(g(n)) = \{ f(n):$ there exist positive constants c and n_0 such that $0 \le f(n) \le cg(n)$ for all $n \ge n_0 \}$. It is the asymptotic upper bound of $f(n)$.

$\Omega(g(n)) = \{ f(n):$ there exist positive constants c and n_0 such that $0 \le cg(n) \le f(n)$ for all $n \ge n_0 \}$. It is the asymptotic lower bound of $f(n)$.

$\Theta(g(n)) = \{ f(n):$ there exist positive constants c_1, c_2, and n_0 such that $c_1 g(n) \le f(n) \le c_2 g(n)$ for all $n \ge n_0 \}$. It is the asymptotic tight bound of $f(n)$.

Besides notations, it is also important to explain two concepts in algorithm complexity:

---

[1] If you want to review basic algorithms, I highly recommend "*Introduction to Algorithm*" by Thomas H. Cormen, Charles E. Leiserson, Ronald L. Rivest and Clifford Stein. It covers all the theories discussed in this section and includes many algorithms frequently appearing in interviews.

Worst-case running time $W(n)$: an upper bound on the running time for any n inputs.

Average-case running time $A(n)$: the expected running time if the n inputs are randomly selected.

For many algorithms, $W(n)$ and $A(n)$ have the same $O(g(n))$. But as we will discuss in some problems, they may well be different and their relative importance often depends on the specific problem at hand.

A problem with n inputs can often be split into a subproblems with n/b inputs in each subproblem. This paradigm is commonly called divide-and-conquer. If it takes $f(n)$ primitive operations to divide the problem into subproblems and to merge the solutions of the subproblems, the running time can be expressed as a recurrence equation $T(n) = aT(n/b) + f(n)$, where $a \geq 1$, $b > 1$, and $f(n) \geq 0$.

The **master theorem** is a valuable tool in finding the tight bound for recurrence equation $T(n) = aT(n/b) + f(n)$: If $f(n) = O\left(n^{\log_b a - \varepsilon}\right)$ for some constant $\varepsilon > 0$, $T(n) = \Theta\left(n^{\log_b a}\right)$, since $f(n)$ grows slower than $n^{\log_b a}$. If $f(n) = \Theta\left(n^{\log_b a} \log^k n\right)$ for some $k \geq 0$, $T(n) = \Theta\left(n^{\log_b a} \log^{k+1} n\right)$, since $f(n)$ and $n^{\log_b a}$ grow at similar rates. If $f(n) = \Omega\left(n^{\log_b a + \varepsilon}\right)$ for some constant $\varepsilon > 0$, and $af(n/b) \leq cf(n)$ for some constant $c < 1$, $T(n) = \Theta(f(n))$, since $f(n)$ grows faster than $n^{\log_b a}$.

Let's use binary search to show the application of the master theorem. To find an element in an array, if the numbers in the array are sorted ($a_1 \leq a_2 \leq \cdots \leq a_n$), we can use binary search: The algorithm starts with $a_{\lfloor n/2 \rfloor}$. If $a_{\lfloor n/2 \rfloor} = x$, the search stops. If $a_{\lfloor n/2 \rfloor} > x$, we only need to search $a_1, \cdots, a_{\lfloor n/2-1 \rfloor}$. If $a_{\lfloor n/2 \rfloor} < x$, we only need to search $a_{\lfloor n/2+1 \rfloor}, \cdots, a_n$. Each time we can reduce the number of elements to search by half after making one comparison. So we have $a = 1$, $b = 2$, and $f(n) = 1$. Hence, $f(n) = \Theta\left(n^{\log_2 1} \log^0 n\right)$ and the binary search has complexity $\Theta(\log n)$.

Number swap

How do you swap two integers, i and j, without using additional storage space?

Solution: Comparison and swap are the basic operations for many algorithms. The most common technique for swap uses a temporary variable, which unfortunately is forbidden in this problem since the temporary variable requires additional storage space. A simple mathematic approach is to store the sum of i and j first, then extract i's value and assign it to j and finally assign j's value to i. The implementation is shown in the following code:[2]

```
void swap(int &i, int &j) {

    i = i + j;  //store the sum of i and j

    j = i - j;  //change j to i's value

    i = i - j;  //change i to j's value

}
```

An alternative solution uses bitwise XOR (^) function by taking advantage of the fact that $x \wedge x = 0$ and $0 \wedge x = x$:

```
void swap(int &i, int &j){

    i = i ^ j;

    j = j ^ i; //j = i ^ (j ^ i) = i

    i = i ^ j; //i = (i ^ j) ^ i = j

}
```

Unique elements

If you are given a sorted array, can you write some code to extract the unique elements from the array? For example, if the array is [1, 1, 3, 3, 3, 5, 5, 5, 9, 9, 9, 9], the unique elements should be [1, 3, 5, 9].

Solution: Let a be an n-element sorted array with elements $a_0 \le a_1 \le \cdots \le a_{n-1}$. Whenever we encounter a new element a_i in the sorted array, its value is different from its previous element ($a_i \neq a_{i-1}$). Using this property we can easily extract the unique elements. One implementation in C++ is shown as the following function:[3]

```
template <class T> vector<T> unique(T a[], int n) {

    vector<T> vec; // vector used to avoid resizing problem

    vec.reserve(n); //reserver to avoid reallocation

    vec.push_back(a[0]);

    for(int i=1; i<n; ++i) {
```

---

[2] This chapter uses C++ to demonstrate some implementations. For other problems, the algorithms are described using pseudo codes.
The following is a one-line equivalent function for swapping two integers. It is not recommend, though, as it lacks clarity.
` void swap(int &i, int &j) { i-=j=(i+=j)-j; };`
[3] I should point out that C++ STL has general algorithms for this basic operation: unique and unique_copy.

```
            if(a[i] != a[i-1])
                vec.push_back(a[i]);
    }
    return vec;
}
```

Horner's algorithm

Write an algorithm to compute $y = A_0 + A_1x + A_2x^2 + A_3x^3 + \cdots + A_nx^n$.

Solution: A naïve approach calculates each component of the polynomial and adds them up, which takes $O(n^2)$ number of multiplications. We can use Horner's algorithm to reduce the number of multiplications to $O(n)$. The algorithm expresses the original polynomial as $y = \left(\left(\left(\left(A_nx + A_{n-1}\right)x + A_{n-2}\right)x + \cdots + A_2\right)x + A_1\right)x + A_0$ and sequentially calculate $B_n = A_n$, $B_{n-1} = B_nx + A_{n-1}$, $\cdots$, $B_0 = B_1x + A_0$. We have $y = B_0$ with at most n multiplications.

Moving average

Given a large array A of length m, can you develop an efficient algorithm to build another array containing the n-element moving average of the original array $(B_1, \cdots, B_{n-1} = NA, B_i = \left(A_{i-n+1} + A_{i-n+2} + \cdots + A_i\right)/n, \forall i = n, \cdots, m)$?

Solution: When we calculate the moving average of the next n consecutive numbers, we can reuse the previously computed moving average. Just multiply that average by n, subtract the first number in that moving average and then add the new number, and you have the new sum. Dividing the new sum by n yields the new moving average. Here is the pseudo-code for calculating the moving average:

S= A[1] + $\cdots$ + A[n]; B[n] = S/n;

for (i=n+1 to m) { S = S − A[i-n] + A[i]; B[i] = S/n; }

Sorting algorithm

Could you explain three sorting algorithms to sort n distinct values $A_1, \cdots, A_n$ and analyze the complexity of each algorithm?

Solution: Sorting is a fundamental process that is directly or indirectly implemented in many programs. So a variety of sorting algorithms have been developed for different purposes. Here let's discuss three such algorithms: insertion sort, merge sort and quick sort.

Insertion sort: Insertion sort uses an incremental approach. Assume that we have sorted subarray A[1, ..., *i*-1]. We insert element A_i into the appropriate place in A[1, ..., *i*-1], which yields sorted subarray A[1, ..., *i*]. Starting with $i=1$ and increases *i* step by step to *n*, we will have a fully sorted array. For each step, the expected number of comparisons is $i/2$ and the worst-case number of comparisons is *i*. So we have

$$A(n) = \Theta\left(\sum_{i=1}^{n} i/2\right) = \Theta(n^2) \text{ and } W(n) = \Theta\left(\sum_{i=1}^{n} i\right) = \Theta(n^2).$$

Merge sort: Merge sort uses the divide-and-conquer paradigm. It divides the array into two subarrays each with $n/2$ items and sorts each subarray. Unless the subarray is small enough (with no more than a few elements), the subarray is again divided for sorting. Finally, the sorted subarrays are merged to form a single sorted array.

The algorithm can be expressed as the following pseudocode:

mergesort(A, beginindex, endindex)

if beginindex < endindex

then centerindex ← (beginindex + endindex)/2

merge1 <- mergesort(A, beginindex, centerindex)

merge2 <- mergesort(A, centerindex + 1, endindex)

merge(merge1, merge2)

The merge of two sorted arrays with *n*/2 elements each into one array takes $\Theta(n)$ primitive operations. The running time $T(n)$ follows the following recursive function:

$$T(n) = \begin{cases} 2T(n/2) + \Theta(n), & \text{if } n > 1 \\ 1, & \text{if } n = 1 \end{cases}.$$

Applying the master theorem to $T(n)$ with $a=2, b=2$, and $f(n)=\Theta(n)$, we have $f(n) = \Theta\left(n^{\log_b a} \log^0 n\right)$. So $T(n) = \Theta(n \log n)$. For merge sort, $A(n)$ and $W(n)$ are the same as $T(n)$.

Quicksort: Quicksort is another recursive sorting method. It chooses one of the elements, A_i, from the sequence and compares all other values with it. Those elements smaller than A_i are put in a subarray to the left of A_i; those elements larger than A_i are put in a subarray to the right of A_i. The algorithm is then repeated on both subarrays (and any subarrays from them) until all values are sorted.

In the worst case, quicksort requires the same number of comparisons as the insertion sort. For example, if we always choose the first element in the array (subarray) and compare all other elements with it, the worst case happens when $A_1, \cdots, A_n$ are already sorted. In such cases, one of the subarray is empty and the other has $n-1$ element. Each step only reduces the subarray size by one. Hence, $W(n) = \Theta\left(\sum_{i=1}^{n} i\right) = \Theta(n^2)$.

To estimate the average-case running time, let's assume that the initial ordering is random so that each comparison is likely to be any pair of elements chosen from $A_1, \cdots, A_n$. If we suspect that the original sequence of elements has a certain pattern, we can always randomly permute the sequence first with complexity $\Theta(n)$ as explained in the next problem. Let $\tilde{A}_p$ and $\tilde{A}_q$ be the pth and qth element ($1 \le p < q \le n$) in the final sorted array. There are $q - p + 1$ numbers between $\tilde{A}_p$ and $\tilde{A}_q$. The probability that $\tilde{A}_p$ and $\tilde{A}_q$ is compared is the probability that $\tilde{A}_q$ is compared with $\tilde{A}_p$ before $\tilde{A}_{p+1}, \cdots$, or $\tilde{A}_{q-1}$ is compared with either $\tilde{A}_p$ or $\tilde{A}_q$ (otherwise, $\tilde{A}_p$ and $\tilde{A}_q$ are separated into different subarrays and will not be compared), which happens with probability $P(p,q) = \dfrac{2}{q - p + 1}$ (you can again use the symmetry argument to derive this probablity).

The total expected number of comparison is $A(n) = \sum_{q=2}^{n}\sum_{p=1}^{q-1} P(p,q) = \sum_{q=2}^{n}\sum_{p=1}^{q-1}\left(\dfrac{2}{q - p + 1}\right)$
$= \Theta(n \lg n)$.

Although theoretically quicksort can be slower than merge sort in the worst cases, it is often as fast as, if not faster than, merge sort.

Random permutation

A. If you have a random number generator that can generate random numbers from either discrete or continuous uniform distributions, how do you shuffle a deck of 52 cards so that every permutation is equally likely?

Solution: A simple algorithm to permute n elements is random permutation by sorting. It assigns a random number to each card and then sorts the cards in order of their assigned random numbers.[4] By symmetry, every possible order (out of $n!$ possible ordered sequences) is equally likely. The complexity is determined by the sorting step, so the

---

[4] If we use the continuous uniform distribution, theoretically any two random numbers have zero probability of being equal.

running time is $\Theta(n \log n)$. For a small n, such as $n = 52$ in a deck of cards, the complexity $\Theta(n \log n)$ is acceptable. For large n, we may want to use a faster algorithm known as the Knuth shuffle. For n elements $A[1], \cdots, A[n]$, the Knuth shuffle uses the following loop to generate a random permutation:

for (i=1 to n) swap($A[i]$, A[Random(i, n)]),

where Random(i, n) is a random number from the discrete uniform distribution between i and n.

The Knuth shuffle has a complexity of $\Theta(n)$ and an intuitive interpretation. In the first step, each of the n cards has equal probability of being chosen as the first card since the card number is chosen from the discrete uniform distribution between 1 and n; in the second step, each of the remaining $n - 1$ cards elements has equal probability of being chosen as the second card; and so on. So naturally each ordered sequence has $1 / n!$ probability.

B. You have a file consisting of characters. The characters in the file can be read sequentially, but the length of the file is unknown. How do you pick a character so that every character in the file has equal probability of being chosen?

Solution: Let's start with picking the first character. If there is a second character, we keep the first character with probability 1/2 and replace the pick with the second character with probability 1/2. If there is a third character, we keep the pick (from the first two characters) with probability 2/3 and replace the pick with the third character with probability 1/3. The same process is continued until the final character. In other words, let C_n be the character that we pick after we have scanned n characters and the $(n+1)th$ character exists, the probability of keeping the pick is $\dfrac{n}{n+1}$ and the probability of switching to the $(n+1)th$ character is $\dfrac{1}{n+1}$. Using simple induction, we can easily prove that each character has $1/m$ probability of being chosen if there are m characters.

Search algorithm

A. Develop an algorithm to find both the minimum and the maximum of n numbers using no more than $3n/2$ comparisons.

Solution: For an unsorted array of n numbers, it takes $n-1$ comparisons to identify either the minimum or the maximum of the array. However, it takes at most $3n/2$ comparisons to identify both the minimum and the maximum. If we separate the elements to $n/2$ pairs, compare the elements in each pair and put the smaller one in group

A and the larger one in group B. This step takes $n/2$ comparisons. Since the minimum of the whole array must be in group A and the maximum must be in group B, we only need to find the minimum in A and the maximum in B, either of which takes $n/2-1$ comparisons. So the total number of comparisons is at most $3n/2$.[5]

B. You are given an array of numbers. From the beginning of the array to some position, all elements are zero; after that position, all elements are nonzero. If you don't know the size of the array, how do you find the position of the first nonzero element?

Solution: We can start with the 1st element; if it is zero, we check the 2nd element; if the 2nd element is zero, we check the 4th element... The process is repeated until the ith step when the $2^i th$ element is nonzero. Then we check the $\dfrac{2^i + 2^{i-1}}{2}th$ element. If it is zero, the search range is limited to the elements between the $\dfrac{2^i + 2^{i-1}}{2}th$ element and the $2^i th$ element; otherwise the search range is limited to the elements between the $2^{i-1}th$ element and the $\dfrac{2^i + 2^{i-1}}{2}th$ element... Each time, we cut the range by half. This method is basically a binary search. If the first nonzero element is at position n, the algorithm complexity is $\Theta(\log n)$.

C. You have a square grid of numbers. The numbers in each row increase from left to right. The numbers in each column increase from top to bottom. Design an algorithm to find a given number from the grid. What is the complexity of your algorithm?

Solution: Let A be an $n \times n$ matrix representing the grid of numbers and x be the number we want to find in the grid. Begin the search with the last column from top to bottom: $A_{1,n}, \cdots, A_{n,n}$. If the number is found, then stop the search. If $A_{n,n} < x$, x is not in the grid and the search stops as well. If $A_{i,n} < x < A_{i+1,n}$, then we know that all the numbers in rows $1, \cdots, i$ are less than x and are eliminated as well.[6] Then we search the $(i+1)th$ row from right to left. If the number is found in the $(i+1)th$ row, the search stops. If $A_{1,i+1} > x$, x is not in the grid since all the number in rows $i+1$ and above are larger than x. If $A_{i+1,j+1} > x > A_{i+1,j}$, we eliminate all the numbers in columns $j+1, \cdots, n$. Then we can search along column from $A_{i+1,j}$ towards $A_{n,j}$ until we find x (or x does not exist in

---

[5] Slight adjustment needs to be made if n is odd, but the upper bound $3n/2$ still applies.

[6] i can be 0, which means $x < A_{1,n}$, in which case we can search the first row from right to left.

the grid) or a k that makes $A_{k,j} < x < A_{k+1,j}$ and then we search left along the row $k+1$ from $A_{k+1,j}$ towards $A_{k+1,1}$ ... Using this algorithm, the search takes at most $2n$ steps. So its complexity is $O(n)$.

Fibonacci numbers

Consider the following C++ program for producing Fibonacci numbers:

```
int Fibonacci(int n)
{
    if (n <= 0)
        return 0;
    else if (n==1)
        return 1;
    else
        return Fibonacci(n-1)+Fibonacci(n-2);

}
```

If for some large n, it takes 100 seconds to compute Fibonacci(n), how long will it take to compute Fibonacci(n+1), to the nearest second? Is this algorithm efficient? How would you calculate Fibonacci numbers?

Solution: This C++ function uses a rather inefficient recursive method to calculate Fibonacci numbers. Fibonacci numbers are defined as the following recurrence:

$F_0 = 0$, $F_1 = 1$, $F_n = F_{n-1} + F_{n-2}$, $\forall n \geq 2$

F_n has closed-formed solution $F_n = \dfrac{\left(1+\sqrt{5}\right)^n - \left(1-\sqrt{5}\right)^n}{2^n \sqrt{5}}$, which can be easily proven using induction. From the function, it is clear that

$T(0) = 1$, $T(1) = 1$, $T(n) = T(n-1) + T(n-2) + 1$.

So the running time is a proportional to a sequence of Fibonacci numbers as well. For a large n, $(1-\sqrt{5})^n \to 0$, so $\dfrac{T(n+1)}{T(n)} \approx \dfrac{\sqrt{5}+1}{2}$. If it takes 100 seconds to compute

Fibonacci(n), the time to compute Fibonacci(n+1) is $T(n+1) \approx \dfrac{\sqrt{5}+1}{2} T(n) \approx 162$

seconds.[7]

---

[7] $\phi = \dfrac{\sqrt{5}+1}{2}$ is called the golden ratio.

The recursive algorithm has exponential complexity $\Theta\left(\left(\dfrac{\sqrt{5}+1}{2}\right)^n\right)$, which is surely

inefficient. The reason is that it fails to effectively use the information from Fibonacci numbers with smaller n in the Fibonacci number sequence. If we compute $F_0, F_1, \cdots, F_n$ in sequence using the definition, the running time has complexity $\Theta(n)$.

An algorithm called recursive squaring can further reduce the complexity to $\Theta(\log n)$.

Since $\begin{bmatrix} F_{n+1} & F_n \\ F_n & F_{n-1} \end{bmatrix} = \begin{bmatrix} 1 & 1 \\ 1 & 0 \end{bmatrix} \times \begin{bmatrix} F_n & F_{n-1} \\ F_{n-1} & F_{n-2} \end{bmatrix}$ and $\begin{bmatrix} F_2 & F_1 \\ F_1 & F_0 \end{bmatrix} = \begin{bmatrix} 1 & 1 \\ 1 & 0 \end{bmatrix}$, we can show that

$\begin{bmatrix} F_{n+1} & F_n \\ F_n & F_{n-1} \end{bmatrix} = \begin{bmatrix} 1 & 1 \\ 1 & 0 \end{bmatrix}^n$ using induction. Let $A = \begin{bmatrix} 1 & 1 \\ 1 & 0 \end{bmatrix}$, we can again apply the divide-

and-conquer paradigm to calculate A^n: $A^n = \begin{cases} A^{n/2} \times A^{n/2}, & \text{if } n \text{ is even} \\ A^{(n-1)/2} \times A^{(n-1)/2} \times A, & \text{if } n \text{ is odd} \end{cases}$. The

multiplication of two 2×2 matrices has complexity $\Theta(1)$. So $T(n) = T(n/2) + \Theta(1)$. Applying the master theorem, we have $T(n) = \Theta(\log n)$.

Maximum contiguous subarray

Suppose you have a one-dimensional array A with length n that contains both positive and negative numbers. Design an algorithm to find the maximum sum of any contiguous subarray $A[i, j]$ of A: $V(i, j) = \sum_{x=i}^{j} A[x], 1 \le i \le j \le n$.

Solution: Almost all trading systems need such an algorithm to calculate maximum run-up or maximum drawdown of either real trading books or simulated strategies. Therefore this is a favorite algorithm question of interviewers, especially interviewers at hedge funds and trading desks.

The most apparent algorithm is an $O(n^2)$ algorithm that sequentially calculates the $V(i, j)$'s from scratch using the following equations:

$V(i, i) = A[i]$ when $j = i$ and $V(i, j) = \sum_{x=i}^{j} A[x] = V(i, j-1) + A[j]$ when $j > i$.

As the $V(i, j)$'s are calculated, we also keep track of the maximum of $V(i, j)$ as well as the corresponding subarray indices i and j.

A more efficient approach uses the divide-and-conquer paradigm. Let's define $T(i) = \sum_{x=1}^{i} A[x]$ and $T(0) = 0$, then $V(i,j) = T(j) - T(i-1)$, $\forall 1 \le i \le j \le n$. Clearly for any fixed j, when $T(i-1)$ is minimized, $V(i,j)$ is maximized. So the maximum subarray ending at j is $V_{max} = T(j) - T_{min}$ where $T_{min} = \min(T(1), \cdots, T(j-1))$. If we keep track of and update V_{max} and T_{min} as j increases, we can develop the following $O(n)$ algorithm:

$T = A[1]; V_{max} = A[1]; T_{min} = \min(0, T)$

For $j = 2$ to n

$\{\ \ T = T + A[j];$

If $T - T_{min} > V_{max}$ then $V_{max} = T - T_{min}$;

If $T < T_{min}$, then $T_{min} = T$;

$\}$

Return V_{max};

The following is a corresponding C++ function that returns V_{max} and indices i and j given an array and its length:

```
double maxSubarray(double A[], int len, int &i, int &j)
{
    double T=A[0], Vmax=A[0];
    double Tmin = min(0.0, T);
    for(int k=1; k<len; ++k)
    {
        T+=A[k];
        if (T-Tmin > Vmax) {Vmax=T-Tmin; j=k;}
        if (T<Tmin) {Tmin = T; i = (k+1<j)? (k+1):j;}
    }
    return Vmax;
}
```

Applying it to the following array A,

```
double A[]={1.0,2.0,-5.0,4.0,-3.0, 2.0, 6.0, -5.0, -1.0};
int i = 0, j =0;
```

```
double Vmax = maxSubarray(A, sizeof(a)/sizeof(A[1]), i, j);
```

will give $V_{max} = 9$, $i = 3$ and $j = 6$. So the subarray is $[4.0, -3.0, 2.0, 6.0]$.

7.2. The Power of Two

There are only 10 kinds of people in the world—those who know binary, and those who don't. If you happen to get this joke, you probably know that computers operate using the binary (base-2) number system. Instead of decimal digits 0-9, each bit (binary digit) has only two possible values: 0 and 1. Binary representation of numbers gives some interesting properties that are widely explored in practice and makes it an interesting topic to test in interviews.

Power of 2

How do you determine whether an integer is a power of 2?

Solution: Any integer $x = 2^n$ ($n \geq 0$) has a single bit (the $(n+1)th$ bit from the right) set to 1. For example, 8 ($= 2^3$) is expressed as $0 \cdots 01000$. It is also easy to see that $2^n - 1$ has all the n bits from the right set to 1. For example, 7 is expressed as $0 \cdots 00111$. So 2^n and $2^n - 1$ do not share any common bits. As a result, $x \mathbin{\&} (x-1) == 0$, where $\&$ is a bitwise AND operator, is a simple way to identify whether the integer x is a power of 2.

Multiplication by 7

Give a fast way to multiply an integer by 7 without using the multiplication (*) operator?

Solution: (x << 3) – x, where << is the bit-shift left operator. x << 3 is equivalent to x*8. Hence (x << 3) – x is x*7.[8]

Probability simulation

You are given a fair coin. Can you design a simple game using the fair coin so that your probability of winning is p, $0 < p < 1$?[9]

---

[8] The result could be wrong if << causes an overflow.

[9] Hint: Computer stores binary numbers instead of decimal ones; each digit in a binary number can be simulated using a fair coin.

Solution: The key to this problem is to realize that $p \in (0,1)$ can also be expressed as a binary number and each digit of the binary number can be simulated using a fair coin. First, we can express the probability p as binary number:

$$p = 0.p_1 p_2 \cdots p_n = p_1 2^{-1} + p_2 2^{-2} + \cdots + p_n 2^{-n}, \; p_i \in \{0,1\}, \; \forall i = 1, 2, \cdots, n.$$

Then, we can start tossing the fair coin, and count heads as 1 and tails as 0. Let $s_i \in \{0,1\}$ be the result of the i-th toss starting from $i = 1$. After each toss, we compare p_i with s_i. If $s_i < p_i$, we win and the coin tossing stops. If $s_i > p_i$, we lose and the coin tossing stops. If $s_i = p_i$, we continue to toss more coins. Some p values (e.g., 1/3) are infinite series when expressed as a binary number ($n \to \infty$). In these cases, the probability to reach $s_i \neq p_i$ is 1 as i increases. If the sequence is finite, (e.g., 1/4=0.01) and we reach the final stage with $s_n = p_n$, we lose (e.g., for 1/4, only the sequence 00 will be classified as a win; all other three sequences 01, 10 and 11 are classified as a loss). Such a simulation will give us probability p of winning.

Poisonous wine

You've got 1000 bottles of wines for a birthday party. Twenty hours before the party, the winery sent you an urgent message that one bottle of wine was poisoned. You happen to have 10 lab mice that can be used to test whether a bottle of wine is poisonous. The poison is so strong that any amount will kill a mouse in exactly 18 hours. But before the death on the 18th hour, there are no other symptoms. Is there a sure way that you can find the poisoned bottle using the 10 mice before the party?

Solution: If the mice can be tested sequentially to eliminate half of the bottles each time, the problem becomes a simple binary search problem. Ten mice can identify the poisonous bottle in up to 1024 bottles of wines. Unfortunately, since the symptom won't show up until 18 hours later and we only have 20 hours, we cannot sequentially test the mice. Nevertheless, the binary search idea still applies. All integers between 1 and 1000 can be expressed in 10-bit binary format. For example, bottle 1000 can be labeled as 1111101000 since $1000 = 2^9 + 2^8 + 2^7 + 2^6 + 2^5 + 2^3$.

Now let mouse 1 take a sip from every bottle that has a 1 in the first bit (the lowest bit on the right); let mouse 2 take a sip from every bottle with a 1 in the second bit; ...; and, finally, let mouse 10 take a sip from every bottle with a 1 in the 10th bit (the highest bit). Eighteen hours later, if we line up the mice from the highest to the lowest bit and treat a live mouse as 0 and a dead mouse as 1, we can easily back track the label of the poisonous bottle. For example, if the 6th, 7th, and 9th mice are dead and all others are alive, the line-up gives the sequence 0101100000 and the label for the poisonous bottle is $2^8 + 2^6 + 2^5 = 352$.

7.3 Numerical Methods

The prices of many financial instruments do not have closed-form analytical solutions. The valuation of these financial instruments relies on a variety of numerical methods. In this section, we discuss the application of Monte Carlo simulation and finite difference methods.

Monte Carlo simulation

Monte Carlo simulation is a method for iteratively evaluating a deterministic model using random numbers with appropriate probabilities as inputs. For derivative pricing, it simulates a large number of price paths of the underlying assets with probability corresponding to the underlying stochastic process (usually under risk-neutral measure), calculates the discounted payoff of the derivative for each path, and averages the discounted payoffs to yield the derivative price. The validity of Monte Carlo simulation relies on the law of large numbers.

Monte-Carlo simulation can be used to estimate derivative prices if the payoffs only depend on the final values of the underlying assets, and it can be adapted to estimate prices if the payoffs are path-dependent as well. Nevertheless, it cannot be directly applied to American options or any other derivatives with early exercise options.

A. Explain how you can use Monte Carlo simulation to price a European call option?

Solution: If we assume that stock price follows a geometric Brownian motion, we can simulate possible stock price paths. We can split the time between t and T into N equally-spaced time steps.[10] So $\Delta t = \dfrac{T-t}{N}$ and $t_i = t + \Delta t \times i$, for $i = 0, 1, 2, \cdots, N$. We then simulate the stock price paths under risk-neutral probability using equation $S_i = S_{i-1} e^{(r-\sigma^2/2)(\Delta t) + \sigma\sqrt{\Delta t}\varepsilon_i}$, where ε_i's are IID random variables from standard normal distribution. Let's say that we simulate M paths and each one yields a stock price $S_{T,k}$, where $k = 1, 2, \cdots, M$, at maturity date T.

---

[10] For European options, we can simply set N=1. But for more general options, especially the path-dependent ones, we want to have small time steps and therefore N should be large.

The estimated price of the European call is the present value of the expected payoff,

which can be calculated as $C = e^{-r(T-t)} \dfrac{\sum_{k=1}^{M} \max(S_{T,k} - K, 0)}{M}$.

B. How do you generate random variables that follow $N(\mu, \sigma^2)$ (normal distribution with mean μ and variance σ^2) if your computer can only generate random variables that follow continuous uniform distribution between 0 and 1?

Solution: This is a great question to test the basic knowledge of random number generation, the foundation of Monte Carlo simulation. The solution to this question can be dissected to two steps:

1. Generate random variable of $x \sim N(0,1)$ from uniform random number generator using inverse transform method and rejection method.

2. Scale x to $\mu + \sigma x$ to generate the final random variables that follow $N(\mu, \sigma^2)$.

The second step is straightforward; the first step deserves some explanations. A popular approach to generating random variables is the inverse transform method: For any continuous random variable X with cumulative density function F ($U = F(X)$), the random variable X can be defined as the inverse function of U: $X = F^{-1}(U)$, $0 \le U \le 1$. It is obvious that $X = F^{-1}(U)$ is a one-to-one function with $0 \le U \le 1$. So any continuous random variable can be generated using the following process:

*   Generate a random number u from the standard uniform distribution.

*   Compute the value x such that $u = F(x)$ as the random number from the distribution described by F.

For this model to work, $F^{-1}(U)$ must be computable. For standard normal distribution, $U = F(X) = \int_{-\infty}^{X} \frac{1}{\sqrt{2\pi}} e^{-x^2/2} dx$. The inverse function has no analytical solution. Theoretically, we can come up with the one-to-one mapping of X to U as the numeric solution of ordinary differential equation $F'(x) = f(x) = \frac{1}{\sqrt{2\pi}} e^{-x^2/2}$ using numerical integration method such as the Euler method.[11] Yet this approach is less efficient than the rejection method:

---

[11] To integrate $y = F(x)$ with first derivative $y' = f(x)$ and a known initial value $y_0 = F(x_0)$, the Euler method chooses a small step size h (h can be positive or negative) to sequentially approximate y values:

Some random variables have pdf $f(x)$, but no analytical solution for $F^{-1}(U)$. In these cases, we can use a random variable with pdf $g(y)$ and $Y = G^{-1}(U)$ to help generate random variables with pdf $f(x)$. Assume that M is a constant such that $\dfrac{f(y)}{g(y)} \le M, \ \forall y$. We can implement the following acceptance-rejection method:

- Sampling step: Generate random variable y from $g(y)$ and a random variable v from standard uniform distribution $[0,1]$.

- Acceptance/rejection step: If $v \le \dfrac{f(y)}{Mg(y)}$, accept $x = y$; otherwise, repeat the sampling step.[12]

An exponential random variable ($g(x) = \lambda e^{-\lambda x}$) with $\lambda = 1$ has cdf $u = G(x) = 1 - e^{-x}$. So the inverse function has analytical solution $x = -\log(1-u)$ and a random variable with exponential distribution can be conveniently simulated. For standard normal distribution, $f(x) = \dfrac{1}{\sqrt{2\pi}} e^{-x^2/2}$,

$$\frac{f(x)}{g(x)} = \sqrt{\frac{2}{\pi}} e^{x - x^2/2} < \sqrt{\frac{2}{\pi}} e^{-(x-1)^2/2 + 1/2} \le \sqrt{\frac{2}{\pi}} e^{1/2} \approx 1.32, \ \forall 0 < x < \infty$$

So we can choose $M = 1.32$ and use the acceptance-rejection method to generate $x \sim N(0,1)$ random variables and scale them to $N(\mu, \sigma^2)$ random variables.

$C.$ Can you explain a few variance reduction techniques to improve the efficiency of Monte Carlo simulation?

Solution: Monte Carlo simulation, in its basic form, is the mean of IID random variables $Y_1, Y_2, \cdots, Y_M$: $\bar{Y} = \dfrac{1}{M} \sum_{i=1}^{M} Y_i$. Since the expected value of each Y_i is unbiased, the estimator $\bar{Y}$ is unbiased as well. If $Var(Y) = \sigma$ and we generate IID Y_i, then $Var(\bar{Y}) = \sigma / \sqrt{M}$, where M is the number of simulations. Not surprisingly, Monte Carlo

---

$F(x_0 + h) = F(x_0) + f(x_0) \times h$, $F(x_0 + 2h) = F(x_0 + h) + f(x_0 + h) \times h, \cdots$. The initial value of the cdf of a standard normal can be $F(0) = 0.5$.

[12] $P(X \le x) \propto \displaystyle\int_{-\infty}^{x} g(y) \frac{f(y)}{Mg(y)} dy = M \int_{-\infty}^{x} f(y) dy \Rightarrow F(x) = \frac{P(X \le x)}{P(X < \infty)} = \int_{-\infty}^{x} f(y) dy$

simulation is computationally intensive if σ is large. Thousands or even millions of simulations are often required to get the desired accuracy. Depending on the specific problems, a variety of methods have been applied to reduce variance.

Antithetic variable: For each series of ε_i's, calculate its corresponding payoff $Y(\varepsilon_1, \cdots, \varepsilon_N)$. Then reverse the sign of all ε_i's and calculate the corresponding payoff $Y(-\varepsilon_1, \cdots, -\varepsilon_N)$. When $Y(\varepsilon_1, \cdots, \varepsilon_N)$ and $Y(-\varepsilon_1, \cdots, -\varepsilon_N)$ are negatively correlated, the variance is reduced.

Moment matching: Specific samples of the random variable may not match the population distribution well. We can draw a large set of samples first and then rescale the samples to make the samples' moments (mean and variance are the most commonly used) match the desired population moments.

Control variate: If we want to price a derivative X and there is a closely related derivative Y that has an analytical solution, we can generate a series of random numbers and use the same random sequences to price both X and Y to yield $\hat{X}$ and $\hat{Y}$. Then X can be estimated as $\hat{X} + (Y - \hat{Y})$. Essentially we use $(Y - \hat{Y})$ to correct the estimation error of $\hat{X}$.

Importance sampling: To estimate the expected value of $h(x)$ from distribution $f(x)$, instead of drawing x from distribution $f(x)$, we can draw x from distribution $g(x)$ and use Monte Carlo simulation to estimate expected value of $\dfrac{h(x)f(x)}{g(x)}$:

$$E_{f(x)}[h(x)] = \int h(x)f(x)dx = \int \frac{h(x)f(x)}{g(x)}g(x)dx = E_{g(x)}\left[\frac{h(x)f(x)}{g(x)}\right]. \text{[13]}$$

If $\dfrac{h(x)f(x)}{g(x)}$ has a smaller variance than $h(x)$, then importance sampling can result in a more efficient estimator. This method is better explained using a deep out-of-the-money option as an example. If we directly use risk-neutral $f(S_T)$ as the distribution, most of the simulated paths will yield $h(S_T) = 0$ and as a result the estimation variance will be large. If we introduce a distribution $g(S_T)$ that has much wider span (fatter tail for S_T), more simulated paths will have positive $h(S_T)$. The scaling factor $\dfrac{f(x)}{g(x)}$ will keep the estimator unbiased, but the approach will have lower variance.

---

[13] Importance sampling is essentially a variance reduction method using a change of measure.

Low-discrepancy sequence: Instead of using random samples, we can generate a deterministic sequence of "random variable" that represents the distribution. Such low-discrepancy sequences may make the convergence rate $1/M$.

D. If there is no closed-form pricing formula for an option, how would you estimate its delta and gamma?

Solution: As we have discussed in problem A, the prices of options with or without closed-form pricing formulas can be derived using Monte Carlo simulation. The same methods can also be used to estimate delta and gamma by slightly changing the current underlying price from S to $S \pm \delta S$, where δS is a small positive value. Run Monte Carlo simulation for all three starting prices $S - \delta S$, S and $S + \delta S$, we will get their corresponding option prices $f(S - \delta S)$, $f(S)$ and $f(S + \delta S)$.

Estimated delta: $\Delta = \dfrac{\delta f}{\delta S} = \dfrac{f(S + \delta S) - f(S - \delta S)}{2\delta S}$

Estimated gamma: $\Gamma = \dfrac{(f(S + \delta S) - f(S)) - (f(S) - f(S - \delta S))}{\delta S^2}$

To reduce variance, it's often better to use the same random number sequences to estimate $f(S - \delta S)$, $f(S)$ and $f(S + \delta S)$.[14]

E. How do you use Monte Carlo simulation to estimate π?

Solution: Estimation of π is a classic example of Monte Carlo simulation. One standard method to estimate π is to randomly select points in the unit square (x and y are independent uniform random variables between 0 and 1) and determine the ratio of points that are within the circle $x^2 + y^2 \leq 1$. For simplicity, we focus on the first quadrant. As shown in Figure 7.1, any points within the circle satisfy the equation $x_i^2 + y_i^2 \leq 1$. The percentage of the points within the circle is proportional to its area:
$\hat{p} = \dfrac{\text{Number of } (x_i, y_i) \text{ within } x_i^2 + y_i^2 \leq 1}{\text{Number of } (x_i, y_i) \text{ within the square}} = \dfrac{1/4\pi}{1 \times 1} = \dfrac{1}{4}\pi \Rightarrow \hat{\pi} = 4\hat{p}$.

So we generate a large number of independent (x, y) points, estimate the ratio of the points within the circle to the points in the square, and multiply the ratio by 4 to yield an estimation of π. Figure 7.1 uses only 1000 points for illustration. With today's

---

[14] The method may not work well if the payoff function is not continuous.

computing power, we can easily generate millions of (x, y) pairs to estimate π with good precision. 1,000 simulations with 1,000,000 (x, y) points each using Matlab took less than 1 minute on a laptop and gave an average estimation of π as 3.1416 with standard deviation 0.0015.

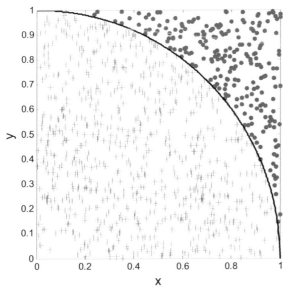

Figure 7.1 A Monte Carlo simulation method to estimate π

Finite difference method

The finite difference method is another popular numerical technique for derivative pricing. It numerically solves a differential equation to estimate the price of a derivative by discretizing the time and the price of the underlying security. We can convert the Black-Scholes-Merton equation, a second order nonlinear partial differential equation, to a heat diffusion equation (as we did in Chapter 6). This new equation, expressed as a function of τ (time to maturity) and x (a function of the price of the underlying security), is a general differential equation for derivatives. The difference between various derivatives lies in the boundary conditions. By building a grid of x and τ and using the boundary conditions, we can recursively calculate u at every x and τ using finite difference methods.

A. Can you briefly explain finite difference methods?

Solution: There are several version of finite difference methods used in practice. Let's briefly go over the explicit difference method, the implicit difference method and the

Crank-Nicolson method. As shown in Figure 7.2, if we divide the range of τ, $[0, T]$, into N discrete intervals with increment $\Delta\tau = T / N$ and divide the range of x, $[x_0, x_J]$, into J discrete intervals with increment $\Delta x = (x_J - x_0)/J$, the time τ and the space of x can be expressed as a grid of τ_n, $n = 1, \cdots, N$ and x_j, $j = 1, \cdots, J$.

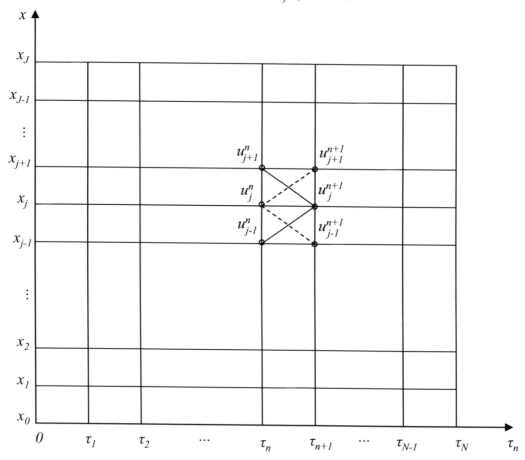

Figure 7.2 Grid of τ and x for finite different methods

The **explicit difference method** uses the forward difference at time τ_n and the second-order central difference at x_j: $\dfrac{\partial u}{\partial \tau} \approx \dfrac{u_j^{n+1} - u_j^n}{\Delta \tau} = \dfrac{u_{j+1}^n - 2u_j^n + u_{j-1}^n}{(\Delta x)^2} \approx \dfrac{\partial^2 u}{\partial x^2}$.

Rearranging terms, we can express u_j^{n+1} as a linear combination of u_{j+1}^n, u_j^n and u_{j-1}^n:
$u_j^{n+1} = \alpha u_{j-1}^n + (1-2\alpha)u_j^n + \alpha u_{j+1}^n$, where $\alpha = \Delta t /(\Delta x)^2$. Besides, we often have boundary conditions u_j^0, u_0^n, and u_J^n for all $n = 1, \cdots, N$; $j = 0, \cdots, J$. Combining the boundary

conditions and equation $u_j^{n+1} = \alpha u_{j-1}^n + (1-2\alpha) u_j^n + \alpha u_{j+1}^n$, we can estimate all u_j^n's on the grid.

The **implicit difference method** uses the backward difference at time t_{n+1} and the second-order central difference at x_j: $\dfrac{\partial u}{\partial \tau} \approx \dfrac{u_j^{n+1} - u_j^n}{\Delta \tau} = \dfrac{u_{j+1}^{n+1} - 2u_j^{n+1} + u_{j-1}^{n+1}}{(\Delta x)^2} \approx \dfrac{\partial^2 u}{\partial x^2}.$

The Crank-Nicolson method uses the central difference at time $(t_n + t_{n+1})/2$ and the second-order central difference at x_j:

$$\frac{\partial u}{\partial \tau} \approx \frac{u_j^{n+1} - u_j^n}{\Delta \tau} = \frac{1}{2}\left(\frac{u_{j+1}^n - 2u_j^n + u_{j-1}^n}{(\Delta x)^2} + \frac{u_{j+1}^{n+1} - 2u_j^{n+1} + u_{j-1}^{n+1}}{(\Delta x)^2} \right) \approx \frac{\partial^2 u}{\partial x^2}.$$

B. If you are solving a parabolic partial differential equation using the explicit finite difference method, is it worse to have too many steps in the time dimension or too many steps in the space dimension?

Solution: The equation for u_j^{n+1} in the explicit finite difference method is $u_j^{n+1} = \alpha u_{j-1}^n + (1-2\alpha) u_j^n + \alpha u_{j+1}^n$, where $\alpha = \Delta t / (\Delta x)^2$. For the explicit finite difference method to be stable, we need to have $1 - 2\alpha > 0 \Rightarrow \Delta t / (\Delta x)^2 < 1/2$. So a small Δt (i.e., many time steps) is desirable, but a small Δx (too many space steps) may make $\Delta t / (\Delta x)^2 > 1/2$ and the results unstable. In that sense, it is worse to have too many steps in the space dimension. In contrast, the implicit difference method is always stable and convergent.

Index

Made in the USA
Lexington, KY
13 January 2016